THE GOLD COAST CHURCH
AND THE GHETTO

THE GOLD COAST CHURCH AND THE GHETTO

CHRIST AND CULTURE IN MAINLINE PROTESTANTISM

JAMES K. WELLMAN JR.

Foreword by Martin E. Marty

UNIVERSITY OF ILLINOIS PRESS

URBANA AND CHICAGO

Unless otherwise noted, all photographs are from
*A Light in the City: A History of the Fourth Presbyterian
Church of Chicago,* copyright ©1990 by the Fourth
Presbyterian Church of Chicago, reprinted with permission.

Library of Congress Cataloging-in-Publication Data
Wellman, James K.
The gold coast church and the ghetto : Christ and culture
in mainline Protestantism / James K. Wellman, Jr. ;
foreword by Martin E. Marty.
p.   cm.
Includes bibliographical references and index.
ISBN 0-252-02489-3 (cloth : alk. paper)
ISBN 0-252-06804-1 (pbk. : alk. paper)
1. Fourth Presbyterian Church (Chicago, Ill.)—History.
2. Chicago (Ill.)—Church history.
3. Protestant churches—United States—Case studies.
4. Christianity and culture—United States—Case studies.
I. Title.
BX9211.C414W48   1999
285'.177311—dc21   98-58127

CIP

1 2 3 4 5 C P 5 4 3 2 1

For Annette,
with whom all things
are well

Contents

Foreword by Martin E. Marty   ix

Preface   xiii

Prologue: From Christianization to Humanization   1

Introduction: From Center to Periphery   7

1. Dealing with Displacement: The Protestant Mainline
   in the Twentieth Century   25

2. The Cultural Protestant Church, 1908–28   40

3. The Cultural Protestant Church in Tension, 1928–61   79

4. The Paradox of the Evangelical Liberal Church, 1961–84   120

5. The Lay Liberal Protestant Church, 1985–98   154

6. Finding a New Center: The Future of the Liberal Protestant
   Mainline   197

Appendixes
   A. Survey Results   221
   B. A Short History of American Presbyterianism   236

Works Cited   243

Index   253

Illustrations follow page 78

Foreword

Martin E. Marty

Mainline Protestantism—the concept did not even exist early in the twentieth century, when James Wellman's story begins. It still lacked a name even at midcentury, when the church Wellman analyzes was at ease in the Protestant Zion that America still appeared to be then.

In those decades the mainline Protestant was simply called "Protestant," as in *"Protestant-Catholic-Jew,"* the three-way division among Americans that Will Herberg identified in his book with that title in 1955. Herberg and most other observers were of course aware that there were other religious cohorts out there somewhere, even within Protestantism. He and they would give a few lines to what later sociologists would call African American Protestantism, a vital sector that receives more attention from them today than the mainline ever would. Herberg noticed fundamentalism at the cultural margins, but the word *evangelical* was just beginning to become a trademark for a huge alternative version of Protestantism that included such fundamentalism. Back then it would typically be dismissed as belonging to the cultural backwaters. It was strong in the Bible Belt, thought to be inhabited by rednecks, hillbillies, Holy Rollers, and other doomed embarrassments in respectable America.

Today the surveyors cut the old three-way religious division and reconfigure it in a four-piece pie chart, each piece containing numerous varieties. Ask a hundred Americans their religious preference, and about a fourth of them answer in ways that can be clumped in sections marked "Catholic," "Main-

line Protestant," "Evangelical," and "Other"—Jewish, Muslim, Eastern Orthodox Christian, Mormon, New Age, new religious movements, or no preference.

In the eyes of most chroniclers the Protestantism that, to be colloquial, ran
the show in the 1950s has taken its place not at the margins—there are no longer
margins pushed off from the center—or as an outsider—there are no longer
simple insiders and outsiders—but as one cluster that shares power and place
with other clusters, none of which runs the show in American culture.

James Wellman accounts for aspects of that decisive power shift, not with
broad sociological generalizations made as if from the distance of a satellite
photograph but with a close-up, which in many ways is more helpful for those
who want to understand American patterns of loyalty and commitment.

In 1952 President-elect Dwight D. Eisenhower was baptized and received not
into his grandparents' churches, which were definitely populated by outsiders at the margins. He became Presbyterian, the denomination with which
Wellman's congregation is affiliated. That choice was noncontroversial. Had
Ike chosen to become Catholic eight years before the election of John F.
Kennedy, he might have been culturally impeached by the Protestant establishment. Had he joined the River Brethren sect that some older Eisenhowers
cherished, he would have lost cultural status and bewildered those who knew
where power and prestige lay. Presbyterian was what someone became if one
wanted to be seen as a believer but not an eccentric one.

Since Eisenhower, Kennedy, and Lyndon Johnson, all the presidents, no matter to which church they belonged, took counsel more readily from evangelicals
of roughly the Billy Graham stripe than from mainliners. The Bible Belt now
has more to encircle than anyone envisioned back in 1952 or 1955. The evangelicals—which includes fundamentalists, Pentecostals, Southern Baptists, other
conservative Protestants, and the like—have become more politically active,
in the public eye, than the mainliners and Catholics ever were. The old establishment has become disestablished, through a series of bloodless coups by
other aspirants to establishment, centrality, and insiderhood. Such a shift has
epic dimensions, but it has lacked its saga-singers. Stories and analyses such
as James Wellman's are important contributions to a grand story that is still
in the making.

To effect such contributions, one must have the knowledge gained by close
acquaintance as well as a sense of distance that comes to those who choose
stances and bring expertise that let them provide perspective. Wellman is
qualified to offer such a vantage and has shown himself to be a helpful expert.

Why need a sense of distance? My answer would be that most of us are too close to the subject of change in American culture and religion to be aware of the adjustments congregations, denominations, social classes, and other groupings have been making. Someone once said that whoever named the water, it certainly wasn't the fish. The wet milieu was too close, too enveloping, too much taken for granted to be identified and named. Naming something "main*line* Protestant"—I would have preferred and long have chosen to write about "main*stream* Protestant" for its fluid and dynamic connotations—was one step in providing identity and perspective. But discerning what was on that line has been needed, and studies such as this one of the Fourth Presbyterian Church in Chicago are welcome.

Those who study this culture and its subcultures up close suffer somewhat from the fact that this enveloping phenomenon is *so* close that it does not inspire much natural curiosity in most of the citizenry. If you wish to draw a crowd on an American campus, you invite someone exotic, like the Dalai Lama, not the moderator of the Presbyterian Church. Transact with religious powers in today's metropolis, and you will find that city hall deals with African American pastors more often than with mainline Protestant leaders. Look for celebrity, and you will feature the pope, Billy Graham, or Louis Farrakhan. Charter historians and sociologists to select their topics as they seek foundation grants, and you will hear more about new religious movements than about older ones, the New Age more than seasoned traditions, Mormons more than Methodists, Amish more than Episcopalians. All that is well and good, but it overlooks high drama disguised as the humdrum familiar story next door. In this scene books such as Wellman's acquire importance that exceeds any ordinary packaging.

Social historians relish the discovery of archival means of close-up access to past cultures. Find the floor plan of a never-built medieval monastery, the legal log of a French village plagued by heresy, the shipping records of slavers, and you have the raw material for revealing stories. They would represent parts, not the whole, of a story, but they would provide some sense, some flavor, of a bigger drama.

If in some distant future an archivist came across Wellman's story of mainline Protestant change, he or she would possess a valuable, even precious, means of understanding something significant about what was going on in the United States in these decades. This, however, is not a distant future. Now is the time for those who have been casual observers of culture to take advantage of the chronicles of change that so many so easily overlook. Wellman has mastered the elements of social theory that help make his detail meaningful, but, one is grateful while saying it, he does not burden the reader with jargon or mean-derings down bypaths. He sticks to the plot of this strategic congregation.

Epics need titanic and heroic central figures. *The Gold Coast Church and the Ghetto* features central characters who, like all their mainline Protestant coun-terparts, were not national celebrities, definers of their age. But the succession of head pastors—Timothy Stone, Harrison Ray Anderson, Elam Davies, and John Buchanan—provides Wellman with leaders who have been powerful in congregation, denomination, and their segment of the culture. We get to know them well, as they knew and know their culture well, and from their actions the story gains coherence, and readers gain comprehension.

If this were simply a whining story of decline and fall or even a triumphal story by enemies of the old mainline, we could easily dismiss it. Or we would relocate it with William Wordsworth's "Solitary Reaper," as dealing with "old, unhappy, far-off things, and battles long ago." Wellman readily talks about decline, but he deals more often with change. He is not an enemy of the main-line, though he never shirks the task of addressing the patriarchy, paternalism, and prejudice that marked even its clerical and laypeople of goodwill. He is trying to make sense of it all and its surrounding culture, and he does so quite convincingly.

While by century's end mainline Protestantism may have become disestab-lished as a national movement, thousands of congregations and millions of lay members remain strong and vital contributors to personal and national life. Not too many metropolitan main streets, such as Chicago's Magnificent Mile, have congregations as booming and bustling as Fourth Presbyterian, which is located on that mile. Somehow, however, the less visible churches like this one attract new constituencies and minister to new seekers.

Fourth Presbyterian has its largest membership ever, people who evidently have not gotten the message that the mainline has no mission, souls who find their spiritual hungers addressed and their impulses to activism inspired by this ministry. Those who care or begin to care about the mainline and its present vocation can pick up clues from this study, subtitled *Christ and Cul-ture in Mainline Protestantism*. Looking over their shoulders will be histori-ans, sociologists, and students of the humanities who will find here something they may well have overlooked or about which they had lacked curiosity. Wellman inspires curiosity and ministers to it. But it is time for introducers to get off stage and see the curtain rise for this drama that tells something of what happens when a Gold Coast church and the ghetto meet.

PREFACE

When we arrived in Chicago in 1990, we were overwhelmed at the diversity of the city. We enjoyed driving up Lake Shore Drive, with mansions to the west and water to the east; the intimacy of Wrigley Field; the blues clubs all over the city; every ethnic dining one could imagine; the array of museums and neighborhood cultural events; and the somewhat gaudy but seductive Magnificent Mile. In the midst of this avenue that celebrated every consumer's dream was a Gothic structure at Chestnut and Michigan—the Fourth Presbyterian Church. We began attending and became enamored with its elegant liturgy and music, the forceful and engaged preaching from the pulpit, and the clear commitment to social service and outreach to the community of Cabrini-Green, a public housing ghetto not more than a mile west of the church. I thought, what could make a more fascinating study than to explore a church that stood at the intersection between the heart of the Gold Coast and the chaos of the ghetto? Moreover, Fourth Presbyterian Church is a thriving church. It is a counterexample of a liberal and mainline Protestant church in decline. I wanted to understand what makes it work. This book addresses answers these questions and seeks to pose possible paths for the mainline Protestant churches in the new millennium. Finally, the book is a celebration of the diversity and the continuing acts of reconciliation between two radically different racial ethnic groups and classes of people.

The more involved I became with this study, the more numerous my debts became. My coadvisers, Don Browning and Martin Marty, were invaluable from the beginning. Don Browning asked me the first and perhaps the most important question of my years at the University of Chicago: What is your question? Martin Marty has played an indispensable role directing my historical work on the church in the twentieth century and has been a constructive critic and friend in the process. Martin Riesebrodt steered me through the maze of social theory in the sociology of religion. I first presented some of this material to a group on September 25, 1994, at Stephen Warner's meeting called the Chicago Area Group for the Study of Religious Communities. Warner's expertise in American religion and in congregational studies was crucial in clarifying many of my own biases. At several points along the way his comments opened the door to new insights. Matthew Price and Elfriede Wedam, respondents at Warner's meeting, provided stimulating input. The staff and congregants at Fourth Presbyterian made this study a joy because of their openness and dedication to ministry. There are many individuals at Fourth Presbyterian who contributed, but Micah Marty, Elam Davies, John Buchanan, Jack L. Stotts, Bob Rasmussen (the archivist for Fourth Presbyterian), David Braskamp, and Ann Rehfeldt were particularly generous. Family members of former pastors of Fourth Presbyterian have been helpful as well, especially Harrison Ray Anderson Jr. and George T. Stone.

I thank the Fourth Presbyterian Church for permission to use material from its archives; Harrison Ray Anderson Jr., Elam Davies, John Buchanan, and the Billy Graham Evangelistic Association for permission to publish excerpts from personal correspondence and interviews with them; and the *Journal of Presbyterian History* for allowing me to use material from my article "The Decentering of the Protestant Mainline: John Timothy Stone in Chicago, 1908–1930," published in volume 76, number 3 (Fall 1998).

The Louisville Institute awarded me a fellowship in 1994. Nancy Ammerman, Jim Lewis, John Mulder, and others encouraged me about the importance of the study in understanding American religion in the twentieth century. I also won the student paper award from the Society for the Scientific Study of Religion (SSSR) in 1994 for a chapter on John Timothy Stone. I have found helpful colleagues in the SSSR and the Religious Research Association, especially Carl Dudley, Bill McKinney, Dean Hoge, and Bill Swatos. Friends along the way from the University of Chicago Divinity School and elsewhere have made the journey enjoyable and fruitful, especially Robin Petersen, Jim Perkinson, and Bill Harper.

In the early stages of the project, comments from Wade Clark Roof, Martha Heller, Terry Schmitt, James Moorhead, and Jon Berquist guided revisions. In the final stages of publishing, Rhys Williams's adroit analytic comments were enormously helpful in moving the text forward. My editor at the University of Illinois Press, Elizabeth Dulany, has been a constant voice of encouragement. Jane Mohraz, associate editor, has made the text far more readable. Mary Johnson's keen eye was indispensable on the page proofs. For all these contributions I give credit, but for any of the book's shortcomings I take responsibility.

My family has played a pivotal part in this process, beginning with my mother, who died in 1996 but the memory of her spirit buoys my own, and my father, whose faithfulness to all things good has been a light and an inspiration. My two children, Constance and Georgia, were born during the research and writing and have been a constant source of inexpressible joy. My spouse, Annette, from the beginning has been my partner in things intellectual, spiritual, and, most of all, in love. For each of them I give thanks.

THE GOLD COAST CHURCH AND THE GHETTO

PROLOGUE:
FROM CHRISTIANIZATION
TO HUMANIZATION

O Master from the mountainside,
Make haste to heal these hearts of pain;
Among these restless throngs abide,
O tread the city's streets again,
Till sons of men shall learn Thy love,
And follow where Thy feet have trod;
Till glorious from Thy heaven above
Shall come the City of our God.
—Frank Mason North, "Where Cross
the Crowded Ways of Life," 1905

THIS CLASSIC OLD PROTESTANT HYMN catches the cultural Protestantism of
its day. It resonates with the theme of Christianization of the city and its people.
The goal of the Christian mission was the same wherever the church was
present—to evangelize all people so that in the end everyone would bow to
Jesus Christ. This relatively innocent hymn rings rather hollow in the pluralistic and contentious cities of our contemporary American society. Nonetheless, it aptly illustrates the ministry of John Timothy Stone, the pastor of Fourth
Presbyterian in Chicago from 1908 to 1928. Two stories of Fourth Presbyterian,
one from the 1910s and one from the 1990s, illuminate the prismatic nature of
the Fourth Presbyterian Church and how I will use it to understand the Protestant mainline in the twentieth century. The stories show the dramatic changes
in the church and culture—how the mission of Fourth Presbyterian shifted
and how its relation to society has become more complex. This book is the
story of the transition of a 4,000-member Protestant church from an early-
century Protestant establishment congregation to a lay liberal church. It pro-

vides a window into the passage of the Protestant mainline from institutional dominance in American culture to but one institution among many competing for the loyalty of individuals.

THE MISSION OF THE PROTESTANT ESTABLISHMENT, 1912

John Timothy Stone ardently bore witness to his deep faith in the power of Jesus Christ. This message affected many lives. Stone, who came from a prominent Protestant heritage, rubbed shoulders with the powerful Protestant leaders in business and politics of his day. He promoted a mission to Christianize his neighborhood, the nation, and the world. One example of Stone's vision for Christian ministry can be seen in the life of William Whiting Borden. Borden and his family were members of Stone's church during the early years of Stone's ministry. The Borden family is emblematic of the hopes and dreams of this Protestant establishment church and how the mission of the church commingled with the establishment culture.

Borden came from a wealthy Chicago family. His father had succeeded in business, and his mother's deep piety influenced her son. Borden went to private boarding schools in his early years and began Yale University in 1905. The year before entering college, he traveled the world, as many young people did at that time. During his travels he met missionaries in several areas of China and the Far East. The economic and spiritual need of those who had not experienced the gospel impressed him. At Yale he started the Yale Hope Mission in a poor section of New Haven. He also became president of Phi Beta Kappa and excelled in various sports, from yachting to golf. His pictures from that time present a handsome young man, groomed for success.

Borden, however, decided to exercise his privileges, in both his person and resources, in a different direction. He attended Princeton Theological Seminary. Borden led various evangelical organizations, including the Student Volunteer Movement, and directed programs for the Moody Bible Institute. Upon graduating from Princeton, Borden chose full-time mission work with the China Inland Mission. He set his sights on evangelizing the more than one million Chinese Moslems.

The *Chicago Tribune* covered Borden's ordination. The January 22, 1912, headline read "Borden Ordained for Chinese Post: Ministers Lead Services for Chicagoan Who Renounced $5,000,000 Fortune." The article reported that John Timothy Stone gave the young man the following charge:

"Be strong. Strong with a strength that the world may not at first recognize. I remember the life of Dr. Cotton in India. I remember how forty Buddhists met in the local chamber of commerce, went in a body to the temple of Buddha, and asked that each might lose one year from his life that it might be added to the life of the Christian physician. That was strength, to make men do such things. I charge you, be a man of apprehension. See ahead a better Chicago, a better New York, a better London. See ahead better things for the suffering in China, in India, in Africa. Keep the spirit of a clean life, keep faith, keep wisdom, keep power."

In early 1913 Borden traveled to Egypt for language education. While there he contracted spinal meningitis and died at the age of twenty-six. His letters to his mother capture his single-minded passion for service and his desire to share the gospel of Christ with the world. Borden often repeated Dwight Moody's famous line, "The world has yet to see what God can do with a fully consecrated man." This young man incarnated Stone's call to Christianize the world. Borden's will distributed more than a million dollars to various organizations. These gifts included $250,000 to the China Inland Mission, $100,000 to Moody Bible Institute, and $50,000 each to Princeton Theological Seminary and the Board of Foreign Missions for the Presbyterian Church U.S.A. Borden's mother, who supported her son throughout his missionary journey, gave Fourth Presbyterian a mission library upon her son's death. The library stocked more than twelve hundred volumes of missionary journals and served to inspire others to mission work. Charles R. Erdman, the conservative Presbyterian pastor who would become the moderator of the Presbyterian Church U.S.A. in 1925, wrote a memorial of Borden's life and mission. He used Borden as an exemplar of a true Christian gentlemen (Erdman, 1913).

The Borden family illuminates many of the elements of the early Protestant establishment and the ways the Fourth Presbyterian Church embodied its hopes. These included access to great wealth; the effect of Protestant establishment families on the broader culture; the drama of choice in the pursuit of a worldly or religious calling; the power of the gospel to lead men and women to sacrifice their privilege; and an exclusivist Christian theology. The fervency of Borden's biography served to inspire many to go into the mission field, but this single-mindedness began to fade as the decades advanced. The cultural matrix that shaped Borden was peculiar to the early part of the century. As the 1920s progressed, the Protestant establishment could no longer claim its early cultural hegemony. The cultural Protestantism of that time began to wane, along with the powerful partnership between the wealthy establishment and the mission of the church. The McCormick family, parent to the International

Harvester Company and integral in bringing Stone to the church, contributed nearly half a million dollars each year in the 1910s to Fourth Presbyterian's mission funds. In the 1920s the funding ended abruptly and with it the wealthy's romance with mission work.

Stone did everything he could to inspire his wealthy congregation to continue the mission to Christianize Chicago and the world, but his ability to persuade his congregation declined in the 1920s. By the middle of the decade American culture was heading in new directions, and the number of Protestant missionaries from mainline churches declined precipitously. Fourth Presbyterian had to adjust. In a sense this transition is the story of the book. In the 1990s Fourth Presbyterian is a church dramatically different from what it was in the 1910s. Nonetheless, in the midst of its metamorphosis there are ties to the past. Those connections are also a part of the focus of this study.

THE MISSION OF A LAY LIBERAL CONGREGATION, 1998

In 1996 John Buchanan, the pastor of Fourth Presbyterian from 1985 to the present, became moderator of the General Assembly—the national ruling body of the Presbyterian Church (U.S.A.). Like Stone, Buchanan leads a church that has a strong membership and financial base. Unlike Stone, Buchanan stands with the liberal side of the denomination. Whereas Stone preached an exclusive gospel that demanded proselytizing, Buchanan has pushed the inclusive side of the gospel and a benevolence-based outreach to the poor of the city. The ordination of practicing homosexuals in the Presbyterian Church (U.S.A.) aptly illustrates the inclusive nature of Buchanan's theology.

Buchanan's tenure as moderator came in the midst of controversy over the passage of an amendment to the Presbyterian constitution that made explicit, for the first time, the constitutional denial of ordination to practicing homosexuals. The new criterion for the ordination as minister, elder, or deacon now explicitly demands that one live in either faithfulness and fidelity in marriage or chastity in singleness. This provision was passed at the end of Buchanan's year as moderator. During his moderatorial tenure Buchanan remained neutral on the amendment, even though most knew he stood against it. When it passed at the 1997 General Assembly and his term as moderator was finished, Buchanan, along with other disappointed Presbyterians, formed an organization—the Covenant Network of Presbyterians—to combat the new constitutional rules. The organization worked to amend the new clause by supporting an amendment that would have replaced the terms "fidelity" and "chastity" with "fidelity and integrity in all relationships." It accommodated a more flexible position on the sexual behavior of potential candidates for ordination. Buchanan came out strongly for the new amendment. Nonetheless, early in 1998 the amendment was defeated by a large majority of the 172 nationwide presbyteries. In the midst of this defeat Buchanan finally broke his silence from the pulpit of Fourth Presbyterian on the ordination of homosexuals. In a sermon on January 18, 1998, entitled "Water to Wine," he stated his case clearly:

> The issue before the church is an important one: what constitutes faithful, responsible intimate behavior. But the issue behind all the discussion is whether or not gay and lesbian persons shall be ordained in the Presbyterian Church (U.S.A.). Those who oppose it do so primarily on the basis of what, for them, is a clear Biblical mandate. For some of us, the Biblical mandate is not clear. For others of us, the Biblical mandate is in the direction of openness and inclusivity and it seems quite clear. I am one of these. I believe in the heterosexual marriage, faithfulness in marriage. I believe the church needs to affirm marriage and teach and encourage responsible sexual behavior for all people. But I do not believe scripture mandates the exclusion of everyone who, for one reason or another, does not live within those norms. And I do not personally believe scripture mandates the exclusion from leadership in our church of faithful gay and lesbian Presbyterians, who are faithful to one another, honest and just in all their relationships, and devoted to following Jesus Christ.

This was neither a confession nor a call to arms. Many in the congregation already understood Buchanan's position. He was not urging the congregation to take a more strident position, as some in the denomination have done by calling themselves "more light" congregations. The "more light" position of churches officially encourages the open ordination of practicing homosexuals and the transformation of the church's policies on the issue. Buchanan has never entertained this option. At the same time, he would not exclude gays or lesbians from ordained leadership in the church. In the midst of all these discussions the clergy and lay leadership of the Fourth Presbyterian Church have educated the congregation on the issue. Moreover, the Fourth Presbyterian session—the ruling board of the church—has taken a position that favors the ordination of homosexuals.

Buchanan's and Fourth Presbyterian's position on homosexual ordination is a far cry from Stone's ministry. In a way Buchanan, unlike any of his predecessors, has put Fourth Presbyterian against the mainstream of the denomination. In its history Fourth Presbyterian has always taken neutral positions on the larger national issues in the denomination. In this instance Buchanan breaks new ground for the church. It is a position of some tension both within the Protestant churches and in American culture (Comstock, 1996:13–14). Although most Americans support gay civil rights, a majority still believe that homosexuality is morally wrong (Wolfe, 1998:74–75).

The position, however, is consistent with the lay liberal congregation that Buchanan has developed and nurtured at Fourth Presbyterian. It is a congregation that values traditional but relevant worship services and seeks biblically based sermons that speak to the issues of the day. It is a church that by any standards provides extensive services to the dispossessed in the city of Chicago. It is a church that is inclusive of others and affirms the religious pluralism of the nation and world. For the second half of the twentieth century Fourth Presbyterian did not actively support missionary outreach in any way that is close to what we saw with Stone and Borden. Mission is now local and service-oriented. To evangelize is to show benevolence toward those with less. It is not a matter of proclaiming one's faith.

This transition, from a cultural Protestant church that used the resources of the establishment to Christianize the world to a church that supports liberal values of inclusion and reaches out to those in need, is a central theme in this study. In this way Fourth Presbyterian has adapted to its circumstance and worked to make the gospel applicable in its context. For Buchanan the model is Christ transforming culture; this is not, however, the culture's Christianization but its humanization. The dream is no longer the city of God but a city for all people, a goal that in the end, at least for lay liberals, may be the same thing.

Introduction:
From Center to Periphery

It [the dilemma] is not essentially the problem of Christianity and civilization: for Christianity, whether defined as church, creed, ethics, or movement of thought, itself moves between the poles of Christ and culture. The
relation of these two authorities constitutes its problem.
—H. Richard Niebuhr, *Christ and Culture,* 1951

But, in a word, culture is what makes religion interesting. Religion is, after all, centrally concerned with beliefs and convictions, with texts and their
interpretation, with the dissemination of the revealed word, with the ways
in which meaning and purpose is constructed, and with the traditions that
accumulate around particular religious communities. To avoid focus on
these aspects of religion would be like trying to understand apple pie without paying attention to apples.
—Robert Wuthnow, "The Cultural Turn," 1997

IN THIS STUDY I try to understand not only the apples but the preparation of
the pie and how it has been served throughout the era that I have analyzed.
This is a story of the Protestant mainline told through the lens of a downtown
Chicago church. The Fourth Presbyterian Church is the vehicle through which
we witness the transition of the Protestant mainline from the center of American culture to but one pillar among many in American society. For some it has
been a journey of decline and defeat. I argue that it has been a necessary adjustment to the facts of the twentieth-century American religious market.

The Fourth Presbyterian Church illustrates the various strategies that the
Protestant mainline used to accommodate and resist the dramatic changes that
occurred in the twentieth century. I do not claim that this analysis of Fourth
Presbyterian explains the full gamut of Protestant mainline experience, but it
does illuminate the ways in which one mainline Protestant church came to
grips with many of the most pressing problems of the century, including eco-

nomic expansion and depression; racial segregation and integration; the shifting currents of populations in American urban centers; the rise of urban poverty; the theological conflicts between conservatives and liberals in the Protestant church; and the relatively recent decline in membership in Protestant mainline churches. All of these trends in American life confronted the Protestant mainline and specifically the Fourth Presbyterian Church.

Using a modified framework of H. Richard Niebuhr's Christ and culture typology, I examine the cultural challenges that confronted the Protestant mainline and Fourth Presbyterian in the twentieth century. How did the formal ideology and theology of Fourth Presbyterian accommodate and resist the rapid societal changes of the century? How did Fourth Presbyterian and its leadership balance its comforting and challenging roles in negotiating issues of race and class in its urban setting? How did this tension between Christ and culture evolve in the midst of the transition of the Protestant mainline from the center of American culture to one church among many fighting for its particular niche in an open religious market?

Two factors make the Fourth Presbyterian useful for examining the travail of the Protestant mainline. First, three of the four pastors in the twentieth century had tenures of more than twenty years, and the last, John Buchanan, has every expectation of fulfilling a similar incumbency. Each pastor and his leadership thus developed a particular theological response to their time and gave the church a relatively coherent perspective to interpret and understand. Each made intentional and energetic attempts not only to confirm but also to challenge the symbolic and social boundaries of the Gold Coast on the Near North Side.[1] Each developed specific strategies to respond to changes in American culture and society; the fluctuations in how Chicago dealt with urban poverty; the shifting demographics of Fourth Presbyterian's urban setting; the racial tensions, particularly at midcentury; the theological fireworks throughout this era that crisscrossed the Presbyterian denomination; and the steady and sometimes dramatic decline in Protestant mainline membership and status during the latter part of this era. Second, Fourth Presbyterian had a relatively stable membership and financial situation throughout this tumultuous period. It offers a picture of a religious institution that has carved out its own niche in an American cultural milieu that no longer supports the Protestant mainline in any official way. Even as Fourth Presbyterian has maintained its membership in recent years, however, it has had to grapple with its own decreased status. This change in status is detailed in the chapters on the church, but two points partially show what this has meant to Fourth Presbyterian. Architecturally, in the early part of the century, Fourth Presbyterian dominated the Near North Side. In its present state, one of the most interesting views of the church is looking down from the hundred-story John Hancock Building across the street. More important, whereas Fourth Presbyterian's pastor and lay leadership were frequently in touch with the political leaders of the city in the past, particularly through the 1970s, the present pastor and leaders have little contact with and no positions in the city government. This Protestant mainline church and its leadership are only one voice among many when it comes to contemporary political and cultural power in the city of Chicago.

My aim is to provoke reflection and thought on the place of the Protestant mainline in our contemporary cultural setting. The Protestant mainline no longer sets the agenda of American culture as it once did. In a sense any contemporary incarnation of mainline Protestantism compared with its former glory seems rather pale. I argue, however, a new era calls for a new church that is no longer nostalgic for the past but learns from it and is ready to move forward. This study is meant to be a learning instrument for reflecting on what has gone before, how it occurred, and what lies ahead. To be sure, the precise course of the Fourth Presbyterian Church has no exact parallel in American religious life, yet as Stephen Warner commented in his study of the Mendocino church in California, "it is within the particular that the general resides" (Warner, 1988:282). This study of Fourth Presbyterian thus offers a heuristic model for other Protestant mainline congregations seeking to adapt to the multiple cultural and social changes at the turn of the century. Fourth Presbyterian has been able to adjust to its own displacement and to come to a new identity in the midst of the changing patterns in American religion and society.

TENSIONS IN RELIGION AND SOCIETY

Defining Christ and Culture

In H. Richard Niebuhr's classic study *Christ and Culture,* Niebuhr begins with what he calls the "enduring problem" of defining Christ and culture and the interaction between the two. He enumerates the dynamics in this interplay and comes up with five types around which various traditions and figures within the Christian tradition can be understood and classified (Niebuhr, 1951:1–11). The tension between Christ and culture, religion and society, accommodation and resistance, comfort and challenge, the priestly and prophetic is the faultline I explore in this study. How has the Protestant mainline, specifically Fourth Presbyterian, negotiated this precipice that shipwrecked many a church and denomination in the twentieth century? In the midst of the rapid changes in our culture and society it is not surprising that the Protestant mainline has struggled to adjust to American culture, which in many ways has left the Protestant main-line behind. Cultural Protestantism, in the form defined by Niebuhr below, no longer exists. Now multiple traditions vie to prioritize the lives of their follow-ers; it is not uncommon for individuals to be loyal to a wide array of commit-ments. Before I develop these tensions between Christ and culture in greater depth, I define these terms using Niebuhr's *Christ and Culture.*

As Niebuhr outlines, to be a Christian is to say that one believes in and fol-lows Jesus Christ. For the believer Christ is the one who brings to the world a new teaching, a new life, and a new community. From the perspective of Chris-tian tradition Jesus embodies a new covenant between God and humankind. This covenant calls forth a new command to love in the sacrificial way of the cross. It is a prophetic challenge to give one's life for the sake of others, to care for enemies, to forgive unconditionally; it is a bracing summons to the believer. The prophetic stance is set in the context of the new life that one has in Jesus Christ. Through the crucifixion and resurrection of Jesus Christ one is made a new person; the old self is past and gone. One's sins are forgiven, and one is promised a new life in this world and in the one to come. This new life is the kingdom of God, and the believer is promised the presence of the Holy Spirit. The final quality of life in Christ is the new community. This is the commu-nity of the church, where one finds fellowship with other believers in the faith. The community of faith is called the body of Christ. It is where the gifts of grace, forgiveness, and reconciliation and the sacraments of the church, bap-tism and communion, are practiced. This new community is Christ's witness to the world that God's incarnate son, Jesus Christ, has come to the world not to condemn it but to save it. In traditional Christian theology these three modes of Christ are classified as prophet, priest, and king. Jesus challenges his follow-ers, brings new life to them, and is their Lord and Savior (Niebuhr, 1951:11–29).

Niebuhr defines culture as a social and human achievement. It involves the realization of temporal and material values, which are conserved and passed on through each generation. Culture is fundamentally pluralistic, as diverse as the people involved in its construction, and it has manifold possibilities. Culture constitutes the habits, ideas, beliefs, customs, social organization, in-herited artifacts, technical processes, and values that people bring to a social setting. Culture is thus a term that encompasses the many strands of human thought, practice, and emotion that are constructed by a group or an associa-tion. The shaping process is reciprocal; that is, the group creates cultural and symbolic boundaries, and these forms also shape the values, attitudes, and habits of the group (Niebuhr, 1951:29–39).

Niebuhr uses five classifications of Christ and culture to describe the patterns of religion and society in Western Christian culture throughout its history. He begins with Christ against culture, which he describes as the model most representative of early Christian communities. This type is exclusive in its perspective on the world and constructs its own cultural identity against the culture of its social setting. It is the model that embodies the greatest tension. The next type, the Christ of culture, is the least tensive of the five. It is most readily understood in the light of modern church history as a form of cultural Protestantism. This type is exemplified in Protestant liberalism in such figures as Immanuel Kant and Friedrich Schleiermacher and in forms of Christian deism in the American context that assert Christ as the implicit goal of the culture. The third type Niebuhr calls Christ above culture. This is a synthetic form of Christ and culture, best reflected in the thinking of Thomas Aquinas and the tradition of medieval Catholicism. Human reasoning is reliable as a guide for human conduct; it cannot do the work of salvation, which is Christ's domain, but human efforts coalesce with divine power in the reconciliation of humans with God. The fourth model is that of Christ and culture in paradox. Niebuhr used the term *dualist* to describe this type. St. Paul and Martin Luther are the great representatives of this model. It tends to emphasize the fallen state of humanity and all of its cultural manifestations. The revelation of God's grace in Jesus Christ redeems individuals from their corrupt condition. The created world is not evil, but the sin of humanity remains despite God's grace. This type picks up some of the tension of Christ against culture yet without the drive to form a separate Christian culture, precisely because all cultures are skewed by sin. In this model some forms of state authority are acceptable because they bind the worst in human nature, as exemplified in both St. Paul's and Luther's instructions to submit to civil authorities. The final type is Christ the transformer of culture. This type is the least Christo-centric. God's work of creation comes to the forefront, in that nature and culture are perceived as divine domains, distorted by sin, yet able to be reformed and reconciled to God. Christ is the savior of fallen men and women. Men and women are thus free to work in the world not only to save individuals but also to reconcile the society and culture to the ways of God (Niebuhr, 1951:39–44).

Niebuhr's typological framework is helpful in categorizing the various ways in which Fourth Presbyterian has negotiated the culture of its time. For this study I use his model as a way of classifying the degrees of tension between the embodiments of the Christian faith and their cultural contexts. I do, however, complement Niebuhr's types by using the analytic categories of symbolic and social boundaries. These analytic tools are useful in analyzing with greater specificity the forms of power used in language and social structure. They are more precise in comprehending the conflicts and tensions over race and class, particularly between Fourth Presbyterian, the Gold Coast, and the ghettos of Chicago's West Side.[2]

The Role of Social and Symbolic Boundaries

I define symbolic and social boundaries as the tools that individuals and groups use to define and identify themselves in relation to other individuals, groups, and in some cases, ideas. They are the instruments of culture that individuals and groups use to differentiate themselves in relation to class and race.[3] The reproduction of social and symbolic differences (or boundaries) are the sources of distinction individuals and groups use to gain, maintain, and sometimes contest social status. These boundary strategies reveal the way in which Fourth Presbyterian dealt with the issues of race and class as it adjusted to its own cultural and social displacement.

Fourth Presbyterian was deliberate in its use of social boundaries during the first half of the century. The church used a pew rental system. Those who could afford to rent the pews in the front of the sanctuary were allowed into the service first; others would wait in the narthex or outside the doors of the church. Pew renters could also exit using the doors immediately to the north side of the sanctuary; this exit was especially reserved for them. These seating arrangements were monitored according to professional interests and economic and social status.

In the contemporary history of Fourth Presbyterian symbolic boundary keeping can be seen in the distinction it makes between conservative and liberal churches.[4] Both Buchanan and lay leaders often voice that Fourth Presbyterian is *not* a theologically conservative church. They frequently state that the theology of conservative evangelical churches is parochial and less sophisticated. In this way, religious boundaries take priority over class or racial boundaries in structuring the church's associations, at least in its public discourse.

Social boundaries, for this study, include the way in which economic and cultural dominance was achieved and shaped by the Protestant establishment in the city of Chicago. I examine the strategies used to gain status for certain racial-ethnic and religious groups. An analysis of the cultural and moral discourse of clergy and laypeople at Fourth Presbyterian reveals how they saw themselves within the social setting of the Gold Coast. The goal is to understand the complex symbolic strategies clergy and laypeople used to negotiate, adapt to, express, and, on occasion, confront the social boundaries of the Near North Side.

I argue that theological symbol systems not only are mirrors and expressions of socioeconomic hierarchies but also can and do challenge social structures of inequality. This is to say that symbolic religious systems can alter social structures (Lamont, 1992; Wuthnow, 1987). The empirical evidence from this study of Fourth Presbyterian indicates that the leadership of the church often went against class interests, not by making virtue out of economic necessity, but because its symbolic and moral traditions challenged the economic and social status quo.

Class and Race in Chicago and Fourth Presbyterian

This is not to say that Fourth Presbyterian did not express and participate in the construction of social inequality in the city of Chicago. It is to say, however, that the process is more complex than simply maintaining that socioeconomic success automatically creates the oppression of lower-class groups.[5] The tensions between Fourth Presbyterian and its social boundaries have changed over time, as it has adapted to the shift in its own status in the midst of American culture, to the changes in the life of the city, and to the broader theological changes in Protestant mainline denominations.

Through much of the twentieth century Protestant theologians and sociologists condemned the Protestant establishment as a mere expression of race and class inequality. In 1929 H. Richard Niebuhr attacked Protestant class boundaries in his *Social Sources of Denominationalism*. He charged the Protestant establishment was an agent in maintaining social inequality. At the end of the 1950s, when the core of the Protestant establishment was coming under intense scrutiny, Peter Berger's *Noise of Solemn Assemblies: Christian Commitment and the Religious Establishment in America* (1961) and Gibson Winter's *Suburban Captivity of the Churches: An Analysis of Protestant Responsibility* (1961) were severe judgments on the state of Protestant churches and their encouragement of social inequality and racial segregation.

In recent decades studies have refuted the claim that religious institutions do nothing more than sanctify social and status differences. Religion, as a political resource, has been used to mobilize political protest, solidify dissent against dominant social structures, and rally the civil rights movement. Rhys Williams's 1996 article "Religion as Political Resource: Culture or Ideology" provides a more nuanced understanding of how culture and ideology can be used to interpret the intersection of religion and society. Religion is a cultural tool that creates meaning and solidifies moral order, but it also can be used as an ideological resource to legitimize power relations or subvert these same processes. As Williams explains, "Religion shapes the identity, the sense of solidarity, and the moral outrage that are integral to social-movement culture. Motivated believers are the core of any collective action. At the same time, religious doctrine and theology can offer coherent and elaborated cognitive rationales that diagnose social problems, prescribe possible solutions, and justify the movement's action—often in the cause of universal verities" (Williams, 1996:377).

Williams's point is that ideology (or symbolic boundaries) should be defined as a neutral term. Ideology can be used by either those in power or those who are resisting power: "Ideologies are belief *systems*—articulated sets of ideas that are primarily cognitive . . . primarily articulated by specific social class/group, that function primarily in the interests of that class or group and yet are presented as being in the 'common good' or as generally accepted . . ." (Williams and Demerath, 1991:426–27). Ideology or symbolic boundaries are transformative systems of ideas based on the interests of a group, proffered as a common good, whether put forth by those in power or those without power. Religion is therefore a set of symbolic tools that can be used culturally to shape associations, resist political power structures, or reify dominant status groups.[6]

The history of Fourth Presbyterian reveals the complex nature of the interrelationship between class, race, and symbolic boundaries. Early in the twentieth century the power of the Protestant establishment was assumed, giving the culture a moral order and a social ethos. Ideologically, there was a pervasive notion that if one became loyal to Protestantism, one would thrive in the economic and cultural environment of the time. In this sense Protestantism was a cultural religion at the center of the society that promoted a symbolic framework of success as a product of the Protestant religion (Weber, 1946). Not only was the power of Protestantism assumed, but also its racial and class superiority were asserted. Few explicit remarks were made by those at Fourth Presbyterian, but boundaries of race and class were maintained in less obvious ways.

In Chicago social and symbolic boundaries of race, class, and religion were constructed and defended with great energy. In the early decades of the twentieth century the Protestant establishment saw the Mafia as the work of recent immigrants and backed by the Roman Catholic Church. There was little or no contact between Protestants and Roman Catholics, a mutual feeling of distrust prevailed, and comments made by Protestants were highly critical of the archdiocese of Chicago (Greeley, 1967). Christianizing the city and its inhabitants meant making Catholics Protestant *and* American. By midcentury the cultural values and norms were changing, and Americans were less tied to their Protestant traditions (Avella, 1992). Moreover, the politics of the city were no longer in the hands of Protestants, and Catholics were less diffident in their dealings with the Protestant establishment (Green and Holli, 1995). Indeed, a wide array of social groups, including the Protestant establishment, used their economic power and solidified their social gains through the segregation of African Americans into the massive public housing projects of Chicago, later called the "second ghetto" (Hirsch, 1983).

Despite the complicity of the Protestant establishment and Fourth Presbyterian in the segregation of African Americans, I argue that Fourth Presbyterian dealt with the social upheavals of the 1950s and 1960s in a more complex way than is often assumed. Even as Fourth Presbyterian and the Protestant establishment participated in the creation of the second ghetto of the postwar years, they were only one among many agents in the segregation of African Americans into Chicago's notorious public housing (Hirsch, 1983). Moreover, Fourth Presbyterian took up a role in working to alleviate the suffering caused by public housing and the poverty of minority groups in the city.

Fourth Presbyterian embodied the contradictions of a powerful status group that achieved enormous economic and social growth at the cost of creating tremendous social inequality. With the rise of the civil rights movement in the 1960s, Fourth Presbyterian began to reach out to local neighborhoods in need. African Americans were not only served but also welcomed into membership. The church, prodded by Elam Davies and his lay leadership, pushed the church to reach out to the many in need in the ghettos of Chicago's West Side. The combination of Davis's preaching and the implementation of new social programs led to the integration of the church across lines of class and race. Symbolically, the message no longer assumed the superiority of class and race but began to challenge the regnant inequality. Davis proclaimed a gospel for the sake of the common good of all people, no matter what their race, ethnicity, or social status.

Christ and Culture at Fourth Presbyterian

Throughout the twentieth century Fourth Presbyterian's leadership nurtured a strong institutional identity that fostered an underlying sense of social privilege. It is a Gold Coast Protestant church. At the same time, the church's leadership challenged its congregants to move beyond status quo social boundaries to contest class interests and racial discrimination. The tension between the prophetic call of Christ and the comforting role of priest changed in each era. For John Timothy Stone, the pastor from 1908 to 1928, it was an evangeli-

cal message that questioned the need for financial security and challenged the
Protestant establishment to missionary work. It was the Christ of culture, a
form of cultural Protestantism wherein the church converts, baptizes, and
shapes the world by means of the gospel. Near the end of Stone's tenure, the
signs of the displacement of the Protestant mainline disrupted the security of
this cultural Protestantism. How Stone dealt with this turbulence is an important aspect of the study. Harrison Ray Anderson, the pastor from 1928 to 1961,
complemented this Protestant culture with touches of the Puritan prophet.
Even as he shaped Fourth Presbyterian in the establishment tradition, he called
forth an ascetic ethos and made a ferocious attack on social excess. Furthermore, in 1942, when many were very suspicious of people of Japanese origin,
Anderson invited Japanese Americans into the church. It was the Christ of
culture in tension. At the end of Anderson's pastorate, American culture was
approaching its most explosive era, a period of change that caught off guard
not only Anderson but also the Protestant mainline. Elam Davies arrived as
pastor in 1961. During his tenure he used his internationally renowned oratorical skills to proclaim a gospel of inclusiveness and challenged Fourth Presbyterian to reach out to the neighborhood of Cabrini-Green, the public housing project only one mile to the west of the church. He opened the doors of
the church to African Americans for the first time. There is no doubt that
Davies transformed the church; his model, however, was Christ and culture
in paradox. He held that the church and the world were not separate but
ontologically the same in their tendency toward self-righteousness. Both were
fallen instruments; they were redeemed by God but never made pure. Davies
maintained this paradoxical understanding without denigrating the church or
the world. His was the most complex vision of the four pastors.

    In the contemporary period John Buchanan, who became the pastor in 1985,
taps the class interests of his upper-middle-class congregation by affirming
them in their privilege while activating their latent need to reach out to those
with less (Wuthnow, 1991; Ammerman, 1997a). For Buchanan it is the model
of Christ transforming culture. Buchanan is fully committed to a church that
serves the world. He is, however, aware, in ways unlike his predecessors, that
Fourth Presbyterian is one among many institutions to which the membership is loyal. He is much less apt to assume that the church is the center of
people's lives and the main focus of their energies. That is to say, at the turn
of the century the Fourth Presbyterian Church is a classic example of lay liberalism, or what Nancy Ammerman has called "golden rule" Christianity
(Ammerman, 1997a). Lay liberals are characterized as those who join a church
to organize their charitable giving and experience a sense of transcendence in

worship. Lay liberalism describes a type of religion that emphasizes how to live one's life instead of a set of rules or doctrines. In this way it is a type of liberal cultural Protestantism. The tension in this type of religion is minimal, and the church is well adapted to the pluralistic setting of American culture. It has come to terms with the decentered nature of the Protestant mainline in the American religious market, and in this way it has constructed a particular type of religious adjustment to its cultural setting.

FRAMING THE FIELD

Outline of the Study

This study is a historical ethnography. The first chapter provides a condensed history of the development and decline of the Protestant establishment and the fate of the Protestant mainline at the end of the twentieth century. It outlines how the Protestant mainline adapted to and resisted its own displacement. It also reflects on the various explanations of this decentering process and the way Fourth Presbyterian fits in this broader picture of American Protestantism. The four chapters covering Fourth Presbyterian coincide chronologically with the tenures of Fourth Presbyterian's twentieth-century pastors. This framework uses Fourth Presbyterian as a lens through which to analyze the history of the mainline Protestant church in the twentieth century, the significant religious and social changes in American culture during this era, and the development of Chicago's Near North Side. Each chapter begins with an analysis of the social boundaries of the Near North Side and how they related to the symbolic boundaries of the leaders and laypeople of Fourth Presbyterian. I examine the relation between the social context and church's social boundaries and the kind of programs and people that the church attracted and produced. The chapters then explore the symbolic boundaries that each pastor developed as he negotiated the cultural and social forces of the era and their impact on the life of the church. The final chapter expands on how Fourth Presbyterian and the Protestant mainline have accommodated and resisted their cultural surroundings in the light of moving from the center to the periphery in American society. It also develops more fully the specifics of Protestant lay liberalism and its place in American culture at the turn of the century.

In presenting the historical chapters, I chose to follow tenures of the ministers for several reasons. First, as mentioned earlier, the tenures of the first three ministers that I studied at Fourth Presbyterian lasted more than twenty years, and John Buchanan is in the middle of his second decade. Each brought to the church a consistent style of leadership and programmatic agenda. Second, the chronological frameworks of each pastor outline significant periods in twen-tieth-century religious and cultural history and thus provide natural breaks. Finally, the preachers in this church were pivotal in constructing the symbolic responses to cultural change in the city, the nation, and the Protestant main-line. Moreover, pastoral leadership was crucial in maintaining the stability of the church's finances and membership. Congregants, particularly in urban settings, tend to be mobile. Since congregational loyalty is evanescent, numeri-cal stability depends largely on the preacher's ability to continue to attract new congregants to the church. In the 1990s if Fourth Presbyterian's preacher had failed to attract 300 new members to the church annually, the church's mem-bership of more than 4,000 would have decreased at a precipitous rate.

John Timothy Stone tripled the membership of the church in less than fifteen years. Stone led the church in a $1 million building program, and the church's downtown Gothic cathedral building on North Michigan avenue was completed in 1914. Stone, a moderate evangelical, avoided controversy and attracted many to the church by his personality and his preaching. In his time he was one the most influential pastors in the Presbyterian Church in the United States of America.[7] In 1914 he became moderator of the General Assembly and in the early 1920s led a reorganization of the national church's governmental structures.

Harrison Ray Anderson continued a strong but more bureaucratic style of leadership that centered on the values of the Protestant ethic. He preached and practiced an ascetic Protestantism. He led Fourth Presbyterian in a tenacious advocacy program for conservative social values in Chicago; he advocated the return of Prohibition and attacked corruption in the police force and city government. He was also a nationally known figure and was a friend of Dwight Eisenhower and Billy Graham.

Elam Davies, a Welshman who embodied the charismatic style of Stone's leadership, helped steady the church during the tumultuous 1960s and 1970s, when many downtown Protestant churches were in decline. Davies combined a theologically evangelical and socially progressive message. He did not, how-ever, support the civil rights movement, and he excoriated antiwar protesters. Davies led the church in outreach ministries to the ghettos on the West Side. He began multiple social service programs, including a tutoring program for African American young people.

John Buchanan, a liberal Protestant, has an activist leadership style. Dur-ing his tenure the church has expanded its membership by more than a thou-sand members. Buchanan has aggressively expanded the church's ministries to Cabrini-Green, with a tutoring program that provides more than five hun-dred young people with individual volunteer tutors each week. He has led

Fourth Presbyterian in a $14 million capital campaign to refurbish the sanctuary and reconstruct the church buildings. In 1996, with Buchanan's successful bid for moderator of the Presbyterian Church (U.S.A.), three of the five ministers of Fourth Presbyterian in the twentieth century had risen to the highest office of the national church. At the end of 1998 Buchanan announced that he would accept an offer to take the part-time position as editor/publisher of the *Christian Century,* a Chicago-based ecumenical weekly magazine of liberal Protestantism.

Historical Ethnography and the Insider

This study picks up on the recent developments in the study of American religious communities, represented in part by Robert Wuthnow's work on restructuring American religion (1988), Nancy Ammerman's social location of religious communities (1997b), and E. Brooks Holifield's essay "Toward a History of American Congregations" (1994). This cultural turn to particular religious communities is well summarized in Penny Edgell Becker and Nancy L. Eiesland's edited volume, *Contemporary American Religion: An Ethnographic Approach* (1997). Becker and Eiesland assert that ethnography promises a better rendering of the American religious narrative in all its diversity and particularity: "Ethnography is a method uniquely suited to challenging conventional wisdom, for subjecting large-scale theories to empirical examination, for generating data on new phenomena, and for generating new theories or insights on the subjects we thought we already knew. Ethnography is a form of rendering an account that does not emphasize formalism or move to theoretical closure in a premature way. It allows for the expression of emergent understandings, partial accounts, and contradiction" (Becker and Eiesland, 1997:19).

This recent focus on ethnography in studying American religion not only allows greater nuance in making generalizations about American religion but also at times challenges the old paradigm (Warner, 1993). It no longer takes for granted the conclusions about the Protestant mainline that have ruled the field over the last generation (Finke and Stark, 1992). It takes a new approach to subjects that some feel have received enough attention already. Another analysis of the Protestant mainline may seem redundant, but when done with new tools and a different perspective, fresh insights can be gained. It is simply not the case that the Protestant mainline, particularly the liberals within that tradition, face inevitable decline. Modernization and secularization theory become unhelpful at the point where the theory no longer fits with empirical research—or in the felicitous phrasing of Ammerman, when theory "disguises reality" (Ammerman, 1997b:357). Fourth Presbyterian is a dramatic example of the vitality of a liberal, mainline church. Furthermore, this is a study that is not nostalgic for the Protestant mainline's past but sees something new in the "old wineskins" of American Protestant churches (Warner, 1988). Indeed, a part of the purpose of this study is to show that liberal Protestant churches have a place in the American religious market and that identity rather than strictness is critical to institutional vitality. As Warner's "new paradigm" work asserts, mainline churches that are sensitive to their surroundings and responsive to their market can and will thrive in American religious culture (Warner, 1993:1057). My study does not attempt a grand new theory but seeks to understand the complexity of the situation in which the liberal Protestant church finds itself. As the chapter on Buchanan makes clear, since congregants use any number of institutional affiliations to construct their identity, any simple analysis that prematurely forecloses an explanation without considering the heterogeneity of modern identity construction does not adequately portray the American religious scene.

Most of the research for this book took place between 1993 and 1996 while I was a part-time minister on the staff of the Fourth Presbyterian Church. In a sense I combined an insider's perspective with intense participant observation. I not only observed events and individuals but also at times helped create events and lead individuals in the congregation. Some will undoubtedly think this crosses the line of objective research, but as scholars have come to think in more complex ways about participant observation, most conclude that scholarship is never finally objective or disinterested (Warner, 1988; Rose, 1988; Dorsey, 1995; D. E. Miller, 1997). Aware of my own tendency to give the church the benefit of the doubt, early on I was critical of the church. When I began to share some of my findings with colleagues, many noted a negative tone in my analysis. I have struggled to reach a balance between observation and critique.

My insider status not only forced me to address my own biases but also allowed me to feel and encounter in visceral forms the ethos of Fourth Presbyterian and its leadership. I felt the pressure to perform well in worship leadership and in ministry to individuals and groups within the congregation. There was continual emphasis on reaching a high level of excellence in every aspect of the ministry. There was an overwhelming sense that the mission of Fourth Presbyterian was more important than the prerogatives and feelings of individual ministers or members. One therefore had to go along with the vision of the pastor and his lay leaders or move out of the church. This is not to say that the leadership was heavy-handed; a remarkable amount of freedom was given to individual ministers as long as they attracted numbers for the programs and developed creative curriculum that was sensitive to the mission of the church to reach out to those with less—to be, in the words of Fourth Presbyterian's mission statement, a "light in the city." To be sure, this ethos was daunting at times but in the main invigorating; mediocrity was not acceptable. This intense pressure to succeed had the earmarks of an Anglo-American institution but also the feeling of a city, Chicago—a city that works or, in the words of Chicago's poet Carl Sandburg, the "City of the Big Shoulders" (Mayer and Wade, 1969; Sandburg, 1994:1). Fourth Presbyterian would be a church of the big shoulders that works—as we witness throughout the history of Fourth Presbyterian in the twentieth century.

This study differs from Becker and Eiesland's ethnography in that history is an integral part of the book. The major focus of the research was Fourth Presbyterian's voluminous archival material covering the church in the twentieth century. In the archival search I examined the church's newsletter, the minutes of session meetings, bulletins, and the pastors' personal papers. A content analysis of each of the pastors' sermons located the themes and social issues directly related to social and symbolic boundaries. To gain a wider context for the church's history, I reviewed research on Chicago's political, cultural, philanthropic, and religious history. This provided a backdrop for understanding the broader picture of social boundaries of the city and how and in what ways Fourth Presbyterian interacted with, responded to, and expressed these changing social boundaries.

In the chapter on the contemporary period my research became more ethnographic in the classic sense of semidirected interviews with present and former clergy; relatives of the former head pastors; lay leadership of the church, some of whom were members during the tenures of Stone, Anderson, and Davies; professional and volunteer leadership in the social outreach departments of the church; and laypeople from various periods of the twentieth century. With rare exceptions I have maintained the interviewees' anonymity, except for the senior ministers of Fourth Presbyterian.

I conducted a church survey of Fourth Presbyterian in April 1994 as a part of my work on the Buchanan era. Questionnaires were distributed to a random sample of 684 congregants from age twenty on up. The sample return was 317, a return rate of 46 percent. The survey was an eight-page, self-administered questionnaire, which included demographic information, questions about the individual's church and religious life as well as religious beliefs, and inquires into the respondent's social and political opinions (see Appendix A).

Throughout the research I reflected on how Fourth Presbyterian fit in the larger picture of twentieth-century American religion. This involved under-

standing the various rhythms, patterns, and growth of the Protestant mainline in the twentieth century. This is discussed more specifically in chapter 1,
which provides background for placing Fourth Presbyterian in the wider terrain of American religion.

NOTES

1. The Near North Side of Chicago is the area north of the Chicago River running
up to North Avenue. The Gold Coast is a part of the Near North Side, east of State Street
to Lake Michigan and north of Chicago Avenue to North Avenue.

2. The best recent critical study of Niebuhr's model of Christ and culture is Stassen,
Yeager, and Yoder (1996). Yoder's essay in particular is a provocative critique of
Niebuhr's bias toward the model of Christ transforming culture. Yeager offers a perspective similar to my own in that she maintains Niebuhr's study needs the complement of a more precise understanding of power structures and their interaction with
culture.

3. Michèle Lamont's study of cultural and moral boundaries in contemporary
American and French culture was particularly helpful in shaping my own work on
social and symbolic boundaries (Lamont, 1992:1–24).

4. It is difficult to be exact in defining liberal and conservative Protestantism because
there is a wide spectrum of belief and action across these ideological lines. For this
study, however, I define a liberal Protestant as one that takes seriously but not literally
the Scripture and the tradition's creeds, emphasizes the importance of inclusiveness
in membership, and acts out one's beliefs through service to others. A conservative
Protestant church makes the Scripture central and interprets it literally; it is a church
that seeks to evangelize others by asking them to believe in Jesus Christ as Savior; it is
more exacting in its creedal demands; and it tends to act out the gospel with a stronger emphasis on traditional personal morality, in contrast to stressing the need for
social justice.

5. Lamont asserts that modern cultural boundaries are not tightly bound, particularly in modern American society. The social mobility of the upper middle class and
the wide range of cultural status signals that it uses effect little consensus in terms of
high-status markers. Consequently there is less potential for the reification of a set of
status signs and emblems to shape the stratification of groups (Lamont, 1992:178).

6. A status group, as Max Weber defines it, is a group that has common interests and
values, that is, a specific "style of life" (Weber, 1978:932).

7. The Presbyterian Church has experienced several schisms in its history in the
United States. The most significant was between the southern and northern Presbyterian churches in 1861. In the following years the southern church was called the Presbyterian Church U.S., and the northern church was known as the Presbyterian Church

U.S.A. In 1958 the Presbyterian Church U.S.A. united with the United Presbyterian Church of North America to become the United Presbyterian Church U.S.A. Following the 1983 reunion between the northern and southern churches, the church was renamed the Presbyterian Church (U.S.A.). See Appendix B for a short history of Presbyterianism in the United States.

1

DEALING WITH DISPLACEMENT: THE PROTESTANT MAINLINE IN THE TWENTIETH CENTURY

I have suggested earlier that much contemporary discussion of "the decline of mainline Protestantism" has been superficial, that historical inspection reveals not so much "decline" as natural, overdue adjustment to the facts of American life. But one can also, of course, raise questions about the extent and genuineness of this adjustment. Has the Protestant establishment now lost its coherence and force, or not?

—William R. Hutchison, *Between the Times: The Travail of the Protestant Establishment in America, 1900–1960,* 1989

IN 1907 A CHICAGO MINISTER, Charles Clayton Morrison, bought a defunct journal that at the turn of the century had been renamed the *Christian Century* (Marty, 1986:164). The name of the journal reflected the optimism of turn-of-the-century modernism and the triumphalist spirit of the Protestant establishment that were so pervasive at the time. The religious leader John Mott spoke of the "evangelization of the world in this generation" (quoted in Marty, 1986:273). The spirit of revival in such evangelists as Dwight L. Moody and Billy Sunday punctuated the air in the early part of the century. This same mood of unlimited capacity suffused John Timothy Stone. Stone had been successful in each of his previous pastorates and was primed to lead Fourth Presbyterian. Fourth Presbyterian had plateaued in membership, even though some of the biggest names in Chicago worshiped there. During Stone's tenure Fourth Presbyterian's membership tripled. Similar growth was not uncommon in Protestant churches across the country. New ventures in mission and evangelism produced results wherever the gospel was preached. Fourth Presbyterian embodied the rapid expansion and exuberant optimism of the Protestant mainline establishment at that time. In this early part of the twentieth century it appeared as if it would be the Christian century.

Not only was the twentieth century to be the Christian century, but it was to be the Protestant century. William Hutchison, in his *Between the Times: The Travail of the Protestant Establishment in America, 1900–1960*, summarizes the ebb and flow of the Protestant establishment in these early decades. Hutchison does not define the Protestant establishment per se, but its power is illustrated in his historical overview of the personal network of Protestant establishment leaders in church, politics, and culture. To be sure, early in the twentieth century the Protestant establishment had an exaggerated sense of its own power. At the same time, its political, cultural, and social muscle was quite real, and its membership outpaced that of other religious groups. Protestant leaders dominated ecumenical and mission forums across the world, even though its membership garnered less than 50 percent of the U.S. population and it was a minority religion internationally (Hutchison, 1989:4–5). These establishment denominations included Congregationalists, Episcopalians, Presbyterians, and the white divisions of the Baptist and Methodist churches. They made up close to 90 percent of the leadership of the National Council of Churches and other major ecumenical bodies (Hutchison, 1989:4). Moreover, early in the century a similar high proportion of the "Who's Who" in American society came from these major Protestant denominations. Protestants were thus overrepresented in America's cultural elite, and their power to influence American culture was quite real.[1]

E. Digby Baltzell defines the Protestant establishment in his classic work *The Protestant Establishment: Aristocracy and Caste in America*. Baltzell's definition is cultural rather than specifically religious and in this way is more helpful. According to Baltzell, the Protestant establishment gained its power because of its influence in maintaining and shaping cultural norms, a political ethos, and a powerful religious culture. Baltzell defines the elite (the establishment) as those who have risen to the top of their professional groups. This does not mean they are morally superior, but they form a ruling class or status group that leads in culture, politics, economics, and the church. For Baltzell an aristocracy is an "open" class that is constantly infused with new elites who come from diverse classes and racial-ethnic backgrounds. In contrast a caste system is dominated by a ruling class that is closed to individuals with talent and is based on arbitrary categories of gender, class, and race (Baltzell, 1964:333). Baltzell's thesis is that the stability and strength of a democratic society depends on whether the social boundaries of the ruling class are open or closed. Baltzell's fear was that by the early 1960s the establishment had become a caste and that it had precipitated a revolt against all forms of excellence and aristocracy he thought necessary for the health of a liberal democracy.

The idea of a cultural and religious establishment in the United States has always engendered intense debate because of the populist undercurrents in American democracy (Hatch, 1989). Some, for instance C. Kirk Hadaway and David A. Roozen, assert that the very notion of a Protestant establishment is antithetical in American religious culture: "It is not possible to be THE church for a pluralistic society that does not permit an established church. Established churches have a taken-for-granted quality" (Hadaway and Roozen, 1995:93). To be sure, the nineteenth century brought the final legal disestablishment of American churches; in 1833 Massachusetts was the last state to cease its state support of religious activities (Hammond, 1992). Churches were forced to compete in an open religious market. More mainline churches had to contend with sectlike religious movements led by independent and entrepreneurial leaders of the early nineteenth century (Hatch, 1989). According to Hadaway and Roozen, "These religious movements compelled the loyalty of followers by creating their own plausibility structures regardless of encompassing cultural sanctions" (Hadaway and Roozen, 1995:93).[2] Nonetheless, by the late nineteenth and early twentieth century, most mainline churches were enormously successful in their ability to be taken for granted as *the* religious institutions in American society.

This cultural establishment would not hold, however. As Robert Handy points out, a second disestablishment came in the 1920s (Handy, 1984:159–84). Up to this time the Protestant establishment made powerful claims on the cultural life of America. Moreover, Protestant leadership pervaded cultural affairs; built hospitals, orphanages, schools, and colleges; and generally shaped the American economic, social, and political terrain. But in the 1920s, with Catholic immigration and changing style and tastes, Protestants were pushed back on their heels (Hammond, 1992; Ernst, 1987). During the 1930s and 1940s the country experienced the depression and World War II. The 1950s featured an explosion in church building and membership growth, but the Protestant establishment would never again set America's cultural norms and values. Phillip Hammond, in his *Religion and Personal Autonomy: The Third Disestablishment in America* (1992), suggests that in the last thirty years a third disestablishment occurred, which entailed a shift away from "collective-expressiveness" and the importance of "primary groups" to an emphasis on "personal autonomy" and the development of "secondary identity groups." Put simply, individuals pick and choose as they create their identity, and they feel less obligated to group norms. The church is no longer pivotal in shaping their sense of self in the community.

The changes in American culture displaced the Protestant establishment.

Protestantism had to adapt to the culture rather than set the culture's vision. The impact on Fourth Presbyterian is clear in the ethnographic chapter on the contemporary period, when church membership remains strong but is clearly influenced by the ethos of personal autonomy. Because members are motivated by intense personal preferences, the church must be particularly sensitive to the needs of its congregants. These waves of disestablishment paralleled and perhaps partly instigated the tensions in the Protestant mainline. Fractures in the unity of the early century became evident in the modernist-fundamentalist controversy of the 1920s.

CRACKS IN THE PROTESTANT MAINLINE CONSENSUS

The modernist-fundamentalist debate disrupted the general consensus of the Protestant mainline. The conflict arose among the elites of the Protestant establishment when conservatives began to resist the incipient accommodation to the cultural milieu. The conservative ideology pushed for greater dogmatic purity; moderates agreed on the essentials yet were less demanding in how beliefs would be negotiated. It is neither helpful nor accurate to use the contemporary dichotomy of liberal-conservative to describe the modernist-fundamentalist controversy. In the early part of the century most Protestants agreed on the standards of moral behavior; the moral ethos of early twentieth-century American culture was conservative and laced with the tonality of America's Puritan past. The conflict in the Protestant mainline centered on the authority and interpretation of Scripture and the degree to which standards of belief would be enforced. In particular it focused on the extent to which the historical/critical method of interpretation would be used in analyzing the Bible. For conservatives, such as J. Gresham Machen, the laissez-faire attitude of liberals toward Scripture and their willingness to question the authority of Scripture were anathema to the faith. Machen, who taught at Princeton Theological Seminary, judged Christian liberalism as heresy.[3]

In 1910 the Presbyterian Church adopted the "five points" of fundamentalism: the inerrancy of the Bible; the virgin birth of Christ; Christ's substitutional atonement; Christ's bodily resurrection; and the authenticity of miracles. These essentials of faith were confirmed over the next fifteen years in the Presbyterian Church. Machen would not tolerate any deviation from them. When Harry Emerson Fosdick, a Baptist preaching at the First Presbyterian Church in New York City in the early 1920s, continued to flout certain of these fundamentals, Machen attacked. Fosdick never changed his mind, and he was forced

to leave the church. Most Protestants would not go as far as Machen in enforc-
ing the fundamentals. In 1924 moderates and many conservatives in the Presbyterian Church gathered and signed the Auburn Affirmation, which affirmed
the five points but allowed for alternative formulas for explaining these doctrines and called for toleration in the denomination. During the next several
general assemblies Machen's contentions were refuted (Balmer and Fitzmier,
1993:191–93; Longfield, 1991:128–61).

The controversy divided American Protestantism. Until then there was a
theological consensus in mainline churches and in the Protestant establishment that produced and supported a conservative and evangelical perspective.
Protestants who were modernists or progressives on theological issues upheld
the social and moral norms of the evangelical camp. Henry Sloane Coffin,
president emeritus of Union Theological Seminary and the arch enemy of
many fundamentalists and evangelicals, wrote in 1947, "Evangelicalism without liberalisms' open mind and constant search for truth becomes obscuran-
tist." At the same time, he asserted, "Liberalism without evangelicalism leaves
the Church impotent and her members chill in heart" (quoted in Wuthnow,
1988:141). For much of the first half of the twentieth century the liberal-conservative divide was less a chasm than a quarrel in the family. By midcentury,
however, the two sides grew further apart, and the conflict became a matter
of two clans in different camps with growing theological differences.

In the 1930s and 1940s open conflicts decreased, but confusion reigned in
American Protestantism. Many commented on the flaccid character of the
churches and the general disarray of the Protestant mission. Much of the en-
thusiasm for mission and service disappeared by the late 1920s. The Student
Volunteer Movement, the Sunday School Movement, the Men and Religion
Forward Movement, and the Interchurch World Movement lost much of their
energy, money, and recruits (Handy, 1984:178). Of course, this was partly because of the depression and World War II. Culturally, however, the mood of
the American people had changed. The rallies of Dwight Moody and Billy
Sunday ceased, and there were few populist Christian figures to take their place.
In the 1940s a new energy spurred the evangelical movement, marked by the
inauguration of the National Association of Evangelicals in 1942, the rise of
Billy Graham throughout the decade, and the opening of the nondenominational Fuller Seminary in Pasadena, California, in 1947. Evangelicalism, which
had always been a part of the Protestant mainline, now beget its own separate
institutions and began to make its presence known in the wider arena of
American religion (Marty, 1996).

A DECENTERED PROTESTANT ESTABLISHMENT

To be sure, the vestiges of the Protestant establishment remained a powerful force in American culture and religion. In 1948 *Time* magazine ran feature articles on the Methodist bishop G. Bromley Oxnam, the Presbyterian John Foster Dulles, and the renowned American theologian Reinhold Niebuhr. They were all associated in one way or another with the World Council of Churches. At the same time, questions about the place of Protestantism in American culture were being explicitly asked. The earlier consensus of the Protestant mainline dissipated. On the one hand, such figures as the Niebuhr brothers called for greater involvement in social justice ministries. They came out early in support of the civil rights movement. This emphasis on social justice infiltrated many mainline bureaucracies by the early 1960s. Eugene Carson Blake, a Presbyterian minister who was stated clerk of the United Presbyterian Church U.S.A. in the late 1950s and general secretary of the World Council of Churches in the 1960s, became a pivotal leader for mainline churches in the civil rights movement (Balmer and Fitzmier, 1993:130–31). On the other hand, in the 1940s and 1950s new church development in the suburbs burgeoned as the mainline sought to keep pace with the baby boomer generation (Bullock, 1991). These new buildings were built in anticipation of the large numbers of young people who were coming of age. In 1958 Fourth Presbyterian completed the Westminster House for students. The irony is that this building was never used for students, a dilemma mirrored across the country as young people began to move out of the church. Moreover, new church development in the Presbyterian Church U.S.A. decreased dramatically as resources were funneled into inner city ministries (Bullock, 1991).

The mainline Protestants faced a double dilemma. New church development anticipated the growth of churches based on the baby boomer generation. These suburban churches, however, failed to retain their young people and were unprepared to deal with the turbulent cultural changes of the 1960s (Hoge, Johnson, and Luidens, 1994). Liberals, who by the 1960s were a part of mainline bureaucracies, pushed their progressive programs based on racial reconciliation and social justice. They came up against more conservative laypeople and in time lost membership and funding. One of the most provocative examples was the dispute over the $10,000 grant from the Emergency Fund for Legal Aid of the General Assembly for the trial of Angela Davis in 1968. Conservatives complained bitterly over the support of a "communist" and forced the blacks in the Presbyterian leadership circles to reimburse the church out of their personal resources (Wilmore, 1990). This trend announced the growing alienation between conservative congregants and the leadership of the Presbyterian denomination—analyzed in Jeffrey Hadden's aptly titled book *The Gathering Storm in the Churches* (1969). During this difficult era Fourth Presbyterian embodied the conservative response to church hierarchy. Elam Davies described the pronouncements of the General Assembly of the Presbyterian Church (U.S.A.) as "meaningless rhetoric, with little relevance to the local churches " (Davies Interview, December 10, 1993).

This double dilemma dislodged an earlier consensus in American Protestantism and in the Protestant establishment. The implicit agreement on the importance of evangelism dissipated as new agendas began to compete for limited mission dollars. Some wanted to fund inner city justice ministries, while others fought for new church development and moneys to send missionaries overseas. Earlier in the twentieth century agreement on personal morality and the church's mission transcended differences and enabled the Protestant mainline to present a unified front, but by the 1960s the ideological differences over mission emphases and the direction of financial resources created a fissure in the mainline churches that continued into the 1990s.

MEMBERSHIP AND AN OPEN RELIGIOUS MARKET

This lack of unity over mission coincided with a decline in church membership. Even as mainline church membership reached an all-time high in the 1950s, growth in mainline and evangelical Protestant churches barely kept pace with the growth of the U.S. population (Roozen, 1993). The decline in the mid-1960s was thus part of a trend that had commenced much earlier. Not only did liberal and moderate Protestant churches lose members in the 1960s, but also conservative Protestants plateaued. The only exceptions in the Protestant family were the Pentecostal/Holiness churches, which grew tremendously in the 1960s and 1970s but declined precipitously in the 1980s. Membership trends improved somewhat for moderate, liberal, and conservative Protestants in the decades following the 1960s, but this increase has lagged far below the growth of the U.S. population. The Roman Catholics led the way in growth, though this expansion can be partly attributed to recent immigrants (Roozen, 1993).

Conservative Protestants are players in American politics and culture. They have not, however, achieved the hegemony of the early Protestant establishment. Conservative Christian interest groups have failed to enforce or persuade large pluralities of the American population to the conservative political and cultural norms that they represent. In the contemporary period no one is able to dominate the center, neither the Christian Right nor the Protestant mainline. The Protestant camp is split into diverse camps that compete in a deregulated religious market, a market in which consumers rule according to the nature of their preferences, making stability a thing of the past for religious institutions.

Two court cases in the early 1960s became emblematic of the decentering of Protestant culture. Protestants could no longer expect civil society to promote and uphold the language of Protestant Christianity. In 1962 in *Engel v. Vital* (370 U.S. 421) the Supreme Court rejected as unconstitutional a prayer prepared by the New York State Board of Regents for use in school. The Supreme Court judged it to be a religious ceremony in a public institution and an act of establishing religion. A similar blow to the cultural foundation of Protestantism came a year later in the case of *Abington Township School District v. Schempp* (374 U.S. 203). The verdict invalidated a Pennsylvania law requiring the reading of ten verses from Scripture without comment, finding that its primary purpose was to promote religion (Handy, 1984:194).

With these decisions the Supreme Court removed the final civil underpinnings of cultural Protestantism. Public Protestantism ceased to be the de facto religion of American public life. Children were now *protected* from the influences of the Judeo-Christian tradition. The decision extracted the Protestant tradition from the center of American public discourse. Needless to say, the separation made religion, specifically Christianity, less taken for granted. Religion became an option for the general populace and less woven into the fabric of public pronouncements and common culture.

THE STRICTNESS DEBATE: EXPLAINING DECLINE

The analysis of the decline of the Protestant mainline church is a cottage industry in contemporary literature on American Protestantism. Study after study attempts to pinpoint how and why the Protestant mainline has fallen on hard times. There is little doubt that the nearly 30 percent loss of membership over the last thirty years just in the Presbyterian Church alone is noteworthy. Authors, however, have used the fact to pursue their own ideological agendas. The book by Thomas Reeves, *The Empty Church: The Suicide of Liberal Christianity* (1996), is emblematic of the Christian Right's attempt to blame the so-called sagging morals of the nation on the liberalization of the Protestant mainline. Reeves reported on polls that showed that Americans see the nation in severe moral decline. Reeves noted that this perception parallels the rise of liberal Christianity (Reeves, 1996:3). The book is a variation on the Puritan jeremiad, a type of sermonic essay that draws a connection between people's immoral behavior, the loss of religious dedication, and the consequent wrath of God. For Reeves the liberal church has caused the decline of American morality and the increase in violent and antisocial behavior.

Conservatives are not alone in designating the causes of Protestant decline. Liberal critics blame liberal Christianity for its inability to create a unique political and religious identity. Benton Johnson's provocative essay in 1982, "End of Another Era," criticized the Protestant church for its failed liberal agenda, an agenda that had stumbled into supporting a bourgeois political program. In 1994 Dean Hoge, Benton Johnson, and Donald A. Luidens published *Vanishing Boundaries: The Religion of Mainline Protestant Baby Boomers*, which analyzed Presbyterian baby boomers who had been confirmed in the church and subsequently left in record numbers as they became adults. They blamed this exodus partly on the vagueness of liberal theology and its inability to stimulate members to maintain their Christian belief system or to bring others into the Christian community.

Another popular rationale for the decline of liberal Protestant churches came from Dean Kelley's 1972 work, *Why Conservative Churches Are Growing*. He asserted that "*strong* churches (that is growing religious organizations) support absolutist creedal systems and demand discipline and strict conformity in belief and practice. *Weak* churches, on the other hand, are relativistic, encouraging diversity and individualism" (Kelley, 1972:78). This strict-church thesis was heatedly debated in the 1970s and lost steam in the early 1980s. It was reinvigorated by Roger Finke and Rodney Stark in their 1992 study, *The Churching of America, 1776–1990: Winners and Losers in Our Religious Economy*. Finke and Stark asserted that complacency set in following the success of mainline churches in the early twentieth century. The Protestant mainline lost its evangelistic drive, accommodated to liberal culture, relativized its beliefs, and failed to inspire and retain the loyalty of its congregants (Finke and Stark, 1992).[4] The gist of the argument is that churches that make firm creedal demands create the strongest religious institutions (Iannaccone, 1994).[5]

This strictness thesis was challenged by more recent research indicating that the largest numerical growth for religious institutions took place when religious standards were weakened (Holifield, 1994).[6] Moreover, Hadaway and Roozen argued, "*Strong churches are demanding*, but they are not strong *because* they are demanding. This change of emphasis, from the demands of a denomination to its *character*, or *strength*, eliminates the dilemma created by Dean Kelley and perpetuated by Roger Finke and Rodney Stark" (Hadaway and Roozen, 1995:104). That is, demands in themselves are not what make churches grow or what bring religious institutions their vitality; it is the constitution and identity of a church that creates a compelling vision and thus engages the loyalty of congregants.

This strong institutional identity can be conservative or liberal in theology. In either case a vision is provided, listeners become followers, and membership increases. Donald Luidens in his "Numbering the Presbyterian Branches: Membership Trends since Colonial Times" interpreted the numbers from the perspective of American religious history. He looked specifically at the Presbyterian Church but compared it with other mainline denominations. He came up with a more complex set of explanations that moved the argument away from ideological horizons and toward a more nuanced understanding of the vagaries of membership growth and decline. Luidens claimed that denominational growth over the last several centuries has fluctuated somewhat unpredictably across mainline denominations. He asserted that no one explanation can be used to elucidate periods of decline or growth because there are simply too many variables and too much unpredictability. Moreover, Luidens showed that, contrary to Kelley's thesis, strictness, at least in the conservative branches of the Presbyterian Church, has led not to growth but in several cases to decline. The old axiom that the drop in Sunday school attendance foreshadows the loss of membership by roughly five years has proven true in short-term analyses, but over the long-term it, too, is not a predictive instrument: "While Sunday school enrollment is probably related to the vitality of a church, it is a very weak predictor of long-range denominational fortunes" (Luidens, 1990:62). Luidens reflected on the fact that the decline in membership is taken as the critical indicator of denominational health and yet in virtually every mainline denomination there has been steady growth in the per capita level of contributions to church causes. Finally, schismatic episodes over the course of church history have not shown to precipitate decline: "In sum, the larger Presbyterian branches have been little affected by schism. For them, the issue of dramatic growth and decline has been directly related to mergers" (Luidens, 1990:63). That is, mergers within denominational groups lead to more dramatic moments of decline or growth.

Luidens's article is helpful in clearing away the ideological biases that are used to interpret the decline or growth of large denominations. The most reliable and coherent book on the subject is C. Kirk Hadaway and David Roozen's 1993 edited volume, *Church and Denominational Growth*. The book specified the reasons for growth or decline by looking at mainline and conservative churches across the United States. They found that both external and internal factors are critical to the growth of a congregation. External factors include the church's neighborhood and whether it is growing; internal ingredients relate to the general health of the institution as an educational facility, the church's commitment to reaching out to new members, and the quality of the preaching. Hadaway's concluding essay, "Church Growth in North America: Religious Marketplace," was far from sanguine about liberal Protestantism. Most liberal Protestant congregants are "consumer-oriented" in their choice of churches. That is, they have no loyalty to denomination; they choose a church almost entirely on the basis of its appeal to their tastes and perceived needs. Conservative Christians are more committed to their churches in the long term, but they still base their choices on their interests.

Hadaway painted a picture of Americans that shows them in an open marketplace, in which tradition and historical loyalties are losing any relevance in the choice of a religious institution. The entrepreneurial aspect of ministry therefore becomes even more important in attracting "customers." Just as the Protestant mainline has been decentered, the church in the United States has been deregulated, monopolies are a thing of the past, and free agency rules the day. As Hadaway put it, "Obviously some churches will be more successful than others in a deregulated religious economy. The research in this book tells us that evangelistic churches are most likely to grow. It also tells us that growth is rapid in new churches and large entrepreneurial congregations. The religious consumer wants a friendly, warm, caring church where he or she can worship God in a meaningful way" (Hadaway, 1993:356). That is, what makes or breaks a religious institution is not whether the belief system has dogmatic principles but whether the religious beliefs are meaningful and provide a sense of identity to individuals in the congregation.

Not only have many Americans become fickle in their choices of churches, but also fewer are attending worship. In a 1996 survey the Princeton Religion Research Center showed that on average 38 percent of the population attended worship, down five points since 1995 and the lowest level since 1940 (*Presbyterian Outlook*, April 28, 1997). Moreover, Americans no longer attach spirituality solely to the church or religion. Wade Clark Roof's 1993 study of baby boomers, *A Generation of Seekers: The Spiritual Journeys of the Baby Boom Generation*, points in this direction, as does Alan C. Klaas's recent book, *Faith in an Unchurched Society:*

> In an unchurched society, most unchurched people have separated the miracle of faith from the act of congregational participation. Virtually all research on attitudes of unchurched people has yielded the same findings. Between 70 percent and 85 percent of unchurched people identify religion as important or very im-

portant in their lives. Between 40 percent and 60 percent of unchurched people report praying to God daily or weekly. These people identify themselves as having faith but choose not to participate in a congregation. (Klaas, 1996:4)

FOURTH PRESBYTERIAN AND THE LAY LIBERAL NICHE

The evidence for the decline of the Protestant mainline church is pervasive. Studies on liberal Protestant churches indicate significant declines in membership beginning in the 1950s and 1960s and a partial leveling off in the 1970s and 1980s (Hoge and Roozen, 1979; Roozen, 1993). The guiding assumption in this research is that liberal Protestantism is an ailing religious form. Not only has liberal Protestantism collapsed, but also congregations whose members were in the highest socioeconomic status were the most likely to decline in church membership during the 1960s and 1970s. According to Wade Clark Roof and William McKinney, "Careful analysis of membership trends shows that the churches hardest hit were those highest in socioeconomic status, those stressing individualism and pluralism in belief, and those most affirming of American culture" (Roof and McKinney, 1987:20).

Nonetheless, the argument against the strict-church thesis is that strong churches, regardless of their ideological perspective, are founded on a distinctive identity and thus are able to attract and maintain members. The ideological debate is in some sense a false screen and not an accurate indicator of decline or growth. American culture through the twentieth century has become more pluralistic and less amenable to religious monopolies. It was therefore inevitable that the Protestant mainline would fail to sustain its status and its influence in the wider culture. The Protestant mainline has struggled to come to terms with its own decentered position in the culture, but it must now compete along with other religious institutions for followers and members, and there is little social reinforcement for those who attend Protestant mainline churches. Fourth Presbyterian has managed to weather this decentering process. It has done so by creating a distinctive church identity, an identity constructed in the tradition of liberal Protestantism. The church has understood the need for adaptation in the midst of momentous cultural changes and the consequent shift in the place of the Protestant mainline in American society.

There is no simple formula for growth, such as a high-demand ethos with a popular style of worship, that will bring large numbers into the church. Fourth Presbyterian is a church that is addressing the needs of many Americans who struggle with meaning and purpose in the midst of a pluralistic culture. Despite the media's focus on conservative churches, most Americans are "lay liberals" in their theological orientation.[7] Lay liberalism means that they attend church for a sense of transcendence but have little denominational loyalty or need for strict doctrine; they also seek an outlet for their charitable giving (Ammerman, 1997a). Moreover, the characteristics of lay liberals describe many of the so-called unchurched Americans. Fourth Presbyterian, particularly in its contemporary incarnation, is a lay liberal Protestant church that attracts these kinds of individuals and counters the claim that lay liberalism is an equation for decline (see, for example, Hoge, Johnson, and Luidens, 1994).

In the first half of the century Fourth Presbyterian was an evangelical Protestant church. In the early part of the century the church mirrored the wider Protestant establishment that was moderately evangelical in tone. By mid-century Fourth Presbyterian took a more public role in advocating for civic righteousness in the city, and in the second half of the twentieth century it became a liberal Protestant church.[8] The demand for theological purity was stronger in the early part of the century; in the second half of the century the priorities of social righteousness and care for those less fortunate became more prominent. Congregants in the 1990s were challenged to transgress social boundaries and reach beyond class comfort zones. Nonetheless, over the course of the twentieth century Fourth Presbyterian has represented a Protestant mainline church slowly losing its hold on the center of power in Chicago and in the nation, and yet it has been able to adapt to these national trends in creative ways leading to institutional stability. The patterns of Fourth Presbyterian's accommodation and resistance to the Gold Coast culture have changed during the century. How its theological symbolic boundaries have interacted with the social and cultural boundaries of the Gold Coast, its urban setting, and the wider Protestant church is at the heart of this study of the Fourth Presbyterian Church.

NOTES

1. The Protestant mainline denominations maintain a similarly disproportionate representation in our contemporary governmental organizations. From 1789 to 1992, 55 of 112 U.S. Supreme Court justices were either Episcopalians or Presbyterians. The 104th Congress (1995–97) contained 68 Baptists (many of whom were from mainline Baptist denominations), 63 Methodists, 63 Episcopalians, and 59 Presbyterians out of a total of 435 congressional representatives (Reeves 1996:2). Ralph Pyle's recent work, *Persistence and Change in the Protestant Establishment* (1996), provides further evidence for a contemporary continuity of powerful influence.

2. In the Troeltschian tradition religious movements become sects if they withdraw from the world; they become denominations when they accommodate to the ethos of the culture (Troeltsch, 1931).

3. Machen attacked the mainline, particularly Christian liberalism, for what he considered its complete accommodation to modern culture (Machen, 1923).

4. Finke and Stark use a rational-choice model of human nature in their research. This "exchange" perspective asserts that human beings make choices on the basis of costs and benefits. Since religion is a "collectively produced commodity" and a "risky good," it needs social proof to make the prize worth the risk. Otherworldly rewards, forms of religious stigma, and sacrifice are the most potent factors to attract followers and develop institutional loyalty (Finke and Stark, 1992:250–55).

5. Roger Stark and Rodney Finke have argued that greater religious pluralism increases church adherence (Finke and Stark, 1988, 1989, 1992; Finke, 1990, 1992, 1997; Finke, Guest, and Stark, 1996; Stark, Finke, and Iannaccone, 1995; Stark, 1997), but Daniel Olson demonstrates this argument is flawed (Olson, [1999]). Olson asserts that Stark and Finke's thesis is based on a calculation error in one of their statistics and is plagued by a multicollinearity problem in their overall equations. Judith R. Blau, Kenneth C. Land, and Kent Redding also dispute Stark and Finke's findings that pluralism actually increases church adherence (Blau, Land, and Redding, 1992; Blau, Redding, and Land, 1993). This debate is explored further in comment and reply by Daniel Olson, Roger Finke, and Rodney Stone (Olson, Finke, and Stark, 1998). At the same time, Olson admits that his point does not contradict other claims Finke, Stark, and others make about the effects of regulation, market share, and competition in the religious environment. Finke, Stark, and Iannaccone have argued persuasively that greater religious regulation decreases religious involvement; that where there is a monopoly of market share (that is, a dominant religious group), member commitment levels tend to decrease; and that where competition is particularly fierce among religious groups, all groups work harder to recruit and retain members (Finke and Stark, 1988, 1992; Stark, Finke, and Iannaccone, 1995; Stark and Iannaccone, 1996; Stark, 1998).

6. E. Brooks Holifield provides evidence that it was only after the admission of "halfway members" into the Puritan churches of New England and the easing of standards for Baptists and Methodists in the eighteenth century that the tremendous rates of church growth were achieved in the nineteenth century (Holifield, 1994).

7. In a June 1996 survey of the American people the Pew Research Center for the People and the Press found that half of all Americans were either white nonevangelical Protestants or white Catholics. These groups are remarkably similar in their religious and political perspectives. They both take moderate views on religious belief, the interpretation of Scripture, and politics (Pew Research Center for the People and the Press, 1996).

8. Liberal Protestantism is commonly interpreted as an internally secularizing tradition. That is, it absorbs modern cultural forms and relativizes theological belief structures as it accommodates to the rationalization of modernity. Ed Farley asserts that

Christian theology has always done this; the Reformed tradition's strength is its ability to adapt and transcend cultural models: "Christianity as a type of religious faith is especially open to both cultural and critical modernism, because of its conviction that no specific cultural form, nation, ethnicity, or gender is necessary to salvation prompts it to appropriate a great variety of cultural forms and worldviews" (Farley, 1990:135). Farley argues that the internal essence of the Reformed tradition does not change but that the theology used to interpret it is modifiable, revisable, open to new information, able to celebrate difference, and social in character (Farley, 1990: 137). Theological change thus does not equal secularization but is a constitutive element in the maintenance of the tradition.

2

THE CULTURAL PROTESTANT CHURCH, 1908–28

Churches mean nothing—people for the most part simply don't go. Certain of them are more or less "fashionable," though, and if one does go it is to St. James, St. Chrysostom's, or to the Fourth Presbyterian.

—Harvey Warren Zorbaugh, *The Gold Coast and the Slum: A Sociological Study of Chicago's Near North Side,* [1929] 1983

HARVEY WARREN ZORBAUGH'S comment, based on his classic ethnographic study of the Near North Side in the early 1920s, though overdrawn was already pointing to the decentered nature of the Protestant establishment. There is little doubt that Fourth Presbyterian had a powerful influence on its social setting. Nonetheless, toward the end of John Timothy Stone's ministry, the telltale signs of Protestant mainline decline were evident. Thus we witness both the story of a Protestant virtuoso, John Timothy Stone, who mastered his cultural domain, and the way in which Stone and his leadership adapted to and resisted the early displacement of the Protestant mainline in American culture.

Stone exemplified the establishment ruling class of his time. He had the ability to blend with this high-status group, and in the process he motivated them to become evangelists, missionaries, advocates for civic reform, and philanthropists for the cause of the church. Stone and Fourth Presbyterian's leadership confirmed and expressed the establishment boundaries of the Gold Coast, the wealthiest neighborhood in metropolitan Chicago, but in subtle ways they also contested the status quo.

Social inequality was a potent force on the Gold Coast in the 1920s. It affected Fourth Presbyterian by shaping the cultural and aesthetic sensibilities the church used to attract its Gold Coast congregation. Even as Stone conformed to the tastes of his cultural milieu, however, he consistently spoke against class interests by imploring his congregation *not* to give their inheritance to their children but to support the church and its mission to the world.

Stone, a nineteenth-century American evangelical, believed that the church's role was to bring individuals into a personal relationship with Jesus Christ. Progress was the Christianization of the Near North Side and the world. It was the Christ of culture, baptizing and transforming the social and symbolic forms of the Protestant establishment in the name of Jesus Christ. The church and Stone's leadership embodied a cultural Protestantism with little pronounced tension between it and its social setting. Stone used the symbols of business to communicate the gospel to his culture. In the first half of his Chicago years it proved effective, but by the end of his ministry the culture itself had shifted. The ideal of the Christianization of culture that motivated so many Protestants early in the century began to fade. The strong institutional identity of the church and the structural tension between the maintenance and transgression of social boundaries had to change with the transition in America's cultural priorities. This transformation furnishes early evidence of the passage of the Protestant establishment from the central role it played in the early part of twentieth century to its later peripheral place in the American cultural terrain.

THE SOCIAL BOUNDARIES OF THE
NEAR NORTH SIDE

The Gold Coast

Zorbaugh's *Gold Coast and the Slum* provides a vivid map of the social boundaries of the Near North Side during the 1920s.[1] At that time the Near North Side was demographically divided in thirds, with the Gold Coast to the east, the slum to the west, and the rooming-house area sandwiched in between the two. It was the most heterogeneous community of any in metropolitan Chicago:[2] "The Near North side has the highest residential land values in the city, and among the lowest; it has more professional men, more politicians, more suicides, more persons in 'Who's Who,' than any other 'community' in Chicago" (Zorbaugh, [1929] 1983:6). A distinctively diverse population of people lived and worked in a relatively small area of land. Separate social boundaries gave each community its identity. At the same time, the heterogeneity of the population brought dramatic vitality to the area, and because of the close proximity of diverse groups, boundaries were inevitably crossed and sometimes became permeable. Stone and Fourth Presbyterian's leadership worked to facilitate a creative blending of these class boundaries.

Nonetheless, the social registry class in the Gold Coast population promoted separation and created a bounded zone in which a high-status group practiced its privilege.[3] The Gold Coast area shielded itself from the violence common in certain parts of the city, such as the African American "black belt" of Chicago's South Side and West Side and "Little Italy," an Italian community on the west corridor of the Near North Side, where more than half of the city's murders occurred (Zorbaugh, [1929] 1983:14). This violent culture stood in stark contrast to the calm of the Gold Coast. The social registry group in the Gold Coast community created stiff social boundaries that were strictly enforced:

> It is about these clubs and hotels, these "events" of the season—assemblies, balls, the opera *premiere*, and the Easter parade—that the formal pageant of "society" moves. Invitations to assemblies and to membership in "smart" clubs are necessary plays in the social game. To some, indeed, they are coveted prizes. But within this pageant the "game" goes on for higher stakes: invitations to certain box parties at the opera, certain "dinners of 100" at the Casino, a dinner and dance at the Saddle and Cycle, to meet the Prince of Wales, at which "the heirs to the city's social throne are chosen"; eventual inclusion in the number of those who are recognized as swaying the destinies of the Four Hundred. (Zorbaugh, [1929] 1983:51)

These social boundaries were impenetrable to many, not just those who lived in the rooming-house district or the slum but also most people on the Gold Coast. Just because Fourth Presbyterian was located in the midst of this area *did not* mean that it shared these exclusive boundaries. The church and its leadership were, however, influenced by this social milieu and had to address these sensibilities to attract and challenge those who lived on the Gold Coast.

The Rooming-House District and the Slum

In the early 1920s the rooming-house district had more than a thousand furnished rooms on the Near North Side. More than 23,000 men and women inhabited this area, an area that separated the Gold Coast from the slums to the west. Sixty-two percent of the inhabitants of the area were single; men made up the majority. Most married couples had no children. The majority of the population was between twenty and thirty-five years of age. Zorbaugh portrayed the rooming-house district as inhabited by isolated individuals for whom community was nonexistent: "The rooming-house is a place of anonymous relationships. One knows no one, and is known by no one. One comes and goes as one wishes, does very much as one pleases, and as long as one disturbs no one else, no questions are asked" (Zorbaugh, [1929] 1983:70–75). Social boundaries were individualized, and identity was atomized. This isolation permeated the slum of the Near North Side as well. The intense poverty and lack of financial resources crippled the west section of the Near North Side: "One alien group after another has claimed this slum area. The Irish, the Germans, the Swedish, the Sicilians have occupied it in turn. Now it is being invaded by a migration of the Negro from the south. It has been known successively as Kilgubbin, Little Hell, and, as industry has come in, as Smoky Hollow. The remnants of these various successions have left a sediment that at once characterizes and confuses the life of this district" (Zorbaugh, [1929] 1983:127).

According to Zorbaugh's door-to-door examination of the slum, this social world was marked by disorder, familial deterioration, loneliness, and despair. The social boundaries of the area cohered only because people were limited by poverty and the lack of mobility. In other words, the solidarity was in large part an external factor. Outside forces limited individuals from moving beyond geographic- and class-determined zones.

The Gold Coast, according to Zorbaugh, was the only area with any sense of community solidarity. In Zorbaugh's study social boundaries are necessary for the creation of community, yet he is critical of the Gold Coast and the boundaries produced by this status group. Contrary to Zorbaugh's view that Fourth Presbyterian was inconsequential to the area, I argue that the church acted as a mediating institution between the isolation of the rooming house and the rigidity of the high-status Gold Coast. Moreover, Fourth Presbyterian served the city by giving it a vision of reaching out in service to many on the Near North Side.

THE SYMBOLIC BOUNDARIES OF THE PROTESTANT ESTABLISHMENT

Stone as Protestant Virtuoso

In 1924 the nondenominational journal *Christian Century,* voice of the Protestant mainline, commissioned a survey to determine the most influential preachers of the day. In response to the survey, 20,000 of the 90,000 ballots were returned (Marty, 1991:49). Most of the twenty-five ministers chosen were white, male, mainline Protestants. John Timothy Stone was one of these. Popular among his peers, Stone achieved the status of a Protestant virtuoso. He mastered the technique and personal style of the Protestant establishment, which meant he felt at home in elite company—educationally, socially, and aesthetically. He exercised the privileges of his class not so much to indulge his own pleasures but to use these resources to spread the gospel.

Stone came from five generations of Congregational ministers. His father died when Stone was eighteen, and a group of four businessmen sponsored his education at Amherst College. At Amherst he put his entrepreneurial skills to work in intercollegiate athletics, at the school newspaper as a paid journalist, and in church as a summertime preacher. Professors at Amherst strongly encouraged him to go into business. He had several lucrative offers in business following college but instead went to Auburn Theological Seminary to pursue the ministry (Shepherd, 1923:67). Upon graduation he pastored two churches in New York in quick succession, and then in 1900, at age thirty-two, he was invited to the Brown Memorial Church in Baltimore. He succeeded the nationally known Maltbie Babcock, who had been called to the Brick Church in New York City.

Stone flourished in Baltimore. Many of the nearby Johns Hopkins University professors attended his church. He began his frequent tours of the college circuit. Later in life he said he spoke at more than five hundred colleges and universities in his career, including Yale, Princeton, and Harvard, as well as numerous other educational and private boarding schools. He often spoke of his visits with prominent leaders in the nation and of a friendship with Woodrow Wilson, when Wilson held the presidency of Princeton University from 1902 to 1910.

Stone accepted the call to the Fourth Presbyterian Church in 1908 only after an ardent pursuit by powerful men of the church and in the city of Chicago. When Stone finally took the call, he turned his energy and passion into a building program for Fourth Presbyterian. The program was completed in 1914. In 1913, at the relatively young age of forty-five, he was elected moderator of the General Assembly of the Presbyterian Church U.S.A. Nominated from the floor of the assembly, Stone was surprised by the selection. There were already four candidates for the position, all of whom had been campaigning for months. The assembly unanimously elected Stone despite his own objections. During that year he spoke nearly every evening while traveling five thousand miles but was absent from the Fourth Presbyterian's pulpit only four times.

A series of achievements in the following ten years brought Stone enormous acclaim. He was the army chaplain for Camp Grant in Illinois from the fall of 1917 to the fall of 1918, during World War I. He spoke at the camp four days a week, three to six times each evening, rallying the troops to what he clearly thought was a righteous cause. As the war was ending, the First Presbyterian Church of New York City pursued him, but Stone decided to remain at Fourth Presbyterian.

In 1919 Stone chaired the General Assembly's reorganization commission. In 1922, after three years of intensive effort, the commission succeeded in a complete reorganization of the church's official structures. It reduced the number of boards from sixteen to four. Stone and his committee faced tough opposition, but through the force of Stone's personality and the comprehensive layout of the commission's plan, he won unanimous approval for the reorganization (*The Continent,* May 4, 1922).

In the midst of reorganizing the bureaucracy of the Presbyterian Church, Stone was elected to resident membership in the Union League Club of Chicago in 1919. The Union League Club, the most prestigious club in the city, enjoyed the membership of the most powerful men in the Midwest. It had as honorary members many of the prominent conservative politicians of the first half of the twentieth century, including Theodore Roosevelt, Herbert Hoover, Calvin Coolidge, and, later on, Douglas MacArthur, Dwight Eisenhower, and Robert A. Taft. Stone was the first and only clergy ever nominated for club president (he lost by twelve votes). His nomination in 1920, as the club's history relates, was advanced because of his ability "as an organizer and his sound business judgment," not because of his affiliation with Fourth Presbyterian. The nomination provoked a major conflict in the club since many were worried that Stone was too much of a "Prohibition man" and would reform the club's unofficial policy of continuing to serve alcohol (Grant, 1955:258–59). During this period Stone was chaplain to the 1916 and 1920 Republican national conventions. Needless to say, Stone maintained strong connections with the Protestant political establishment of the time.

A portrait of Stone drawn from a 1923 interview provides insight into the persona of the man:

> At first contact the business side of Dr. Stone is disconcerting. You are speaking with a man of handsome physical aspect, clear-eyed, firm-lipped, hard-headed and outspoken. Coming across him in the business world, in Wall Street, in New York, in the grain exchanges in Chicago or in the shipping business in California, you would know you had encountered a superior business man who was making a success of his life, who was master of his environment and who took leadership when it was not readily granted him. (Shepherd, 1923:67)

A current woman elder of Fourth Presbyterian, who was an active young adult at the church in the last two years of Stone's tenure there, vividly recalled him: "He was a dominating figure and a patriarch. . . . He was very successful at this church. He was successful nationally as well. Because he was a dominant person, things were going to be successful" (Interview, March 30, 1994). Stone, a traditionalist on gender issues, nonetheless taught and supported the Business Woman's Bible Study throughout his pastorate at the church; single working women made up the majority of the group's membership.

The Protestant Establishment Pastor

Stone preached powerfully. He was in constant demand as a speaker, and he received numerous job offers from other churches, some of which were the most prestigious in the nation. These included the Brick Church of New York, the Tenth Presbyterian Church of Philadelphia, and the First Presbyterian Church of Germantown, to name only a few. He was by his own definition a preacher who preached for "decision." His sermons were not tightly reasoned or even theologically sophisticated literary pieces; they were evangelical speeches, aimed at the emotional needs of his hearers and enticing them to follow Christ and to share the gospel.

For Stone the preacher was to be a no-nonsense arbiter of human issues as they related to everyday life. Stone did not explore internal issues, either his congregants' or his own: "I had doubts in seminary days, I have always had them; who has not? But let me ask you this honest question, young man: Who wants to listen to your doubts or mine, anyway? Every man has enough of his own, and what he is trying to do is to get rid of them" (*Fourth Church*, February 1916).[4] There is never a hint of doubt or any real struggle in Stone's sermons or his private writings. They all reflect a self-possessed man who was comfortable with himself and his beliefs about the Christian faith.[5]

Stone went along with the more conservative and evangelical wing of the Presbyterian Church. This meant that he could affirm the "five essential" doctrines that were created by the General Assembly in 1910 and reaffirmed in 1916 and 1923. They became the "famous five points" of contention for Presbyterians in the 1920s (Fitzmier, 1991:87), but Stone refused to enter the theological controversy.

Stone's harshest words were reserved for those whom he thought were doing away with the concept of sin and the reality of God's judgment. These were powerful doctrines, which for him compelled all to repent and created the necessity of God's saving act of sending his son Jesus Christ to die on the cross, as Stone asserted in a November 5, 1932, sermon, "The Confidence of a Firm Faith":

> The man who will not regard law is not a man who is going to be free from the justice of God in his true judgment. There is such a namby-pamby sort of religion floating around us. Its name is legion. It says "Love everybody, and never

mind about justice. Never mind what sin you do. All is forgiven. Just smile and look happy and sin all you want to, and wreck all the homes you want to wreck, and never mind the heathen. Let them die in their heathendom. Just let your religion be the convenient thing. Do what you want to do. If you have to handle mud, put on religious gloves. It is all lovely. Sin is not real anyway. WE only think it exists!" No, it is not! And the generation in which we live is revealing that it is not. Great laws and judgment are eternal. Leave judgment out of religion, out of faith, and we have taken the iron out of the blood which leaves nothing but white corpuscles to live on. (*Fourth Church*, May 1923)

For Stone humanity at its most basic level was created by God and had fallen from grace. Trapped in sin, men and women needed a savior, and that salvific figure was Jesus Christ. As Stone said in a February 17, 1924, sermon, "Why God Sent His Son," knowledge would not save the world; only a savior would:

> Christ the Ideal will never save a world. The knowledge of good has never made people good, nor a knowledge of evil has never kept people from sin. The world never had a higher standard of philosophy nor of the ethics of life than many of the ancient nations, but they went farthest in immorality. Knowledge will not save man. But "God sent His Son into the world, not to condemn the world but that the world through Him might be saved." God in Jesus Christ died for all who believe in Him, and secondly to give man the power to overcome sin. (*Fourth Church*, August 1926)

Stone's symbolic boundaries were framed around the sin of humanity and its need for salvation. This equation was a tightly managed one from which he never wavered. Stone did not emphasize or debate such issues as the inerrancy of Scripture and the belief in miracles. Theologically, Stone incarnated the Protestant establishment; he was certain about Scripture, salvation, and the need for those with resources to work to Christianize the city, nation, and world.

The Presbyterian Establishment

The description of Chicago in the early 1900s as "pre-eminently a Presbyterian city" may not have been accurate numerically, but it was true in terms of Presbyterians' power in financial and industrial arenas.[6] The Chicago Sunday Evening Club embodied this power and influence. Clifford Barnes started the club in 1908. Barnes, a civic activist and a Protestant minister, had served as an assistant minister to Stone. Barnes gathered a group of bankers, lawyers, and businessmen at the Union League Club to create "an organization of Christian businessmen to promote the moral and religious welfare of the city" (Heidebrecht, 1989:6).

The club met every Sunday night to listen to speakers on the moral and civic issues of the day. Many of the speakers were nationally known figures or social activists from the community. A partial list gives a flavor of those who addressed the Protestant establishment during these years: Jane Addams of Hull-House spoke five times; George Sherwood Eddy, secretary of the YMCA, spoke six times; Harry Emerson Fosdick, Protestant minister and professor at Union Theological Seminary in New York, spoke twenty-six times; Franklin D. Roosevelt, assistant secretary of the navy at that time, spoke once; Robert E. Speer, a member of the Presbyterian Board of Foreign Missions, spoke twenty-six times; and John Timothy Stone of Fourth Presbyterian spoke eight times (Heidebrecht, 1989:271–79).

A list of the fifty trustees of the Sunday Evening Club from 1908 to 1920 included twenty-one Presbyterians, four of whom were members of Fourth Presbyterian. The vast majority of the trustees were members of a Protestant church. The list is a "Who's Who" of prominent Protestants in industry, banking, and law in the city of Chicago and included Charles Bartlett, president of Chicago Title and Trust; Eugene Buffington, president of Gary Land Company; Jacob Dickinson, secretary of war from 1909 to 1911; Thomas Donnelley, president of R. R. Donnelley Company; Albert Harris, president of Harris Trust and Savings; Cyrus H. McCormick, president of International Harvester; and John Shedd, president of Marshall Field and Company (Heidebrecht, 1989:249–79).

The Sunday Evening Club informed and challenged the Protestant establishment about the issues of the day. It mobilized enormous resources to make things happen for civic life in the city of Chicago. Religious rhetoric justified all moral reform. This was cultural Protestantism in its most puissant form. The Chicago Committee of Fifteen, an activist "anti-vice" group of the era, was the product of both the Sunday Evening Club and Clifford Barnes.

The Committee of Fifteen originated in 1911. Self-appointed, the group funded itself with the purpose of fighting civic corruption in Chicago.[7] Its activities illustrated the ethos and ethics of the Protestant establishment of that time. This high-status group took as its vision the Christianization of Chicago. Again, moral and religious boundaries blurred; few balked at the religious rationale for their moral campaigns. Fourth Presbyterian and its leadership worked hand in glove with this group to clean up the city.

The committee focused on houses of prostitution. It targeted prostitution for several reasons. First, the vice districts were assumed to be the cause of police corruption. Second, the committee's efforts functioned in tandem with larger national efforts against what was called the "white slavery" movement, a phenomenon in which hundreds of young girls, lured by money and hopes for the future, were induced into prostitution. Finally, during this period a collaboration existed between prostitution and saloons; thus, to attack one was to slow down the other. The campaign forced saloon keepers to close on time, thus keeping them from staying open all night as a meeting place for prostitutes or their clients (Heidebrecht, 1989:17–18).[8]

Walter Lippmann, in his book *A Preface to Politics,* first published in 1914, described the Chicago anti-vice campaign as an illustration of what he thought was wrongheaded political policy and narrow-minded social analysis. Lippmann argued that the campaign, led by the Committee of Fifteen, made the elimination of lust its central goal: "No one can read the report [Chicago Vice Report] without coming to a definite conviction that the Commission regards lust itself as inherently evil. The members assumed without criticism the traditional dogma of Christianity that sex in any manifestation outside of a marriage is sinful" (Lippmann, 1969:101).[9] He went on to condemn the report for its emphasis on "taboos" and the unqualified repression of the sexual impulse by the imposition of greater police and institutional monitoring. "Spying, informing, constant investigations of everybody and everything must become the rule where there is a forcible attempt to moralize society from the top," he asserted (Lippmann, 1969:112).

Lippmann used a class analysis in his conclusion to declare that if the committee were truly interested in ameliorating the destitution of the working class, it would look to solutions that would transform the working place and the living conditions of these people: "Had the Commission worked along democratic lines, we should have had recommendations about the hygiene and early training of children, their education, the houses they live in and the streets in which they play; changes would have been suggested in the industrial conditions they face; plans would have been drawn for recreation; hints would have been collected for transmuting the sex impulse into art, into social endeavor, into religion" (Lippmann, 1969:114).

Lippmann pushed a progressive liberalism that in time triumphed over the moralistic and puritanical sanctions of the Protestant establishment. The Protestant ruling class sought to purify its social setting. Religion functioned as a tool of redemption for those caught in "social evil" and a prophylactic against future moral corruption. When moral persuasion failed, Protestants were not shy about suggesting external sanctions in the effort to maintain order in society. Progressive liberals, such as Lippmann, were more accepting of human indiscretions and viewed the Protestant establishment as self-righteous and provincial. Progressives believed people would change as social environments improved and progress was made in the working conditions of the lower class.

The 1919 election of William "Big Bill" Thompson as mayor of Chicago de-railed the Committee of Fifteen campaign. Thompson opposed the commit-tee and thought that the efforts were part of a "puritanical narrow-minded-ness" among a group of elite hypocrites (quoted in Heidebrecht, 1989:18). Thompson, however, was no high-minded liberal. He benefited personally and politically from the corruption of city bureaucrats, workers, and police (Bergreen, 1994).

The Partnership of Business and Religion

In a 1924 edition of an illustrated weekly magazine called the *Christian Her-ald,* Stone was venerated as a "business man in religion, a practical man" (Shep-herd, 1923:67). For the author of the article this meant that Stone focused not on the organization and its bureaucratic processes but on the "results" of the organization.[10] The best illustration of this is that what hung on Stone's office walls were not his honorary degrees but portraits of all the men and women who had gone into Christian service as missionaries or as ministers during his pastorate at the church. More than sixty men and women went into church or mission work during Stone's tenure at Fourth Presbyterian.

This result-oriented logic pervaded the American Protestant church in the 1910s and 1920s. Many in the clergy used the market language of product and outcome as markers for success. Roger Babson, a prominent businessman and researcher of the time, wrote several books on how the church must use the model of business to test its productivity: "The best religion is that which makes its people most efficient, most productive, most useful, and most worth-while. This is the test which men demand in business and our religion must pass the same test. . . . The best religion is the religion which gives the best results both to the individual and to the group. The real test of a religion is whether its followers are healthy, happy, and prosperous" (quoted in Lundén, 1988:93).

Stone upheld Babson's perspective, and he was not alone in this support. Babson was championed by some of the most liberal and modernist theolo-gians of the time. Shailer Mathews, the well-known dean of the Chicago Di-vinity School, wrote that people who do not know business should not criti-cize it:

> Business does more than wait for others to make its moralities. It evolves its own,
> for it is not a machine, but a social operation. What else than trade could have
> taught men to be honest? How else have women standardized their right to be

treated as persons? How else would men have been taught self-control and fore-sight which spring from thrift and the desire to produce new wealth. . . . When businessmen talk of rendering service they are not hypocrites, for they do serve their day. . . . For business does more than make money. It makes morals. (quoted in Lundén, 1988:36)

Leaders in business and religion felt strongly that business and religion benefited each other. Religion gave business a sense of direction and moral uplift; the more religious men and women were, the more efficient and pro-ductive they would become. Business provided religion with a sense of effi-ciency and methods by which the church could go out and succeed in bring-ing others to the gospel. For Babson Christianity created better workers for business and a more productive and happy labor force. Babson argued for religion because it was useful in business.

An Exemplar of the Protestant Establishment

Henry Parsons Crowell exemplified the Protestant ruling class. He was a significant leader of Fourth Presbyterian and Stone's close friend. Crowell manifested the Protestant ethic and its "worldly asceticism" as it continued to be a potent force in early decades of the twentieth century (Weber, 1958). The Protestant ethic demanded industry and an austere lifestyle. Crowell wove together this peculiar mix of intense piety with enormous discipline in busi-ness and a talent for making money. As president of the Committee of Fifteen from 1915 to 1927, he advocated puritanical moral boundaries. At the same time Crowell exercised his entrepreneurial skills in the fields of business and reli-gion. He transferred his success strategies developed in business into his reli-gious life. This combination blossomed in his relationship with Stone and in Crowell's eventual leadership of the Moody Bible Institute.

Crowell acquired his wealth as a businessman at the Quaker Oats Company. He, along with Robert Stuart, bought the company from Ferdinand Schu-macher, the founder, in an aggressive takeover in 1899. Following Crowell's takeover, the company's average profit increased to $1 million a year in the first decade of the twentieth century and to $2 million annually in the 1910s (Mar-quette, 1967:78–79). Crowell was called an "autocratic" leader.[11] He invented sales promotion in the world of advertising. He developed the method of "con-stant exposure" in consumer goods. He took the Quaker Oats Company and made it a commonly known brand throughout the nation and the world, as Arthur F. Marquette pointed out:

Until Crowell's pioneering broke the prejudice, reputable manufacturers shunned the use of advertising space as a vehicle for an effective selling message as something identified with patent-medicine charlatanry. The dignified way was to offer an announcement card of their line of business without any sales story whatever. It fell to Crowell to explore the persuasive magic of words in advertising. Crowell made people want what he had to sell. He created a market. He inspired a demand, then satisfied it. His advertisements were—some subtly, some bluntly— arguments to convince the consumer he or she could not do without Quaker Oats, a concept on which the entire modern advertising technique is based. (Marquette, 1967:55)

Crowell, by his own account, was a nominal Christian until he and his wife had a "born again" experience in 1898 (Day, 1946:157). This transformation altered Crowell's life. In 1901 he was elected to the board of the Moody Bible Institute. In February of 1904 he took over the presidency of the board, a position he retained until his death in 1944.[12] Crowell forced through new leadership at Moody when he brought in James M. Gray as dean. Gray ran the Moody Bible Institute for the next thirty-five years, a period of major expansion and growth, financed largely by Crowell himself.

Fourth Presbyterian remained Crowell's home church until the end of his life, but the Moody Bible Institute took much of his time, passion, and resources (Day, 1946:188). While committed to Moody, Crowell made warm personal remarks about Stone, and his commitment to Fourth Presbyterian was substantial. He gave $100,000 to the building fund for the new sanctuary in 1912 (Day, 1946:190).[13] He was an elder on the session, the ruling board of the church, from 1911 to 1943. He was also Stone's closest ally in developing an invitation committee of Fourth Presbyterian. This committee called on nearly three thousand men each year as part of the evangelical outreach of the church to the Near North Side. In a 1924 book honoring Stone's fifty-sixth birthday, members of the invitation committee wrote letters celebrating Stone's leadership; however, men from across the nation and world consistently referred to Stone *and* Crowell as the motivating forces behind the committee. Crowell also participated in national Presbyterian executive councils. Stone sought Crowell's presence and leadership at every level of the church's government and ministry. As Stone said in an interview about Crowell, "He was a man of God! He was the strongest influence in my life" (quoted in Day, 1946:190).

Stone had an eye for talented men and women, and he did not hesitate to ask them to help him in his enterprise. Stone, like Crowell, saw the Near North Side as an open market in which he could sell his goods. The product was the gospel, and the best method of passing on this product was through personal contact whereby one individual asked another for loyalty to the gospel and to the church. Stone used this form of market language to convince business-people to join his efforts.[14] The logic of Stone's leadership included an effective sales pitch, the closing of the deal, and the consequent reproduction of the product. This logic paralleled and transmuted the strategies of the modern businessperson. In Stone men and women in business found a partner in the enterprise of expanding markets and producing profits. Stone envisioned these endeavors as strategies to build the kingdom of God and transform the Near North Side, the city of Chicago, and the world. Crowell, like Stone, was a master salesman, and he teamed with Stone to triple the membership of Fourth Presbyterian in a matter of fifteen years.

CHRISTIANIZATION: THE MISSION OF THE GOLD COAST CHURCH

Reproduction and Fourth Presbyterian's Market

In a 1919 address entitled "God's Niagara Rushes Past," Stone asserted, "The test of great faith is that it is reproducing" (quoted in *Fourth Church*, January 1920). This motto marked his entire ministry. He was passionately dedicated to the reproduction of his faith and the Christianization of his Gold Coast congregation, the rooming-house district, and mission fields around the world. He co-opted the methods and metaphors of business to expand the influence of Fourth Presbyterian and the gospel. In doing so, he ran the risk that these strategies might dominate the message. During the 1910s and early 1920s Stone balanced the tension between accommodation and the prophetic voice of the Christian tradition in such a way that he obtained his desired results. The culture could be challenged with the Christian message without disrupting the culture's fundamental economic and social structures. Christianization meant that the heart of the individual was transformed so that individuals would use their status for different ends. Instead of using their social capital for themselves, they exercised their status and financial means for the sake of spreading the gospel.

Stone's ability to identify with and speak to his upper-class congregation illustrated his powerful leadership skills. He transmuted cultural traditions and motivated individuals toward goals that were, at times, incongruent with the upper-class objectives of the Gold Coast. He used the language of the culture to convert and mobilize his Gold Coast congregation to evangelize in a city setting that had its own particular challenges.

In 1913 Charles Stelzle asked a central question of Fourth Presbyterian's identity as a quintessential city church: "Can the church make good in the modern city with its pressing social problems and its acute religious situation?" The main task that Stelzle foresaw for Fourth Presbyterian was "Christianizing the conditions in a community which has in it every problem confronting any church in our great metropolitan district" (quoted in *Fourth Church*, March 1913).[15] Stelzle was responding to a 1911 church survey sponsored by Fourth Presbyterian and the Chicago Church Extension Board. Approximately a dozen students from McCormick Theological Seminary studied the neighborhood within Fourth Presbyterian's close proximity and found conditions similar to what Zorbaugh discovered ten years later. A large majority of the 47,906 population in the Twenty-first Ward were Protestant, young adult males. The recent immigrants to the eastern half of the Near North Side had come largely from England and Europe.[16] Fourth Presbyterian was in a district with a high percentage of Protestants and a small supply of churches to meet the needs of the community. Stelzle reported, "It is said by the social workers who are familiar with the conditions that many of the worst dance halls are found in this district. These are visited every night by young people who live in the boarding houses and apartments nearby. It is quite apparent that one of the most important groups to which Fourth church has to minister is found among these young men and women. . . . Ninety saloons are battling against five churches, and the saloons are among the most demoralizing" (quoted in *Fourth Church*, March 1913).

Fourth Presbyterian entered a market ripe with possibilities for substantial growth in church affiliation. The church, before moving to Chestnut and Michigan Avenue in 1914, was located at Rush and Superior. A condition of Stone's acceptance of the call to the church in 1908 was the leadership's commitment to a new building. Stone turned down the church's initial offer. In response the pastoral nominating committee, led by Cyrus H. McCormick Jr., the son of the founder of International Harvester Company, offered one dollar for every two dollars raised by others for a building campaign. McCormick, in conjunction with his mother, Nettie Fowler McCormick, made an initial pledge of $100,000. These promissory notes persuaded Stone to come.[17]

At the time of new church's construction, North Michigan Avenue was a muddy road still referred to as Lincoln Parkway. Some questioned the elders' decision to build on North Michigan Avenue, but it quickly became evident that it was a propitious decision. By the turn of the century many wealthy Chicagoans had moved north to the Gold Coast. Harold M. Mayer and Richard C. Wade observed in their study of Chicago, "Among the most spectacular residential changes of the period was the shift of Chicago's social elite to the Gold Coast on the Near North Side. Presaged by Potter Palmer's move to Lake Shore Drive in the 1880s, the exodus from the Avenues became a stampede after 1893" (Mayer and Wade, 1969:252). Fourth Presbyterian's move to North Michigan Avenue not only was a wise real estate investment but also landed the church in the midst of a social setting primed for Stone's aggressive outreach and leadership.

The church edifice that Stone challenged the congregation to build at Chestnut and North Michigan Avenue sacrificed nothing in terms of aesthetic and technical advances. "Chicago's first real attempt to rival in cathedral architecture the world's masterpieces in that art, is in the construction of the new church edifice and parish property of the Fourth Presbyterian congregation," the *Fourth Church* reported in September 1913, proclaiming that the church was a "beautiful reflection of Gothic art." The church's sanctuary resonated with the taste of elegance, sophistication, and the ambiance of the boardroom: "The ceiling is ridged and will be finished in fumed oak, of which wood the pews and other church furniture will be designed." The sounds of the church were to be magnificent as well. Ernest M. Skinner built the organ, which was funded by Mrs. Emmons Blaine, a daughter of Cyrus H. McCormick. The choir director, Eric De Lamarter, was a foremost musician in the nation. In 1918 he was elected to the position of assistant conductor of the Chicago Symphony Orchestra.[18]

The cultural ethos of the Gold Coast expressed an upper-middle-class milieu. Stone and the Fourth Presbyterian leadership understood the tastes and aesthetic style that maintained these cultural boundaries and social dominance. To attract the Gold Coast patronage to the church, Stone appealed to these *"socially formed"* dispositions (Bourdieu, 1977:124). This appeal to taste and culture was an explicit aspect of Stone's strategy in building the Fourth Presbyterian sanctuary and church complex. Stone understood his market and created an enticing product to which many responded. Moreover, Stone knew that in a patriarchal culture, men were key in reproducing the faith.

Evangelization: Winning Men for Christ

In the early twentieth century a new movement arose focusing on the development of masculine traits (A. Douglas, 1977). This came in many forms, from the Boy Scouts in 1908, with its "man-making" instruction in outdoor activities, to the Men and Religion Forward Movement, a nationwide ecumenical venture that began in 1911. Stone served as the chairman of this ecumenical movement for a short while.

Quite early, Stone was aware of the feminization of the clergy role. In a February 1913 article in *Fourth Church* Stone recalled an admonition from an elder in the church concerning the man's son: "Don't spoil a splendid business man by trying to make my boy a minister." By way of response Stone celebrated the calling of ministry and the masculinity of the vocation throughout his tenure at Fourth Presbyterian.[19] He esteemed constant industry and viewed the church as a corporation that demanded discipline and productivity. His most damning comment was that a man lacked "virility" or that he "lacked the punch." For Stone persistence and industry marked someone who was on the way to success. "Ceaseless, constant never-ending devotion to duty insure success," he declared in the January 1923 issue of *Fourth Church*. Success, whether in business or in religion, was symbolized by production and results. This inner logic of the Protestant establishment paralleled and expressed the culture's business motivations, giving the church cachet in the corporate world.

Stone spoke again and again of his passionate desire to "win all men for Christ." Although conventional for the era, this gender-exclusive language also denoted Stone's particular interest in reaching out to men. He thought that the success of his ministry depended on his ability to convince the "powerful men" of his congregation and city to join him in the cause of sharing the gospel of Jesus Christ. One result of this focus was that on any given Sunday morning the sanctuary of Fourth Presbyterian had more men than women sitting in its pews (Shepherd, 1923:67).[20]

At the same time, Stone was uncomfortable with the "club-like" atmosphere of the church and later wrote:

> From the worldly point of view—social position, financial standing, recognized leadership—all was encouraging, but the church was little more than a religious club, somewhat self-satisfied, and eager to find in the pulpit intellectual and moral direction. But I did not feel the heart-throb to reach the souls of men. In fact, I felt that many disapproved, and were critical of "over-emotional efforts in evangelism," and some frowned upon emphasizing that form of service. "Let the Moody Institute, the Church Tabernacles, the Evangelists, the multitudinous new sects and churches do that sort of work." (Stone, 1936:52)

Stone contested the complacency of Fourth Presbyterian's Gold Coast symbolic boundaries by challenging the church and its leadership to invite others to church and to lead them into a relationship with Jesus Christ. This form of evangelization is more often identified with the religious style of the middle class (McLoughlin, 1955:294–95), but this did not keep Stone from pushing his Gold Coast constituency to pursue evangelical goals.

The session minutes of Fourth Presbyterian during Stone's tenure provide evidence of the seriousness with which membership was taken at the church. Each person who applied for membership was interviewed by a pastor and brought before the session. It was only after "careful examination" that he or she was accepted into membership. Many of the descriptions depict individuals confessing faith in Jesus Christ as a "personal Savior." The language is clearly evangelical, pious, and intimate. Celia Zolg's entrance into membership in 1916 serves as a representative example:

> [She] appeared before the Session and confessed her faith in the Lord Jesus Christ, and her acceptance of Him as her personal Savior, affirming her appreciation of the privilege to benefit by direct personal communication with the Lord Jesus Christ and God the Father. After careful examination, on motion duly seconded and carried she was received into the membership of this church, and at her request it was directed that the ordinance of baptism be administered immediately preceding the communion service to be observed at the close of the morning preaching service. (Session Minutes, November 15, 1916)

This kind of care and concern for personal piety runs throughout the records of Stone's tenure. Stone's recruitment of Crowell into the Fourth Presbyterian's leadership in 1911 helped inaugurate this change. Stone fully supported Crowell's passion for the conservative, evangelical Moody Bible Institute. Crowell chaired the Committee on Spiritual Resources at Fourth Presbyterian. In the session minutes Crowell consistently pushed for higher standards in examining candidates for membership. Stone shared this evangelical piety and often called for religious revival. He led Fourth Presbyterian in becoming an organizational arm for Billy Sunday's revivals in Chicago in 1918.[21] Stone was chairman of the campaign, and in his unpublished autobiography he spoke of his love for Billy Sunday. It was at Sunday's request that Stone took part in the revivalist's funeral in 1935. Stone wrote that the Fourth Presbyterian session only reluctantly supported the Billy Sunday revival in 1918. In terms of numbers, the revival's effect on Fourth Presbyterian was counterproductive. Even so, Stone stood by Sunday to the end.[22]

Stone was aware that the privilege of this upper-middle-class church could lead to indifference and inevitably to decline. Early in his ministry at Fourth Presbyterian he developed an invitation committee, whose sole purpose was to invite other men to worship and to win them by personal persuasion to Christ. The group would report weekly on the progress of their invitational efforts. In Stone's litany of advice to this group, men were told that without them God would have no instrument, that it was "only through you" that God was able to do his work. They were to be patient, confident, good listeners, and willing to ask for a man's allegiance without fear (Stone, 1936:57).

Stone practiced this fearless and aggressive style himself. Frank J. Loesch, a prominent railroad attorney in Chicago, was one of Stone's early recruits. Loesch became an elder on the session of Fourth Presbyterian in 1913 and was the Men's Bible Class leader throughout Stone's tenure. The two first met after an address by Stone. Stone immediately asked Loesch to come hear him preach for a year. Loesch agreed. This invitation by Stone was typical. There were any number of men that he challenged to come to the church to hear him preach. After the year was up, Stone and Loesch met again, and Loesch immediately joined the church and supported Stone with his leadership and his pocketbook. Stone recalled that the lawyer immediately presented him with a check for $1,200 for the new church. Thereafter, Loesch, like Crowell, became Stone's close associate at every level of leadership in the church.[23]

Creating Christian Ladies and Gentlemen

The Church Extension Survey reported that there were 15,000 to 18,000 men and women living in a half-mile radius of Fourth Presbyterian. In the 1910s and 1920s rooming houses were only one block west of the church. Invitation committees were formed to recruit both men and women. The invitation committee's task was to invite to worship as many young men and women in the church's vicinity as possible. Stone intentionally kept the committee's work confidential. Only after leaving the church did Stone write about it.[24] He said, "It transformed the life of our church more than any other one agency, and, unconsciously, influenced the entire church" (Stone, 1936:62).

These committees functioned as feeders for the men's and women's clubs at Fourth Presbyterian. Stone's vision included not only an evangelical outreach but also a facility to shape the social dispositions and values of the men and women who came to Fourth Presbyterian. An integral part of the original design of the church's building plan was a men's and women's club: "The club building on Chestnut Street will be used for recreation, study, social entertainment and various meetings" (*Fourth Church*, September 1913). These club rooms were created in the same architectural elegance as the sanctuary. They included oak-paneled parlor rooms, a dumbwaiter, locker rooms, a gymnasium, and space for a future bowling alley. The stated purpose of these clubs was to reach out to the rooming-house neighborhood: "While the congregation includes many wealthy members, there are also many of very moderate means and it is for these especially that the men's and women's club features will serve their intended purpose" (*Fourth Church,* September 1913). More than 60 percent of the men and women in the 15,000 to 18,000 Church Extension Survey were from out of town. Fourth Presbyterian envisioned the clubs as a "home away from home" and as a way of further Christianizing the neighborhood.

Stone and his handpicked leadership put enormous effort into this outreach. They reached beyond the comfortable symbolic boundaries of their high-status group. To be sure, they used the cultural aesthetics of their upper-middle-class setting to attract these individuals, yet it was done not to exclude individuals of the lower and middle-classes but as a way to include them. The purpose of the clubs was to produce men and women in the mode of the Protestant ethic: a disciplined individual, willing to work hard, ready to delay gratification, and eager to honor the person of Jesus Christ.

This process of religious and cultural reproduction is illuminated in *Fourth Church*'s descriptions of three men who had come to a Men's Club meeting in 1914. The first was a twenty-four-year-old. New to the city, he wanted to "improve" himself through education. A member of the invitation committee heard his story, told him of the club, and asked whether he was a Christian. The man responded, "I don't know." According to the account, they proceeded upstairs, and he "gave his heart to Christ, without reserve" (*Fourth Church,* November 1914). The other two men were also new to the city, one having an alcohol problem and the other needing friendship. The following description of the first young man's condition sums up the response of the club to these men in general:

> Now there were a number of problems this young man faced as he arose for work the next morning. He had led a careless and dissipated life. He needed badly the right kind of friendship and advice. He needed an uplifting place to spend his evenings. Systematic exercise would not come in amiss. And he was unquestionably in need of the education for which at first he had sought out the club. The Men's Club met each of these needs completely, with its Christian fellowship and splendid equipment for mental and physical upbuilding and its opportunities for wholesome recreation. His growth in character has been rapid. (*Fourth Church,* November 1914)

The invitation committees not only evangelized the men and women in the neighborhood but acted as a social service agency as well. The committees met their responsibilities to social conditions by building a catalogue of the best rooms—the cleanest and most sanitary—in the rooming-house district. They also became an employment agency, through which "hundreds of youth found employment" (Stone, 1936:62).

This system of cultural reproduction contested rigid social boundaries between the Gold Coast and the rooming-house district. The condition of acceptance into the club was neither class nor status but a willingness on the part of the men and women to be helped and to help themselves. Stone and the church's leadership sought with great energy and passion to give young adults shelter, work, and a sense of identity, meaning, and friendship.

At the same time, there is little doubt that Fourth Presbyterian was a step up the class and status ladder. In the cultural Protestantism of this era Christ and culture worked hand in hand. One's conversion to Christ meant the transformation of one's social and cultural habits; that is, one became an active participant in middle- and upper-middle-class culture. This was a reflection of not only the ways of the church but also the pervasive impact of Christianity on the culture. Protestantism was *the* culture, and to be a member of it, one had to convert to Christ. There was thus an overwhelming emphasis on the spiritual life of the individual and the necessity of personal piety and morality.

The Women's Club at Fourth Presbyterian had the same mission of reaching out to women in the district. Although the number of interviews performed by the women's invitation committee remained hidden as well, it is clear the committee functioned with a similar zeal. Their Tuesday night club averaged a hundred women throughout Stone's era. Not every individual who came to Fourth Presbyterian, however, found the situation quite so amenable. Zorbaugh's recording of one woman's account of her experience in Chicago and with Fourth Presbyterian is a revealing picture of Chicago in the 1920s. The young woman had come from Emporia, Kansas, to make it in music in the city. She moved into the rooming-house district. Her experience of failure and finally poverty was traumatic: "In all this city of three million souls I knew no one, cared for no one, was cared for by no one. . . . My room-mate had been going to Sunday night services at the Fourth Presbyterian Church, over on the Lake Shore Drive. She told them about me, and one day some pastor's assistant's assistant came to call on me. I went one night after that. I was greeted with ostentatious and half-hearted civility. It was all so impersonal. . . . I never went back; and no other church ever took an interest in me" (quoted in Zorbaugh, [1929] 1983:80). Zorbaugh intends this account to reflect the impersonality of the city and the isolation of young people. It showed the exclusive social boundaries of the Gold Coast and the churches in the area. What is remarkable, however, is that Fourth Presbyterian was the only church to attempt to reach out to this lonely young woman. That she found the church pretentious does not obviate Fourth Presbyterian's willingness to offer itself to others.

Church and the Mission Field

For Stone the church's purpose was to proclaim the gospel. Sharing the Christian message with the world, whether at home or abroad, was Stone's primary passion.[25] In the July 1924 *Fourth Church* a chart illustrated the world missions of the Presbyterian Church. It was entitled "The Projection of the Gospel through Presbyterian Enterprises." This corporate language of enterprise, as noted earlier, became a central metaphor for describing the mission of the Presbyterian Church. The chart used a graphic of a camera to represent the church's mission. The rays of light, labeled the "light of God," shined out of the camera on various mission outposts, including North America, Africa, Europe, and Asia. Numerically, 1924 was a peak year for the Presbyterian Church U.S.A.: there were 1.8 million members; 9,979 ministers; 9,700 churches; and 1,545 foreign missionaries. The total church budget reached fifteen million dollars. The church would never have more foreign missionaries. As an international campaign, it financed modern farming technology, introduced a model of capitalist economy, and presented the Christian gospel—all in an effort to Christianize the world.

In this foreign missionary enterprise cultural practice and religious belief combined in an effort to reproduce the cultural and social infrastructure from which a Christian response could be anticipated. The Christianization campaign attempted to bridge social conditions and subjective dispositions. Cultural reproduction in this domain is the fit between the environment and consciousness that in time functions hand in glove. Pierre Bourdieu describes it this way: "Social reality exists, so to speak, twice, in things and in minds, in fields and in habitus, outside and inside agents. And when habitus encounters a social world of which it is a product it is like a 'fish in water': it does not feel the weight of the water, and it takes the world about itself for granted" (Bourdieu and Wacquant, 1992:127).

Nonetheless, many foreign missionaries found the attempt to create appropriate social conditions frustrating. Letters between Sam Higginbottom, a Fourth Presbyterian missionary in India, and Stone illuminate this frustrating attempt to shape social structures. Higginbottom worked hard to improve the agricultural situation in India in the 1910s and 1920s, but several communications reveal his disappointment with the poor agricultural methods of the country and his disgust with the caste system that he felt hindered both economic expansion and the Christianization of the people. Higginbottom's comments on Gandhi in particular reveal the connection that many Protestants promoted between the gospel and the West's economic practice:

Mr. Gandhi is a thoroughly good man, a good lawyer. His trial was a remarkable spectacle. He pleaded guilty. He has been used by evil men to further their own ends, often destructive ends. Mr. Gandhi is also not up on economic law and like some people and some governments, feels that if moral and spiritual law is observed, economic law will take care of itself. I believe the next great lesson the world has to learn is that economic law is as much God's law as moral or spiritual law, and whoever breaks it will suffer for breaking it. (quoted in *Fourth Church,* September 1922)

The link between Protestant religion and capitalism was a well-developed principle of Protestant leaders in the early decades of the twentieth century, though some Presbyterian leaders commented on technology's negative effects on foreign societies. Robert E. Speer, the senior secretary of the Presbyterian Board of Missions and former moderator of the General Assembly, surveyed China in the spring of 1927. China, in the midst of great civil unrest, had come under the sway of the communist regime. Speer, commenting on the growing "anti-Christian" movement in China, described how the introduction of Western technology by Christian missionaries had caused the anti-Christian movement: "The same reproach which Christianity suffers lies also against medicine and surgery and electricity and all the science and invention of the west. There is no escape from this reproach. The churches must simply live it down and naturalize China not by China-izing Christianity but by Christian-izing China" (quoted in *Fourth Church,* May 1927).

Speer assumed it was possible to separate the technology and culture of the West from the message of the gospel. This critical distinction was at the heart of the discussion of the 1932 Hocking Commission report, *Re-Thinking Missions.* The report emphasized ecumenicity, toleration of other traditions, and a mission strategy that took into account the nuances of an increasingly complex world (Fitzmier and Balmer, 1991:123). These critics of American imperialism and cultural chauvinism challenged the self-confidence of Christians. Moreover, the so-called foreigners, who were the objects of mission, began to question the assumption of cultural superiority within and behind the missionaries' message. In response many missionaries doubted their own legitimacy.[26]

The cultural contradictions of Christian capitalism came out most decisively when the ideals of Christian missionary service were up against the cultural trends of the Gold Coast. From 1925 onward the advertisements in *Fourth Church* became more exotic in their visual cues as well as in their tag lines. The Martha Weathered Shop, which advertised in the *Fourth Church* during this period, had its Gold Coast clientele in mind. Two ads in 1928 marked the incongruence between the sacrifice of the missionary and the excesses of wealth.

One portrays an elegantly dressed man and woman at a football game. The camera points at them, and the line of "silent admiration" is used to describe those looking at the couple. The spectators, of course, are of similar class and attire (*Fourth Church*, November 1928). Opposite this page is a letter from a missionary that describes the hardship of reaching out to loggers in the forests of Alaska. Another ad in the May 1928 *Fourth Church* shows a woman, again in a sophisticated outfit, standing with her golf club in hand; the spectators again look on in "silent admiration." Only nine pages earlier is a notation that two thousand books had been borrowed from the Borden Missionary Library at Fourth Presbyterian during the previous year. According to the library's record all of these works described mission outreach in foreign lands.[27]

The advertisements contradicted one of the principles behind the Protestant Puritan culture: that one could have possessions but should not enjoy them. This contradiction and the ensuing tensions punctured the surface of Fourth Presbyterian's establishment culture throughout the 1920s. In this era the cultural establishment was less apt to support the pietistic ideals that had permeated the cultural Protestantism of the 1910s. The growing tension between Christ and culture began to dislodge and even displace the cultural Protestantism of early twentieth-century American culture.

SIGNS OF PROTESTANT DISESTABLISHMENT AND DECLINE

The Blind Spots of the Protestant Establishment

The subtle signs of displacement appeared early in the twentieth century. Tensions in class and race began to percolate, particularly in the cities. The ideology of cultural Protestantism pivoted around the effort of the individual to reform and transform his or her environment. This individualistic ideology worked well when one was a part of certain Anglo-American and Euro-American ethnic groups, but it clearly was bankrupt when it came to African Americans and those in the working class. It became clear as the century moved along that cultural Protestantism expressed the interests of certain classes and groups and not the ethos of the entire nation, much less the needs of minorities in urban areas.

Stone continued to proclaim the triumph of individual success, however. He did not preach on the social and structural conditions in his city and nation. To be sure, in this he was no different from his peers, but compared with his successor, Harrison Ray Anderson, Stone was chary in addressing social injustice. His rationale followed the conservatives of the time: society does not change individuals; individuals change society. "The state," he declared, "cannot be better than the citizen. Improved social conditions cannot create individual character, but individual character must create proper social conditions" (*Fourth Church,* April 1914). Consumed by passion to convert the hearts of others to Christ, Stone believed that this conversion would Christianize the city of Chicago and the people of the world.

In one of the crucial moral and social issues of the day, Prohibition, Stone took an ambiguous stand. He supported the act not from a position of moral principle but because it was a matter of law and thus something one was obliged to obey. Stone's timidity on the issue is difficult to understand other than to say that for him moral and spiritual change demanded personal transformation to the exclusion of external circumstance. His critique of reformers was patronizing in his January 27, 1924, sermon, "The Winning of Life":

> This is the trouble with many reformers today (God bless them in all their earnest and conscientious purpose) but here is their great error. To say "make environment better and you will have better children, better homes and the millennium" is short-sighted and untrue. Jesus Christ said the opposite—make the heart better and you will then have better environment, better communities. "Keep thy heart with all diligence for out of it are the issues of life." A nation can never be made great by merely enacting laws, no matter how fine they may be. For instance, we may believe in the Volstead Act, and our defense of it may be very helpful, but unless men are willing to give up drinks, the law will not overcome the evil. (*Fourth Church,* April 1924)

Stone might have been right about Prohibition in that the law itself would not keep people from drinking, but his evangelical ardor diverted him from a forceful attack on the social corruption that was ubiquitous in Chicago during the 1920s. Stone not only was blind to the moral and political corruption in the city but also ignored Chicago's slums and the plight of African Americans.

The Slum and Fourth Presbyterian

The proximity of the slum to Fourth Presbyterian was noted in the 1913 church-sponsored survey: "Directly to the west of the community are to be found some of the worst housing conditions in the city" (quoted in *Fourth Church,* March 1913). This neighborhood was noteworthy for its lack of children and the prominence of Anglo-Saxons, but surveys stated that there were well over a thousand African Americans living in the area (Zorbaugh, [1929] 1983:37). At that time there were far more whites than African Americans living in poverty in Chicago; African Americans made up only 2 percent of Chicago's population. Nonetheless, in a separate study conducted by Sophonisba Breckenridge and Edith Abbott in 1912, the authors described the plight of the African American in Chicago: "The color line as it appears in Chicago's housing problem is too important to be overlooked" (quoted in Mayer and Wade, 1969: 254). They portrayed a scene of stark segregation and exploitation by landlords and real estate agents. In contrast to other ethnic immigrant groups who moved into slum areas and worked themselves out of poverty, African Americans suffered a systematic strategy of racial discrimination. Even those African Americans who had greater economic resources could not escape the slum. They moved to other areas only after whites had exited. Moreover, vice districts appeared, often with official political sanction, next to the slums, thus making the neighborhoods breeding grounds for crime and disease (Mayer and Wade, 1969:254).

Between 1916 and 1920, 50,000 African Americans settled in Chicago as a part of a massive exodus from the South. The African American work force in Chicago increased from 27,000 in 1910 to 70,000 by 1920 (Heidebrecht, 1989:94). As the African American population increased, the strength of segregation heightened proportionally. The tension between the African American and white population erupted in July 1919 with the Chicago riots. The July melee was preceded by preliminary skirmishes. "At the edge of the ghetto, a kind of guerrilla warfare broke out—in 1919, twenty-four bombings occurred, directed at new Negro residents or at real estate agents who dealt in transitional property," Mayer and Wade reported in their study (Mayer and Wade, 1969: 284). The July rioting ended with 38 dead (15 whites and 23 blacks) and 537 injured. "Peace was restored," Mayer and Wade observed, "but the scars could not be easily erased, for the grim affair left deep wells of guilt and remorse, hate and bigotry. Worse still, conditions did not change, and the ghetto continued to expand and fester" (Mayer and Wade, 1969:290).[28]

Fourth Presbyterian remained on the sideline of this crisis of race and class. The only mention of the riots was a Chicago Church Federation report reprinted in the August 1919 *Fourth Church*. The blame was evenly distributed between the whites and the African Americans: "While the recent riots have witnessed the most sickening brutality on the part of colored people, the whites have been no less cruel; in a great number of instances the stronger race has fallen upon the weaker with ferocity and without mercy and without cause. . . . There is no higher or clearer statement of our duty towards our dark brothers than the rule laid down in a very ancient decision which has never been overruled—one which we usually refer to as the Golden Rule."

The report assumed that African Americans were the "weaker" race, and the golden rule was proffered as *the* solution to the overwhelming conditions of poor housing and unemployment. This did little to ameliorate the unhealthy and tragic conditions of life in the slum, nor did it address the psychological oppression that African Americans suffered in the wake of systematic injustice in every area of their lives.

Comments on race relations by Stone, as with most Protestant establishment pastors of the time, were infrequent. We can infer that he paid little attention to the harsh conditions of African Americans in Chicago since he never spoke of their conditions and rarely mentioned this group in his sermons or other writings. This social boundary of race remained impermeable at Fourth Presbyterian and in American culture until the 1960s.

Christian Patriotism

Blind to the disparities between the rich and poor, the minorities in the city, Stone heralded the melding of nationalism and the Christian faith as World War I began. His cultural Protestantism reached its peak during the war. It combined a nationalistic fervor with the Protestant call to sacrifice oneself for a worthy cause. Stone emphasized the masculinity of the call to war and the test of the war as a challenge of faith. His efforts did not go unnoticed. In February 1917 Stone received a note of grateful thanks from President Woodrow Wilson for his support of the war efforts. Stone quoted a poem by the bishop of Exeter called "Give Us Men." It was the essence of a masculine Christian patriotism:

> Give us Men!
> Men who when the tempest gathers,
> Grasp the standard of their fathers
> In the thickest fight: Men who strike for home and altar,
> Let the base crowd cringe and falter,
> God defend the right!
> True as true, though lorn and lonely,
> Tender, as the brave are only;
> Men who tread where saints have trod,
> Men for Country—Home—and God:
> Give us Men!
> I say again—again—
> Give us such men!
>   (*Fourth Church*, May 1917)

This torrid rhetoric was followed by action on the part of men and women at Fourth Presbyterian. In 1918, at the height of the war, 240 men from Fourth Presbyterian were serving in the armed forces. The women of the church were involved in providing the Red Cross with hundreds of knitted articles and surgical bandages. For Stone Christianity and patriotism coalesced. This was the civil religion of a cultural Protestantism in its most unadulterated form. "It is not enough," he declared, "to be a member of the church of Christ but Christianity demands of the patriotic citizen that he be a consistent member of society as well as of the church. We do not believe in the union of church and state in this land of ours, but we do believe that the church and the state should work hand in hand as brothers for the reign of righteousness and or-der" (*Fourth Church*, July 1919).

Stone saw the war as an opportunity for Christianity to prove its superior-ity. The faith prepared men for war and heroic sacrifice. Christianity galvanized the nation as a force for righteousness against the enemy. Stone's enormous output of energy, both in rhetoric and in action, signaled his single-minded belief that a nation that was loyal to a Christian God could achieve victory at any cost.[29]

Stone manifested the logic of the cultural Protestantism of his period that linked loyalty to God with success in the business realm and victory in war. In this way, like many in the Protestant establishment, Stone's ministry assimi-lated the ethos of the Protestant ethic and its undiluted allegiance to the Ameri-can way. This fusion of Christ and culture, evangelism and business logic, church and nation came apart in the postwar era. The center of the Protes-tant establishment would not hold.

The Problem of Prosperity

After Armistice Day, November 11, 1918, Stone immediately pushed to capital-ize on the energy and idealism of the war effort. The Gold Coast was at a fe-ver pitch of development. The North Michigan Avenue bridge was completed in 1920. The Drake Hotel, completed in 1921, along with many high-rise apart-ments in the area of the church, served the wealthy who wanted to live close to the Loop. The New Era Movement, an enterprise sponsored by the Presby-terian Church U.S.A. and its Mission Board, had three goals: (1) to capitalize on the idealism from the war, (2) to work for Americanization to bring "unity" to America, and (3) to bring stability to society. These goals mirrored Stone's vision flawlessly. The New Era Movement met for the first time in Chicago. Stone, revealingly, compared the meeting with a business conference, from which the leaders of business houses could "gather their representatives from far and near to an earnest conference about the possibilities of better methods, more faithful service and larger business" (*Fourth Church,* February 1919). As the business life of the country caught fire, Stone energetically used corporate rhetoric to fuel the flames of his passion for spreading the Christian gospel.

This Christian corporate fanfare, however, failed to translate into more missionaries or enlarged mission budgets; indeed, the opposite was the case in the 1920s. The number of individuals entering religious vocations dramatically declined. In 1920, 2,700 students had volunteered to be Protestant missionaries abroad; by 1928, the number had fallen to 252. Moneys to foreign mission projects decreased substantially. Moreover, most city missions that began as evangelical outposts became social service agencies (Lundén, 1988:32). Fourth Presbyterian experienced this diminution in missionary zeal as well. The benevolence budget for the church in the 1910s averaged an annual pledge of $400,000; the annual benevolence budget in the 1920s peaked at $100,000.[30]

Prosperity became problematic for this Protestant establishment church. In January 1921 Stone gave the fiftieth anniversary sermon of Fourth Presbyterian, in which he asserted that one of the key priorities for the church must be to increase the endowment fund from $600,000 to no less than $2 million to secure the church in its social setting. Stone spoke out against the capital interests of his class and challenged families to leave their money to the church, not to their children. He spoke of inherited wealth's danger to the ethical life of the family. He attacked it fervently: "I believe the children and family should have their right place in the gifts which care for them, but I have never seen a case where money was left by a father or mother in large amounts to children, where there was not left with it Christian character to control it and use it aright that did not do harm rather than good. I know this will trouble some people and their children" (*Fourth Church,* January 1923).

Stone trespassed on what was, for many, the sacred ground of financial privacy. His willingness to challenge this social taboo was more controversial than anything he could have said about the social conditions of the neighborhood. Stone reached into the subtle dynamics of his Gold Coast church and pressed his congregants to resist their own need for financial security.

Emile Durkheim voiced a similar cautionary note concerning inherited wealth. For Durkheim inherited wealth "invalidated the whole contractual system at its roots." It would lead to class distinctions based on unjust distributions of capital:

Now inheritance as an institution results in men being born either rich or poor; that is to say, there are two main classes in society, linked by all sorts of intermediate classes: the one which in order to live has to make its services acceptable to the other at whatever cost; the other class which can do without these services because it can call on certain resources, which may, however, not be equal to the services rendered by those who have them to offer. Therefore as long as such sharp class differences exist in society, fairly effective palliatives may lessen the injustice of contracts; but in principle, the system operates in conditions which do not allow of justice. (Durkheim, 1957:213)

Durkheim addressed issues of class and the creation of social inequality. For Stone the issue of inherited wealth involved moral character more than it did social justice. Symbolic boundaries were personalized and kept separate from issues of society. Stone affirmed the upper-middle-class social boundaries of his church, but he also challenged it to be responsive to the wider needs of Christian character. Stone's willingness to confront this taboo challenged his congregation to count the "cost" of membership at Fourth Presbyterian. Stone would accommodate only so far to the cultural movement of his era. The friction between Christ and culture ignited over the issue of character and wealth; similar tensions stirred over the question of Sabbath-keeping in the life of the family.

Keeping the Sabbath

Throughout his tenure at Fourth Presbyterian Stone admonished families to keep the Sabbath and parents to care for and nurture their children. In January 1913 Stone condemned the "'socializing' and 'societyzing' of the Sabbath by the socially active classes" (*Fourth Church*, January 1913). *Fourth Church* reported, "There was no bitterness in Dr. Stone's address. It was a plea for salvation of the home life of the wealthy father—the home life on which, Dr. Stone said, Sunday social activities had made such inroads—that this one day when he could meet and enjoy the company of his children and wife virtually had been taken away from him" (*Fourth Church*, January 1913).

Numerous references in Stone's sermons and essays refer to the importance of reproducing character within the family. Living in a patriarchal culture, Stone believed that the father was the source of health for society and the family. The family was the basic unit of the social contract, and if it deteriorated, society would fall apart. An anecdote from one of Stone's sermons in February 1924 reveals Stone's position:

A few weeks ago a number of men were talking on important business and a splendid little lad about twelve years of age came into the group and touching his father's arm said: "Dad, may I speak to you a minute?" And, much to the surprise of the other members, the man courteously excused himself from the others and withdrew. One of the men in a surly way said: "The little shaver—what right has he to come in here and interrupt this meeting?" The other men sympathized with him. The man came back shortly and said: "Men, I am sorry to have broken in upon this meeting in this way, but there is no business in my life or anything of so much importance to me as what that lad wants. I overheard the remark made as I went out of the room. I do not criticize any of you for making it, but let me tell you something: That boy and I are life-partners. His errand was a most important one, and if you men knew what it was, you would be grateful for a lad who would come to his Dad in such a time of real need. The little lad's mother is not living." (*Fourth Church,* February 1924)

Undoubtedly, this was a sentimental story, one shaped by class and wealth, but it graphically disclosed a powerful theme in Stone's preaching. Business success meant much, but a strong family with Christian character was just as important. Throughout Stone's pastorate he drew the connection between Sabbath observance, high Christian character in the family, and prosperity. Late in the 1920s Stone used a Roger Babson quote to invoke this equation of prosperity: "The three greatest institutions, or the three greatest forces in the world's history, have been the Church, Sabbath observance, and Family prayers" (quoted in *Fourth Church,* January 1928).

Stone understood the power of practice and ritual to bind individuals to each other, to a common purpose, and to a common social institution. He believed that belief cut off from spiritual practice would die. Stone resisted the social and cultural forces that separated belief and practice. These forces included golf on Sunday, the father's working harder and spending less time with his family, the inheritance of money without conditions, and the repeal of Prohibition.

The ability of the Presbyterian Church to guide and control the habits of its congregant's private lives diminished as the 1920s came to a close. Prohibition was soon repealed. Sabbath observance by mainstream Protestants declined. The postwar financial boom reached its zenith. The center of power in cultural influence had changed. In the final years of Stone's tenure at the church, his pronouncements and sanctions against the private behavior of his congregation nearly disappeared.[31]

Stone's gamble that the church could use the language of business to increase its efficiency and production had mixed results. When the language of the church resembled that of its social setting, the tension between the church and its context faded. The church became less influential in its social setting not only because of its accommodation to the status quo but also because the culture took on a life of its own. Market values increasingly drove American culture. The force of the Protestant ethic, its ethos of discipline and delayed gratification and its goal of sharing the gospel, diminished. Stone's strategic use of corporate language to influence the marketplace had little effect toward the end of his ministry. Indeed, the homogenization process was such that the church became one more component of the rationalization of the modern economy.[32]

The relationship between religion and American culture changed in the 1920s. The use of business methods that had succeeded in the 1910s reached a plateau by the mid-1920s. Religious leaders had a difficult time carving out distinctive social and symbolic boundaries in the midst of a booming economy and a changing cultural milieu. Institutionally, the church lost some of its tensive character; it became languid and indistinguishable from other institutions. The cultural Protestantism embodied in the Protestant establishment lost its moral suasion over the cultural ethos of American society.

The Gold Coast Church in Decline?

The question of Fourth Presbyterian's institutional stability or decline weighed on Stone at the end of his pastorate. In 1910 the total membership was 746. In 1920 it was 2,028, a gain of 1,282. In 1930 the church rolls stood at 2,651, less than half the gain of the previous decade. The substantial decrease in giving to church benevolence has already been noted. The decline in membership growth was not due so much to a decline in new affiliations. New members by examination and by transfer remained fairly constant from 1910 to 1930, averaging 160 and 125, respectively. What grew was the number of those who left the church. Stone made a number of references to the fact that many members were moving north and away from the church. These signs of decline came to a head in 1925. At that time the church had its largest congregation in its history, 2,656, and yet it was unable to meet its benevolence goals. This deficit was called a "crisis." Stone put the legitimacy of his leadership on the line several times, challenging the congregation by saying he could not feel good about being the church's pastor if the church did not give away as much as it spent on itself (*Fourth Church*, September 1925). The congregation came through for Stone, but a clear plateau had been reached in financial growth and new membership.

Signs of decline were apparent in the national church as well. An article from the Board of National Mission of the Presbyterian Church U.S.A. detailed the situation of the decline in the number of clergy candidates. In 1926 the church had a candidate for the ministry for every 1,489 communicants; in 1896 there had been a candidate for the ministry for every 626 communicants (*Fourth Church*, May 1926). Locally, the neighborhood of Fourth Presbyterian experienced rapid expansion of high-rise luxury apartments, and fewer young, single adults lived in the immediate area. The Men's Club, which had traditionally met on Thursday nights with three hundred in attendance in the 1910s, stopped meeting altogether by the early 1920s.

In the midst of Fourth Presbyterian's diminished growth, requests for money from the pulpit and the *Fourth Church* became more regular. Numerous articles on tithing, defined by the church as the giving away of 10 percent of one's income, appeared in the 1920s. An article from the *Presbyterian Magazine* refuted those who were accusing the church of "worldly" and "mercenary" strategies of fund-raising: "Money makes the church go and is one form in which our faith and faithfulness expresses itself as truly as our prayer and praise. Money is our incarnated spirit, our toil and very life blood minted into coin. We cannot separate our money from our Christian faith and service any more than we can our truthfulness and honesty. . . . This business is the business of the Lord, and we depreciate it at the expense and honor of our Lord himself" (quoted in *Fourth Church*, March 1926).

As the habits of spiritual practice began to fade with the loss of Sabbath observance, the diminishment of family worship, and the reluctance of congregants to tithe to the church, belief in the institution leveled off. Stone's 1921 vision of attendance at 5,000, an endowment of $2 million, and a progressive Christianization of the neighborhood had to be modified. One of the key goals that he outlined in 1921 was the elimination of the pew rental system. At that time, members who rented pews could have their pews held until five minutes after the 11:00 A.M. service began. Stone asserted, "The pew rental system of this church and every church ought to be a thing of the past. You cannot have a growing, Christian, democratic spirit where you have a pew rental system" (*Fourth Church*, February 1921). Stone lost this battle. In the June 1930 *Fourth Church* the committee on pew rentals encouraged the congregation to rent as many pews as possible. During Stone's tenure the pew rental system received annual revenues of approximately $35,000, a third of the church's operating budget.

In the September 1928 *Fourth Church* Stone outlined his priorities: (1) greater spiritual practice on the part of individuals, (2) greater participation in worship, and (3) an increase of the $600,000 endowment to $1 million. "Our church is so located that as the years go by we are becoming more and more a downtown church. Transient conditions surround us increasingly. No one who does not call constantly in this neighborhood realizes how rapidly we are changing. This last week out of some fifty or sixty calls made in this neighborhood I found that twenty-one families had moved since I went on my vacation last July," Stone wrote (*Fourth Church*, September 1928).[33] Stone's 1928 goals reflected a much reduced vision. The cultural changes as well as the controversies and conflicts in the church in the 1920s took their toll on the confidence of many in the Protestant church.

CONCLUSION

What had changed in American culture in the 1920s? The universities were questioning traditional religious perspectives, Prohibition was attacked in the press, and Puritan values came under intense scrutiny.[34] Even in the Protestant church, modernist perspectives on the authority of Scripture made significant inroads through such leaders as Harry Emerson Fosdick. Missionaries second-guessed the certainty of their calling and the righteousness of their cause (Fitzmier and Balmer, 1991). With the economic boom more people began to spend their resources on interests broader than those of the church. The symbolic life of the United States was less shaped by its Puritan heritage and less bound by the Protestant ethic. Just as the centripetal forces of Protestantism dominated the 1910s, the centrifugal energies of the 1920s caused a splintering in the culture's values and interests.[35] These changes marked the decline in the Protestant establishment's influence. In the postwar years the Protestant establishment no longer set the agenda for the culture.

In the 1910s and early 1920s Stone embodied the bold and aggressive leadership of Protestants in every aspect of culture, politics, economics, and religion. He used the methods and strategies of the business world to exploit the market of his social setting. Early in his ministry the Near North Side teemed with single young adults from rural areas who were ripe for evangelization. Stone and the leadership of Fourth Presbyterian capitalized on these opportunities. In the 1920s the Near North Side became more prosperous, and fewer young adults could afford to live in the area. Moreover, walk-up buildings gave way to high-rise apartments that did not allow for visitation and were built for greater privacy (Stamper, 1991). Access to individuals thus became more difficult. Not only did the social ecology of the Near North Side change, but the values of the American Puritan past no longer animated the culture. Business and the ambition to get ahead displaced the values of the church. Stone attempted to adjust to this by continuing to utilize the business strategies of such friends as Roger Babson to motivate his lay leadership to evangelize and Christianize the Near North Side, the nation, and the world. These strategies, however, failed to produce the kind of results that Stone had accomplished in the prewar years. The changes in the local setting and the shift in the cultural terrain affected Stone and the church, forcing them to lower their expectations for growth and to shift to conserving the institution by expanding the church endowment. In the end Stone wrestled with social and cultural movements beyond his control.

The decline of the Protestant mainline that is often described as an event of the 1960s was already an ongoing process in the 1920s. All of the signs were there at the time: the weakening of missionary zeal; the dwindling of financial resources for church growth; the decrease in human resources for the mission field; the decline of religious practice, including Sabbath observance and family prayers; and the general cultural shift toward consumerist-oriented values. Stone resisted the changes in the culture partly by challenging wealthy families to refrain from passing their capital on to their children. Stone's admonitions misfired at the end. The displacement of the Protestant establishment was far from final, but its heyday was clearly in the past.

As Stone moved on to become president of McCormick Theological Seminary, Fourth Presbyterian's new pastor, the thirty-six-year-old Harrison Ray Anderson, sought to sustain the church's place in Protestant culture. Beginning in 1928, Anderson would fight for the next thirty-three years to maintain the Puritan Protestant symbolic boundaries of the Protestant mainline. Anderson would continue to work toward a form of cultural Protestantism, but this would be an uphill battle against trends in the culture no one foresaw in 1928.

NOTES

1. The Near North Side's population in 1920 was approximately 90,000.

2. Zorbaugh's 1920 demographic breakdown of the Near North Side classified 28 percent of the population as "foreign nationalities" and the rest as "native-born population" (Zorbaugh, [1929] 1983:45).

3. Two thousand of the total six thousand people whose names were on the social registry in the city and suburbs lived on the Gold Coast. As Zorbaugh points out, these Gold Coast inhabitants were the acknowledged leaders of this society (Zorbaugh, [1929] 1983:47).

4. *Fourth Church* was the Fourth Presbyterian's newsletter, published monthly from 1910 to 1940. The newsletter was renamed *The Fourth Church* in 1941 and was published on a bimonthly basis until 1961.

5. Stone's papers include a series of sermon notebooks from 1916 to 1922, averaging each year more than 1,500 pages of typewritten notes on speeches and sermons that he was preparing. They are not scholarly, but they reflect a preacher who was intent on pious evaluations of biblical texts. None of these writings comments on current events or the theological controversies of the time.

6. Andrew Stevenson, president of the Young Men's Presbyterian Union of Chicago, used the title *Chicago: Pre-eminently a Presbyterian City* in a 1907 book that described three Presbyterian institutions in Chicago: the McCormick Theological Seminary, Lake Forest University, and the Presbyterian Hospital (Stevenson, 1907).

7. The originators of the group were Henry P. Crowell, Quaker Oats chairman and elder at the Fourth Presbyterian Church; A. C. Bartlett, an industrialist; Julius Rosenwald, founder of Sears; and Jane Addams, a Fourth Presbyterian Church member and the founder of Hull-House in Chicago.

8. The 1912 Chicago Vice Report on prostitution in Chicago makes it clear that this "social evil" was not a small problem. The report described a study made of a group of 1,012 women identified as working prostitutes. These women received more than 15,000 visits a day, which meant over 5 million visits a year. The report estimated that there were probably five times the number of women in the group studied working in prostitution in metropolitan Chicago. A conservative estimate is that Chicago prostitutes had well over 20 million visits annually (Lippmann, 1969:98).

9. The report to which Lippmann was referring is the Chicago Vice Report. It was written by a Chicago Commission in 1912 and reflected the influence and thinking of the Committee of Fifteen.

10. In an apt coincidence there is an advertisement for Quaker Oats beside the article about Stone in the *Christian Herald*. This placement underlines the intimate relationship not only between Stone and Henry Parsons Crowell, the head of Quaker Oats, but also between the efforts of clergy and American business.

11. Crowell's biography, written with his cooperation, was called *Breakfast Table Autocrat* (Day, 1946).

12. Crowell was a financial backer behind the publication of *The Fundamentals* in 1909. This was a set of twelve volumes of conservative scholarly writings that delineated the principles behind the fundamentalist movement of the 1910s and 1920s. The most significant doctrines included the inerrancy of Scripture, the atonement of Christ for the sins of the world, and the need for a personal commitment to Christ. These volumes were distributed free to three million people in the United States and around the world (Heidebrecht, 1989:176).

13. After Crowell's transformation in 1898, he adopted a habit of tithing that included giving 65 percent of his annual income to the cause of the Christian gospel and the church.

14. Stone's recorded response to a businessman who was reluctant to give money to the church's cause exemplifies the language Stone used: "Well, old man, I am in

business, too, but I am in business for another Man, and I am after more business and money to make that business go, and my Master has told me to push it into the world. If you will pull down your old Bible, I will show you my orders" (*Fourth Church*, July 1915).

15. Stelzle was a minister and social activist who had been born into poverty in New York City's Bowery in 1869. According to Randall Balmer and John R. Fitzmier, "In 1903 he was commissioned by the Presbyterian Board of Home Missions to begin work with urban workers. The ministry grew as both the church and the nation became aware of the social problems of urbanization. The Presbyterians were the first denomination to form a separate department to deal with these problems; in 1906 Stelzle became the first superintendent of the Presbyterian Department of Church and Labor. As head of the new department he lectured, took surveys that formed the basis of the church's overall strategy to address the needs of urban laborers, and attended labor union meetings and councils" (Balmer and Fitzmier, 1993:220).

16. Fourth Presbyterian, during Stone's tenure, sponsored three mission churches on the Near North Side: Christ Church (Affiliated), the Carter Memorial Assyrian Persian Chapel, and the Hubbard Memorial Bohemian Church. In two cases Fourth Presbyterian enabled the churches to build sanctuaries. In each case the churches were supported by Fourth Presbyterian benevolence funds. There were reports on the churches in each *Fourth Church* during the 1910s and 1920s. By the late 1920s the churches were accepted into the Chicago Presbytery of the Presbyterian Church U.S.A. Stone was committed to the Czech-speaking Christians and Christian Persians, each of whom had significant populations on the Near North Side.

17. The building contract was fully subscribed by the congregation at $650,000. The actual total, along with extra moneys for maintenance, was $740,575. The McCormick family contributions totaled more than $300,000 by the end of the campaign.

18. "Our city," the *Fourth Church* declared, is proud of the distinction of being the first in the country to elect an American-born conductor, and the Fourth Presbyterian is glad to lend her distinguished and genial organist and director for this patriotic service" (*Fourth Church*, October 1918).

19. Ann Douglas's explanation for the decline of the Protestant minister's power is apt: "American Calvinism possessed in the seventeenth and eighteenth centuries, and lost in the nineteenth, a toughness, a sternness, an intellectual rigor which our society then and since has been accustomed to identify with 'masculinity' in some not totally inaccurate if circular sense" (A. Douglas, 1977:18).

20. Nationally and in the Fourth Presbyterian Church, women outnumber men by two to one in membership and attendance.

21. Crowell and Nettie McCormick were major contributors to the Billy Sunday revival in Chicago (McLoughlin, 1955:115).

22. As William G. McLoughlin describes in his biography of Billy Sunday, 1918 was the turning point in Sunday's popularity. In the 1920s many abandoned Sunday's dramatic style of evangelism. Sunday became increasingly ideologically conservative and

racist toward the end of his life (McLoughlin, 1955:295). It is illuminating that Stone's respect for Sunday remained strong; Stone apparently tolerated Sunday's crudeness and bigotry because of Sunday's overwhelming passion for the gospel.

23. Loesch also became Crowell's close confidant. Loesch put together the complex trust funds that Crowell left to the Moody Bible Institute. These trusts had theological conditions that if broken disallowed the release of funds (Day, 1946:275).

24. As I worked through the archives, reading through the monthly newsletters from 1913 to 1930, I found only five references to the invitation committee's work. The 1914 annual report notes that the invitation committee had interviewed 1,118 young men in the district. In 1916, it reported 3,474 interviews; in 1922, 3,000 were interviewed; in 1928, 1,500 were interviewed.

25. Stone was thoroughly committed to foreign missions and the process of transforming society and the individual. In every *Fourth Church* there were several pages devoted to letters from foreign missionaries. In the late 1920s the missionaries of Fourth Presbyterian, whose annual number averaged thirty during Stone's tenure, were always listed in *Fourth Church*.

26. A 1922 letter from William Wiser, a Fourth Presbyterian missionary to India, captures the transformation that was taking place in many missionaries' understanding of their purpose. Mission was becoming a reciprocal learning experience: "The Indian Christian church is slowly shifting from its relation of dependence on the west to a position of independence. There are many discouraging features about the transition but with the leadership of Christ it will all come right. One feels as one watches the processes that some day not far distant we may come to India to learn as well as to teach. The troublesome feature of all the reconstruction is that we missionaries have more or less considered ourselves appointed by God to come here and tell these people the way in which they are to go. When they were like so many children we had very little difficulty in making them believe that we were in the right. We have educated them and we have taught them their independence in Christ. Now when suddenly they seem to have 'gone beyond themselves' they simply are expressing that independence which we urged upon them. The shocking part for many is that they go so far as to say that our western civilization has been developed along wrong lines and they quoted instance after instance to prove it. To say the least they have got some of us guessing. . . . Frankly it is no small education to get thousands of miles away from home and try to look at oneself through oriental eyes" (quoted in *Fourth Church*, March 1922).

27. The Borden Library had no less than twenty missionary journals from across the world, including *China's Millions; Missionary Link; Philippine Presbytery; Guatemala News;* and *Neglected Arabia*. It reported that in 1928 three thousand volumes were borrowed from the Borden Library (*Fourth Church*, May 1928).

28. The riot was preceded by conflicts over labor relations and the segregation of African Americans in a limited housing area. "But resentment," Paul Heidebrecht points out, "had been growing in the stockyards where blacks comprised 32 percent of the work force. Particularly galling to the white laborers was the unwillingness of

blacks to join the unions (which continued to require segregated locals) thus giving employers significant leverage against them. Blacks, on the other hand, confined to severely overcrowded sections of the city, grew increasingly restless about their housing conditions and inadequate schools. Also, many Chicago blacks had fought in the War (including the heroic, entirely black 8th Illinois regiment) and returned with a distinct inclination to fight back against white aggression" (Heidebrecht, 1989:95).

29. This triumphalist spirit was shared by most Protestants of the era but not by all. Harry Emerson Fosdick, who was as dedicated as Stone in cheering on the troops, made an unqualified commitment to peace after the war. Fosdick was nationally known as a key figure in the pacifist movement in the interwar years (R. M. Miller, 1985:496–97).

30. Nettie Fowler McCormick contributed $250,000 annually to missions through the Fourth Presbyterian Church during the 1910s (Day, 1946:189).

31. Benton Johnson makes the point that religious ritual and practice are the essential building blocks for a vital religious tradition: "But it is not a trivial thing when we remind ourselves that spiritual practice is one of the three pillars of a religious tradition, the other two being its teaching and its morality." Moreover, without practice the habits of religious belief and behavior are lost: "Without teaching and spiritual practice the will to live by the moral code of a faith fades away" (Johnson, 1990b:107).

32. Walter W. Powell and Paul J. DiMaggio further explicate the idea of homogenization by defining it as a form of isomorphism: "The concept that best captures the process of homogenization is *isomorphism*. . . . [It is] a constraining process that forces one unit in a population to resemble other units that face the same set of environmental conditions" (Powell and DiMaggio, 1991:66).

33. Another sign of the changing neighborhood and the need for greater degrees of privacy in American life was the fact that by 1929 addresses of new members were no longer printed in *Fourth Church*.

34. As Martin E. Marty has pointed out, "The tearing apart of Protestantism in the twenties, then, is one of the major incidents of American religious history" (Marty, 1991: 158).

35. R. Stephen Warner observes that as the Protestant mainline continues to speak to the whole society, its message has little particularity or persuasive power in the pluralistic and competitive market of American religion (Warner, 1993:1044–93).

John Timothy Stone
1908–28

Harrison Ray Anderson
1928–61

Elam Davies
1961–84

John Buchanan
1985–present

Fourth Presbyterian Church ministers, 1908–present

Fourth Presbyterian's English Gothic structure shortly after its dedication in 1914.

This 1914 photo of Fourth Presbyterian's sanctuary illustrates the traditional features of the church and its classical elegance.

The tympanum over the main entrance to Fourth Presbyterian, with the inscription "The Master is here and calleth for thee."

Fourth Presbyterian's chancel, largely unchanged throughout the years, features the fumed oak of the original design.

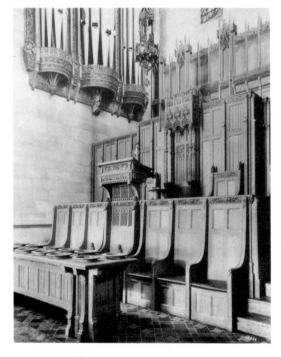

Blair Chapel, named in honor of the Blair family, longtime members of the church, is pictured here as it appeared in 1971, before it was moved to its current location on Delaware Avenue in 1996. It seats 125 and is used for special services and educational activities.

In 1923 Fourth Presbyterian, pictured just beyond the Water Tower at the left of the photo, held its own among the buildings on North Michigan Avenue. (Photo by the *Chicago Daily News;* courtesy of the Chicago Historical Society, photo no. DN-76816)

This 1990 shot portrays the way the church is now overshadowed by high rises on North Michigan Avenue.

Fourth Presbyterian in the 1990s, "A Light in the City"

3

THE CULTURAL PROTESTANT CHURCH
IN TENSION, 1928–61

With its scanty respect for the common people and their causes, Presbyterianism united the rigorous Calvinistic discipline, designed to free men
from the sins of luxury and sensuality rather than from the evils of injustice and inequality. Like its Genevan prototype it was without any real
awareness of the social evils which oppressed the common people, while
the sober kingdom of God on earth which it sought to found was not
designed either to excite the hopes or enlist the energies of those for whom
temptation to luxurious living was, to say the least, an abstract and remote
contingency.

—H. Richard Niebuhr, *The Social Sources of Denominationalism,* 1929

IN THE 1920s Fourth Presbyterian was labeled the "Millionaires' Club" (Zorbaugh, [1929] 1983:184). To be sure the tag fit, but Stone had evangelized not only
the wealthy but also the single young adults in the rooming-house district on
the Near North Side. Although powerful Protestant establishment figures ran
the church, it was populated by middle- and upper-middle-class individuals.
Nonetheless, at the end of Stone's tenure the church had plateaued in membership and money, despite his efforts. The Protestant establishment no longer had
a stronghold on the political, economic, and particularly the cultural and moral
ethos of the culture. Fourth Presbyterian had entered a precarious period.

Harrison Ray Anderson became Fourth Presbyterian's pastor in 1928. Anderson, more than Stone or Anderson's successors, embodied the ethos of what
Max Weber would call the "Protestant ethic" (Weber, 1958:80–81). This tradition honored work and sobriety and condemned luxury and sensuality. Anderson made few compromises with the social registry class of the Gold Coast.
Indeed, Anderson and the church's leadership carried out a moral crusade
against every form of civic and moral corruption. They censured the bootleg-
gers and the New Deal politicians of the pre–World War II era. They attacked

the police corruption and sexual immorality of the postwar period. Purified moral boundaries took priority over other concerns, even the maintenance of theological orthodoxy in the wider Protestant church.

Anderson and the church's leadership valued the power of discipline in the economic sphere, even as they channeled these interests toward moral purity and the fight for civic righteousness. Anderson thus confirmed the social boundaries of the Gold Coast and at the same time passionately pursued a vision of a sober social order based on Puritan moral norms. Anderson's cultural Protestantism was carved out in the midst of a culture opening to a new consumerism, especially in the post–World War II years. Anderson and his leadership contested moral boundaries at every point. Ironically, even as they led the fight against immorality and corruption, they overlooked the segregation of class and race that flourished in the 1940s and 1950s in Chicago. They ignored lower-status groups except as they judged their moral standards and ministered to them as objects of charity. By midcentury, issues of social justice took center stage in the moral discourse of Protestant theologians. The concern for racial and class injustice displaced the focus on moral boundaries and individual virtue. This displacement paralleled the decentering of the Protestant establishment and its loss in cultural and political leadership. Despite these changes, up until the early 1960s the ascetic Protestantism of Anderson and his church challenged the people and leadership of Chicago.

CHICAGO'S SOCIAL BOUNDARIES, 1928–44

The Prosperous Decade

In the 1920s wealthy investors led commercial development on North Michigan Avenue, creating an avenue of dreams. This production of high-status goods collided with the ascetic tradition of the Protestant ethic. Gratification won out over austerity as the era's economic prosperity produced more clubs to serve the needs of the wealthy, *not* more missionaries for the church. Within a three-year period three prestigious clubs were erected on North Michigan Avenue. The Illinois Women's Athletic Club was built in 1927 at 820 North Michigan Avenue; the Woman's Chicago Athletic Club was completed in 1928 at 626 North Michigan Avenue; and the Medinah Club, a select men's club and the most ambitious project of them all, opened at 505 North Michigan Avenue in 1929. Each of these clubs boasted magnificent multistory buildings. Membership was exclusive, based on gender, class, and ethnicity (Stamper, 1991:136–37).

This culture of enjoyment in the 1920s challenged Puritan moral norms.

Fourth Presbyterian was not immune to this celebration of the high life. The church's monthly newsletter supported itself with advertising. One of the ads was emblematic of many. It pictured a woman in fine clothing, and the caption read, "Distinction: Defined—worthy material and nicety of workmanship" (*Fourth Church*, February 1929). These ads were opposite the listings of missionaries and letters from men and women in the mission field, letters that described the hardship and the glory of sharing the gospel.

The placement of symbols of sacrifice next to advertisements for the upper class flags the inherent tension between Christ and culture in the ethic of the Protestant establishment. As Max Weber suggested, when discipline was exercised in a professional calling, there was a propensity to create capital; in time, however, the power of ascetic Protestant sanctions diminished, and individuals began to take advantage of the rewards of their labor (Weber, 1958:176–77). Anderson made no compromise with this kind of temptation. Throughout his tenure he supported temperance, Prohibition, observance of the Sabbath, and family worship. To the end of his ministry he attacked behavior outside these moral parameters.

Nonetheless, the focus of Fourth Presbyterian's theological boundaries were this-worldly. In Anderson's public rhetoric and preaching, salvation was not so much a matter of eternity in the world to come but a new and enhanced life in the present world.[1] Religion functioned not as an end in itself but as a means to empower one's life. This utilitarian turn was in full swing in the 1920s, as religious rhetoric began to mirror the logic of the era's economic interests. Religious leaders used the language of business to improve the efficiency and productivity of the church, but this strategy had ambiguous results. The number of missionaries and resources for their going into the foreign field declined. The vision of Stone and the passion of William Whiting Borden no longer expressed the dreams of the Protestant mainline.

Prosperity surrounded Fourth Presbyterian to an unprecedented degree. High-rise luxury apartment buildings became common. Landlords charged anywhere from $350 to $1,000 a month for rent (Zorbaugh, [1929] 1983:7). Advertisements for these buildings were included in the *Fourth Church*, with tag lines that read "restricted tenancy." This meant not only restrictions on those unable to afford the rents but also racial and ethnic exclusions. There was no official restriction against African Americans at Fourth Presbyterian, but there were no African American members during Anderson's tenure.[2] These kinds of exclusions, though not official, defined the social boundaries of the Fourth Presbyterian Church.

Sources of Pollution

Groups carve out their identity through those they exclude. Throughout the 1920s and 1930s the Protestant establishment produced its boundaries by using labels. Fourth Presbyterian and its leadership spoke of crime organizations in Chicago as progenitors of moral and cultural pollution. The conflict between the Protestant establishment and organized crime, however, was based not only on differences in moral norms but on ethnicity and religion as well. Protestants represented themselves as "native-born" Americans and identified criminals as new immigrants and Catholics.

Economically, the social boundaries were clear. Since the Protestant establishment controlled much of the corporate business ventures of the time, more recent immigrants fought over control of the underworld.[3] Bootlegging and the sale and distribution of alcohol brought in enormous financial rewards. In 1927 the legendary Al Capone and his illegal businesses took in an annual income of $105 million (Bergreen, 1994:236). Capone manipulated the city government and the police through bribery; he was an antihero to many Chicagoans, particularly those in the lower classes.[4]

In the late 1920s Fourth Presbyterian worked with Frank J. Loesch to oppose organized crime. Loesch was head of the Chicago Crime Commission in the late 1920s and early 1930s and was a key figure in Capone's eventual public vilification. Loesch had come to Fourth Presbyterian at the invitation of Stone. He became a close ally of Anderson and a tireless worker for law and order. President of the congregation from 1930 to his death in 1944, Loesch embodied Anderson's ideal: a man who came from humble roots, achieved professional success, witnessed for the gospel, and ardently supported civic virtue in Chicago.

As head of the Chicago Crime Commission, Loesch uncovered and prosecuted corruption during the Republican primaries of 1928. He indicted sixty-three men, most of whom were convicted and fined. Capone became his main target. Capone was said to be "the head center of the devilment afflicting Chicago" (Bergreen, 1994:294). Loesch organized a face-to-face meeting with Capone to solicit his cooperation in the 1928 Republican primaries, or, as Loesch put it, to ask if he would keep "his damned Italian hoodlums out of the election this coming fall" (quoted in Bergreen, 1994:294).[5] Capone, apparently sensing no advantage for himself in the elections, agreed to Loesch's demand. At the time of the elections, Capone ordered the police to protect the polling places. Loesch called it the "most successful election in Chicago in forty years" (quoted in Bergreen, 1994:295).

This reveals not only the tremendous power that Capone had over the city but also the willingness of Fourth Presbyterian and Protestant establishment figures, such as Loesch, to battle civic corruption. Anderson, unlike Stone, confronted problems of crime and civic dishonesty. To be sure, these civic battles had an admixture of racial and class bias, but the fights also took enormous energy and courage. The depression and World War II curtailed the moral crusades of Anderson and his leadership as the economic and world crisis took center stage.

The Depression and World War II

On October 24, 1929, the stock market crashed and ruptured the security, comfort, and luxury of those living on the Gold Coast. In 1930 apartment rentals were 50 percent of the rates charged in 1928; leases on commercial property decreased by 90 percent. Real estate plummeted in value, losing 75 to 90 percent of its original price in a five-year period. Twelve of the major commercial buildings foreclosed during the early 1930s alone.[6]

This overexpansion was mirrored across the country in almost every area of the economy. As William Leuchtenburg summarized in examining the depression in *The Perils of Prosperity, 1914–32*, "The crash exposed the weaknesses that underlay the prosperous economy of the 1920s—the overexpansion of major industries, the maldistribution of income, the weak banking structure, and the overdependence of the economy on consumer durable goods" (Leuchtenburg, 1958:247). In 1932 alone 660,000 jobless men and women walked the streets of Chicago. In 1933 the unemployed in the nation numbered approximately 16 million, almost a third of the working population. Herbert Hoover lost in 1932 to Franklin Roosevelt, not because of Roosevelt's program proposals but because people needed a change (Leuchtenburg, 1958:267).[7] Despite the economic downturn the Gold Coast and Fourth Presbyterian continued in their conservative patterns. Anderson, to the end of his ministry, hearkened back to Hoover as a man of honor and great competency, and he often complained that Hoover had gotten a "raw deal."

Anderson, while a conservative, was no isolationist—nor was he a pacifist.[8] When the United States entered the war in December 1941, he had the session write a paragraph in full support of the effort, in part justifying Anderson's support of the war: "As Christian citizens we believe in the righteousness of our nation's cause and pledge our support to it. We call upon all to gird themselves for the long grim days that are ahead" (Session Minutes, December 12, 1941). Navy midshipmen from Abbot Hall on the Northwestern University campus regularly attended worship services. Support of the war effort was unflagging at Fourth Presbyterian throughout the conflict. At the same time, as we will see later in the discussion on Anderson's theological boundaries, Anderson, unlike Stone, warned against the coercive nature of the state and understood the church as a bulwark against overweening power of the state.

CHICAGO'S SOCIAL BOUNDARIES, 1945–61

Urban Renewal and the Second Ghetto

The development of urban renewal and the creation of postwar public housing in Chicago give a vivid expression of social inequality. The Protestant establishment was in part responsible for these developments. Fourth Presbyterian's role, however, in the construction of the ghetto is a complex story. Anderson and his leadership concentrated their efforts on the moral life of the city. Civic order and economic enterprises took much of their energy. The ghettos of Chicago were objects of charity. The sources of Chicago's ghettos, however, were never investigated. The ideology of cultural Protestantism rationalized this blindness: economic success, often at whatever price, justified the segregation of certain populations. Minority groups were judged less productive and an impediment to the expansion of civic and corporate endeavors. The Protestant establishment supported corporate expansion at every turn and assumed that groups and individuals unable to take advantage of economic opportunities were morally inferior and thus unworthy of prosperity. This began to change in the 1960s, but these symbolic boundaries made the construction of public housing in some ways inevitable.

As the economy picked up following the war, national prosperity failed to translate into better living standards for African Americans in Chicago. Most lived in slums on the South Side and West Side. The 1940s began with a strong liberal impulse in which groups exerted pressure against racial bias, particularly in their opposition to restrictive covenants. In 1948 the Supreme Court rendered all restrictive covenants unenforceable (*Shelley v. Kraemer*). This movement for greater equality for ethnic groups and particularly for African Americans was short-lived and had ironic consequences in Chicago. It precipitated a slow exodus of middle-class African Americans away from the slums of the city. This trend further isolated those at the very bottom of the economic ladder; public housing was built to house this destitute population.

In the immediate postwar years slums surrounded the Loop business district. At the same time, the Loop experienced tremendous economic expansion. The leaders of Chicago's business district worried about the vitality of the downtown area. As it was, the slum dweller populated the area around State Street. To avoid the flight of businesses and whites from the downtown, the Loop business leaders demanded urban renewal, which in the end was simply slum clearance.

This process, as Arnold Hirsch described it in *Making the Second Ghetto: Race and Housing in Chicago, 1940–1960,* was initiated by two Protestant businessmen. One was Milton C. Mumford, an assistant vice president of Marshall Field and Company. The other was Holman D. Pettibone, president of the Chicago Title and Trust Company. Both were small-town, midwestern Protestants. Each had come from modest circumstances and had risen to the top of his profession. Both shared strong ambitions to continue to expand their business interests. Their strategy, however, was to work behind the scenes and to avoid as much as possible the "race problem." Neither was specifically related to Fourth Presbyterian, but their concerns and strategies are representative of the perspectives and behavior of ministers and laypeople at Fourth Presbyterian.

This avoidance of the race problem became clear in the complex negotiations that preceded the plans for clearing the slum areas. The Chicago Housing Authority (CHA), whose primary task was to build public housing, was not trusted by Republican politicians at the state level or by the business elite in the city. The governor's office demanded the creation of the Chicago Land Clearance Commission. Its purpose was "to purchase, condemn, clear, and resell slum properties to private developers" (Hirsch, 1983:110). This new development was critical because the CHA operated publicly owned housing and had a nondiscriminatory tenant selection policy. The back-room political maneuverings were cemented by two legislative enactments essential to this urban renewal movement. In 1947 the state legislature passed the Blighted Areas Redevelopment Act and approved the Urban Community Conservation Act in 1953. Each of these pieces of legislation enabled private developers to clear slums legally and, with private and public moneys, to rebuild commercial and public institutions in the area around the Loop. They hoped to attract middle- and upper-middle-class whites to the city. They promised displaced families public housing near the area from which they had been removed.

The CHA, which in the 1940s was a progressive group that challenged the status quo, by the early 1950s had become, through political pressures, the servant of business interests of the Loop. Politicians and the CHA acceded to the demands of established ethnic groups. These ethnic parties did not want and would not allow African Americans to live in their communities. In time the CHA became the primary actor in building the second ghetto.[9]

Mumford and Pettibone were not oblivious to the race problem. In speaking to Martin Kennelly, mayor of Chicago, they hoped to keep the state legislation entirely free of any reference to racial distinctions or restrictions (Hirsch, 1983:111). They took shelter in the separate but equal doctrine of the time, which, considering the results of public housing development in the 1950s and 1960s, was tragic, as Arnold Hirsch pointed out:

> Of thirty-three projects approved between 1950 and the mid-1960s, twenty-five and a substantial portion of another were located in census tracts containing a black population in excess of 75 percent. Of the remaining seven developments, six were located in areas undergoing racial transition. By the time the projects were actually completed, only one of the thirty-three was situated in an area that was less than 84 percent; and all but seven of the developments, when actually completed, were located in census tracts that were at least 95 percent black. . . . There was little doubt that the CHA, as critics later charged, was building almost a solid corridor of low rent housing along the State Street and nearby streets from Cermak Road (22nd Street) to 51st Street. This policy of intensive centralization led simply to the pyramiding of existing ghettos and the concentration of a host of urban ills. (Hirsch, 1983:242–43)

The second ghetto was produced by not only the Protestant business interests but also the city's ethnic populations and even some African American politicians. William L. Dawson, an African American member of the U.S. House of Representatives at the time, is the classic representative of this group. His rise to prominence coincided with the building of the second ghetto. Dawson would not risk confrontation with city officials over the segregation of African Americans because he benefited from the officials' support and won elections because of the centralization of his constituents. Dawson therefore agreed to the development and segregation of public housing for African Americans in the city of Chicago.

The creation of social inequality in Chicago was thus the product of a combination of interests that included the Protestants, various ethnic groups, and leadership in the African American community. They all had a common interest in securing their privilege and power and safeguarding their futures. In this way the groups resembled one another across race and ethnicity; each worked to consolidate class boundaries. The result for African Americans was segregation into public housing. Compounding the social isolation of public housing was the slow but steady movement of middle-class African Americans away from their poorer counterparts. These combination of forces created the new underclass of African Americans. Moreover, industries followed the middle class to the suburbs, further divesting the city of economic resources and the blue-collar jobs that had drawn so many African Americans to Chicago in the first place. The isolation and the lack of resources devastated the African American community. Poverty, crime, and family disintegration reached an all-time high.[10] This concentration of conditions within the cramped confines of public housing resulted in social chaos, particularly in the 1970s and 1980s (Wilson, 1987:20–62).

As the second ghetto was being built in the late 1940s and 1950s, Fourth Presbyterian continued to grow and prosper. The church did not resist this social movement, but neither Fourth Presbyterian nor any other Protestant bodies worked to integrate African Americans into mainstream American culture. This was a de facto policy of separate but equal. The rhetoric of separate but equal was toothless, however, and was used to mollify tensions and to pacify those displaced in the process of the economic expansion on the Magnificent Mile.

Slum Clearance and the Magnificent Mile

Prosperity and growth returned to North Michigan Avenue following World War II. While some organizations failed because of the depression, such institutions as the Wrigley Building, the Tribune Tower, the Palmolive Building, and Fourth Presbyterian all survived the depression and did well because they carried no debts. The upside to urban renewal was the clearance of slums and the opportunity for neighborhood transformation from the South Side to the Near North Side. On the Near South Side both the Michael Reese Hospital and the Illinois Institute of Technology (IIT) decided to remain in the city in the late 1940s because of slum clearance. They used the land around them to expand and build. Moreover, luxury apartment complexes were constructed all around IIT and the Michael Reese Hospital in the early 1950s, thus completing the gentrification of the area.

This development coincided with the building of massive public housing projects that included the Robert Taylor Homes and the Stateway Gardens, to name just two. These two projects were strategically placed along the South Parkway (which in the 1960s was renamed Martin Luther King Jr. Drive) to segregate the African American community. The segregation was further secured in the early 1960s with the clearance of slums and the building of the Dan Ryan Expressway. The expressway separated ethnic white neighborhoods to the west from the public housing complexes and African American population to the east (Hirsch, 1983:244). These public works programs, spearheaded by the Daley administration, accomplished multiple tasks: the creation of jobs, more secure social boundaries for ethnic groups, and the further segregation of the African American population in Chicago.

These same processes of slum clearance and urban renewal took place on the Near North Side with the LaSalle redevelopment project and the building of the Carl Sandburg Village apartments. Developers cleared African American slum areas for what were intended to be mixed-income housing units. These apartments, however, were eventually rented to middle- and upper-middle-class individuals (Mayer and Wade, 1969:388). Urban renewal helped further secure the prosperity of the Gold Coast, as Mike Royko pointed out:

> Urban renewal was the greatest deceit. True, slum property was being cleared. But it wasn't being replaced by housing for those who were dispossessed. The poor were moved into other marginal neighborhoods, and highly profitable upper middle-class developments replaced the slums. The most glaring example was the Sandburg Village high-rise development, about twelve blocks north of the Loop. It was supposed to have been moderate-income housing. It became one of the most popular places for young, well-off moderns to live, if they could afford the $200-plus rents. On the West Side, where conditions were the worst, nothing was being built, although large tracts of land were available. (Royko, 1971:148)

A major revisioning of North Michigan Avenue began in 1947. Arthur Rubloff called this project the Magnificent Mile. The idea was to develop the area on the basis of human-scale architecture. Low-rise stores and office buildings were to line the avenue. Rubloff proposed the renovation of old buildings, the addition of a park, and more efficient traffic and parking to develop the area's commercial and shopping potential (Stamper, 1991:206).

Rubloff's vision failed because real estate developers wanted larger buildings so they would get a greater return on their investments. This large-scale development began with the construction of the Prudential Building in 1955 at Randolph Street north of Grant Park. It was followed by the Equitable Building at the northeast corner of the Michigan Avenue Bridge Plaza in 1965. In 1969 the hundred-story John Hancock Building was completed. The Hancock Building towered over the Fourth Presbyterian Church. During the 1960s and 1970s the average height of North Michigan Avenue buildings was sixty-five stories—hardly low-rise, human-scale architecture (Stamper, 1991:215).

The Protestant elite in the postwar period feared that Chicago would lose most of its white upper-middle-class population. Suburbs were expanding dramatically, but Chicago's population remained stable until the 1960s. In 1950 the metropolitan population reached nearly 5,600,000; Chicago's population of 3,621,000 represented a moderate 6.6 percent increase over 1940 figures. In 1960 the respective populations of 6,794,461 and 3,550,404 represented a small loss for Chicago that would increase dramatically in the 1960s and 1970s. Nonetheless, the social boundaries of the Gold Coast and Loop business district were secured by the extensive construction of upper-middle-class commercial and residential buildings. This development insulated the Gold Coast from the ghetto and ensured the stratification of class and race in Chicago.

Fourth Presbyterian's prosperity mirrored the prosperity of the Gold Coast. The church paid little or no attention to the changing economic and social conditions of the era. Anderson and his leadership interpreted social and structural problems as matters of personal moral exigencies. When they attacked wider public issues it was with reference to the corruption of moral norms and the defense of Protestant cultural patterns.

THE SYMBOLIC BOUNDARIES OF A RIGHTEOUS CHURCH, 1928–61

Formation of a Protestant Establishment Pastor

In the 1920s businessmen found a home at Fourth Presbyterian, where John Timothy Stone was the quintessential "businessman in religion" (Lundén, 1988:66). Stone asked Anderson to come to Fourth Presbyterian in 1928 to be his co-pastor. Anderson, in a letter to the session, warned the session that he was a theological "conservative" (Session Minutes, June 12, 1928). Stone knew the kind of man he wanted to succeed him and run his church, and no one objected to this ideological bias.

Anderson was born in 1893 in Abilene, Kansas. Midwestern values of land and heritage deeply influenced him. He graduated from Kansas State University in civil engineering, and for three years worked on the Los Angeles aqueduct. He then enrolled at McCormick Theological Seminary. As a seminarian, he was a student minister under his mentor, John Timothy Stone, at Fourth Presbyterian. Not long after his graduation in 1917 Anderson went overseas to serve as a chaplain for the 103d U.S. Infantry. He was twice cited for meritorious service during the war.[11]

Anderson's experience in war profoundly affected his life. In 1957, at his seminary's fortieth class reunion, Anderson put it this way: "I lived daily with death. In spite of it all, the war did something great for me. I saw what was real and what was phony. I knew Jesus Christ and his gospel were adequate" (Seminary Reflections, 1957). At the 1979 memorial service for Anderson, his son spoke of how the war was "*the* major influence on his life and theology." The war took from him any illusions of imminent human progress and the optimism of turn-of-the-century liberalism. Anderson's childhood and early adult experiences shaped within him profoundly conservative values that venerated loyalty to country, obedience to God, and a passion for purity and honesty in every aspect of life.

Anderson also admired the wealthy and influential. He joined the Union League Club and the University Club of Chicago and was a thirty-third degree Mason, which was the highest position in this secret society, a society valued among upper-middle-class people at that time. Anderson developed friendships with Herbert Hoover and Dwight Eisenhower, whom he respected as moral leaders with conservative and traditional visions. Anderson used these connections to gain a platform for himself and for the issues of civic righteousness that he pursued untiringly.[12] In time honors came his way. In 1952 he was elected moderator of the General Assembly of the Presbyterian Church U.S.A. Anderson was chaplain for the 1944 Democratic National Convention and for the 1956 Republican National Convention.[13]

Enemy of the Working Man

In a interview with a former elder of Fourth Presbyterian, who had known Stone and had worked closely with Anderson, the elder told a story about Norman Swenson. After World War II Swenson managed the church's administration for more than thirty years. Swenson came to Fourth Presbyterian as a young man in the 1920s. Swenson's father, a carpenter and strong union man, warned Norman against Fourth Presbyterian. Dr. Stone was an "enemy of the working man." Stone was, the elder explained, from "the old tradition that you worked, you didn't bargain to work, you just worked" (Interview, April 19, 1994). Stone and Anderson took Swenson under their wing, and Swenson became one of Anderson's most important colleagues at the church and later one of Elam Davies's most trusted confidants. Neither Stone nor Anderson advocated directly for the concerns and causes of working people, but they were both often cited for their ability to relate to individuals at all levels of society.

Anderson followed in this conservative political tradition throughout his ministry. He consistently proclaimed that work was the best protection against the moral corruption of the lower and middle classes. Even as late as 1959 he complained in a sermon entitled "The Answer to Life's Monotony" about the reduction of the work week to five days. Anderson was not speaking to working people at Fourth Presbyterian. His congregants were privileged professionals. Their social status gave them the choice about what they would do with their personal and professional lives. Moreover, Anderson showed little empathy for those suffering as a result of the depression. As he said in a pastoral letter to his congregation, they should not complain: "What we are facing in a wave of depression other people have faced forever, until it is normal with them. To be underfed and cold and to suffer is a normal condition for millions of men. Our definition of depression would be their definition of prosperity" (*Fourth Church,* December 1930). Anderson could not have said these words to a working-class congregation in which most families were out of work and without shelter. He could say this to people who continued, on the whole, to maintain employment and roofs over their heads.

Anderson interpreted social crises as caused by moral failures. When hard times came to people, he called for moral uplift and repentance. No one, particularly from the Fourth Presbyterian congregation, had the right, in Anderson's worldview, to complain about conditions in the United States. Moreover, working people had no right to strike or disrupt the social order of society. Anderson repeatedly sided with his Kansas Republican roots that supported the consistent observance of law and order and attacked the immorality of labor organizers. As Robert Moats Miller put it, "Not only did the churches defend the gulf between the rich and the ragged, they unconsciously perpetuated this inequality by denouncing as unchristian all talk of class hatred. After all, Christ preached a gospel of love, and the workingman who expressed unlovely sentiments toward his employer was being un-Christlike. Above all, strikes and industrial violence was to be abhorred, for the only true solution to disputes was Christian charity and sweet reasonableness" (R. M. Miller, 1958:206).

Anderson took for granted social boundaries of class inequality. There is nothing mentioned about these issues in the session minutes of Fourth Presbyterian or the sermons during Anderson's tenure. This inattention was a function of upper-middle-class culture. Stone's and Anderson's avoidance of these issues was hardly unusual for their class, nor were they extraordinary in standing up for the least fortunate in their social setting.

Social prophets in American religion during the 1920s were rare. One of the few voices against social inequality was Reinhold Niebuhr. Niebuhr consistently attacked the overwhelming power of business interests and stood up for working men and women in the labor movement. Niebuhr first took his stand in Detroit, the city of his pastorate in the 1920s. At the height of Henry Ford's popularity, Niebuhr mounted a ferocious assault on Ford's character:

> It is difficult to determine whether Mr. Ford is simply a shrewd exploiter of a gullible public in his humanitarian pretensions, or whether he suffers from self-deception. My own guess is that he is at least as naive as he is shrewd, that he does not think profoundly on the social implications of his industrial policies, and that in some of his avowed humanitarian motives he is actually self-deceived. The tragedy of the situation lies in the fact that the American public is, on the whole, too

credulous and uncritical to make any critical analysis of the moral pretensions of this great industry. (quoted in R. M. Miller, 1958:180)

Anderson would have found this attack misplaced. In a June 26, 1938, sermon entitled "A Christian and His Money," he deemed business and professional success in the world as a sign of God's favor that implied the responsibility to give away a part of one's earnings (*Fourth Church*, September 1938). Yet Anderson could, when provoked by moral transgressions and character flaws, judge those who had succeeded. He vilified Andrew Carnegie's lack of support for Christian institutions and Carnegie's behavior in his rise to success. Anderson said in a sermon of 1932 that his family had befriended the Carnegie clan when they were struggling financially. Anderson reported that even though Carnegie's mother was a remarkable Christian woman, Carnegie had turned away from the faith. This lack of religion corrupted Carnegie's character and caused him, as Anderson said in a January 10, 1932, sermon, "On Learning How to Live on Each Side of the Street," to lose his sense of humanity:

> Carnegie's ideals were mastered by his passions and his passions were for gold. Then as he becomes a success after the pattern of men, see him secluded in a wooden glen of Scotland where news cannot reach him, and then see that bloody industrial battle fought at Homestead, Pennsylvania. See one after another of his partners broken and thrown aside. See a great group of men and women and little children fed into his furnace of steel and gold. He was a modern pirate sailing an industrial sea. Pray God he may be the last of the tribe and that with him that era of America closes. (*Fourth Church*, March 1932)

When provoked, Anderson's convictions rose to the surface; he pounded his own class and its interests with great ferocity. For Anderson the elite had a responsibility, given by God, to serve the interests of common people and to be their moral guides. It was an intentionally paternalistic relationship. Moreover, he rationalized economic inequality with the doctrine of stewardship: all wealth belonged to God, and the rich were merely stewards of God's capital. They were to dispense with this capital in accordance with the Lord's plan (R. M. Miller, 1958:206). Anderson spoke again and again of his class's obligation as stewards of God's blessings and as exemplars of old-fashioned Christianity.

Defending Old-Fashioned American Christianity

Anderson opposed the use of alcohol and strongly supported Prohibition. A summary of moral admonitions of the 1931 General Assembly of the Presbyterian Church U.S.A. mirrored the key issues that Anderson and his leadership upheld. These began with the affirmation of Hoover's call for greater observance of the law; support for the U.S. entrance into the World Court;[14] and enthusiastic approval for temperance, Prohibition, and Sabbath observance as "fundamentals of old-fashioned American Christianity" (quoted in *Fourth Church,* June 1931). Anderson encouraged restrictions against the commercialization of the Sabbath by professional sports and motion pictures. He proclaimed the sanctity of marriage as a cornerstone value and denounced the evils of divorce. In matters of social justice he upheld the two traditional admonitions against lynching and mob violence (*Fourth Church,* June 1931). What is perhaps most remarkable about this vision of Christian conscience is that Anderson pursued it for the next thirty years of his ministry. His regard for Hoover never changed; his dedication to the temperance movement never wavered; his loyalty to Sabbath observance was consistently strong; and his support of marriage and the traditional family persisted throughout his ministry. The only valid reason for divorce was adultery; throughout Anderson's tenure Fourth Presbyterian maintained the rule that only the innocent party in the divorce could remarry.

For Anderson the world and social structures could be reduced to individual moral circumstances. Adultery was an individual's moral failure, not a function of a problematic relationship or family system. Social oppression was caused by the corruption of civic officials, not powerful systems that unintentionally oppressed people and had tragic results. As Anderson explained in a January 1, 1933, sermon, "New Life in Christ," "The problems which the world presents are the problems which the individual presents multiplied" (*Fourth Church,* January 1933). There was therefore no way for Anderson to interpret the political and financial corruption resulting from Prohibition and the depression as anything other than personal moral failures on the part of individuals, as he proclaimed in a March 9, 1930, sermon, "Needed—A Real Cure": "Chicago's problem is not that she is bankrupt financially, but that she is bankrupt morally and spiritually. Her economic failure grows out of a character failure. She has lost her standing at the Bank of Heaven and her position before God needs to be restored as well as her standing before men" (*Fourth Church,* March 1930).

Anderson belittled all arguments for the repeal of Prohibition based on allowances for the weakness of human character or the advantage of taxes from a legal alcohol industry. He claimed these were specious rationalizations and accommodations to human corruption. Anderson often self-righteously scolded his Roman Catholic brethren in Chicago. He despised the hypocrisy of the church that continued to serve sacramental rites to the murdered members of Italian gangs, as he pointed out in his March 9, 1930, sermon: "It is to the everlasting shame of the organized church in this city, Roman and Protestant, that from her pulpits a mighty voice of thunder does not roll out against the wrong and for the right. Have we divorced religion and righteousness? Can men be members of the Church of Christ and kill and cheat and defraud?" (*Fourth Church*, March 1930).

In speaking for this old-fashioned principle Anderson and the Fourth Presbyterian leadership moved away from the agenda of the social registry class of the Gold Coast and the preferences of the American middle and upper middle class. Prohibition, observance of the Sabbath, and family worship had all lost their appeal to many Americans by the 1930s (Johnson, 1990a, 1990b). Anderson, however, continued to advocate for these ideas and movements following the repeal of Prohibition in 1933 and for the rest of his pastorate at Fourth Presbyterian. This stern and sober vision signaled his prophetic admonition to his congregation and to the Gold Coast—an iron fist in a velvet glove.

The Labeling of Social Pollution

Loesch took up Anderson's cudgel. In 1930, at the age of seventy-eight, Loesch attacked Capone as the source of moral and social pollution in Chicago. For Capone, as Laurence Bergreen writes, Loesch was "a toothless dragon backed by a bunch of rich gin-swilling hypocrites whose campaign against racketeers carried distinct overtones of racial and ethnic prejudice" (Bergreen, 1994:365). In a speech given at Princeton University in March 1931 Loesch said, "The American people are not a lawless people. It's the foreigners and the first generation of Americans who are loaded on us." When Loesch was pressed for an explanation, he explained, "The real Americans are not gangsters. Recent immigrants and the first generation of Jews and Italians are the chief offenders, with Jews furnishing the brains and the Italians the brawn" (quoted in *New York Times*, March 23, 1931).

Loesch's undiluted racism met with apparent impunity among his Fourth Presbyterian colleagues. It is not to say that Anderson shared these bigoted assumptions. However, Anderson regarded Loesch as a man of honor and moral character, and, to a degree, Loesch reflected the prejudiced definition of a true American held by members of the Gold Coast community and this Protestant church.[15]

Loesch, nonetheless, was no paper tiger in the conflict with Capone. Since Capone had such power with the police, city officials, and public opinion in Chicago, Loesch created a strategy to attack Capone where he was most vulnerable: his public appeal. Loesch ordered the Chicago Crime Commission to bring him a list of the top twenty-eight known murderers and gangsters in Chicago, which he had published on the front page of the *Chicago Tribune*. This was the public enemies list, with Capone as public enemy number one. This phrase originated with Loesch and became a part of the American lexicon, as Bergreen pointed out:

> The label struck a chord in a nation racked by the Depression, and Capone now became the scapegoat for all sorts of social ills. No longer was he indulged as a symptom of these ills; he was now perceived as the *cause*. Thanks to Loesch's publicity stunt, Al Capone became the first great American criminal of the twentieth-century, and as befits a modern criminal, he was an organization man, not a highway robber or lone killer, but a racketeer, the leader of an illegal fraternity. Conventional wisdom decreed that he and his organization had corrupted society as a whole, and the corruption was spreading fast. (Bergreen, 1994:367)

This stigmatization of criminals and, more insidiously, the tarnishing of racial and ethnic groups as inherently criminal began with Loesch's public relations defeat of Capone. Both Anderson and Loesch labeled good and evil in unambiguous terms. This rhetoric worked with great efficiency in the marketplace of public opinion. To be sure, this symbolic labeling defended them against an anomic threat. Whether the threat is the imposition of different racial and ethnic populations or the intrusion of foreign moral norms and customs, the preservation of symbolic and social boundaries is a bulwark in the maintenance of cultural and class identity.[16] Loesch excelled in using this stigmatization strategy, and he had the ear of powerful Protestants across the nation. He sat on the Presidential Commission on Crime in the 1920s and was in close communication with Herbert Hoover. J. Edgar Hoover, the director of the FBI, employed the public enemy strategy in the creation of the most-wanted list. Loesch utilized these connections to reinforce and advocate for the values of his Protestant civic vision.

Christianizing the Nation and World

Anderson was an evangelical Christian who continuously stressed the importance of converting others to Jesus Christ. The end, however, was not so much eternal life but fulfillment in this life. Having attended seminary in the 1910s, Anderson had been shaped by the intense missionary impulse of the early part of the century. In 1930 he said that the job of the Presbyterian Church U.S.A. was "to evangelize the 100,000,000 people in foreign lands who were without Christ" (*Fourth Church*, January 1930). But the 1930s brought change and decline into the foreign missionary effort. Theologians and missionaries questioned the legitimacy of mission work, which partially precipitated the decline in the numbers of men and women entering the mission field.[17] As Anderson's ministry progressed, less stress was placed on mission work in foreign lands and more emphasis on the conversion of those in the United States.[18]

Anderson stepped into a difficult period of leadership at Fourth Presbyterian. Economic challenges and a decline in the confidence of the Christian faith marked the decade of the 1930s. Hints of this are evident in Anderson's comments to the congregation: "The thrill to win hearts to Christ has disappeared in some quarters. The parish plan will help instill the motivation to go out and win others to Jesus Christ" (*Fourth Church,* August 1931). Anderson conceived of a plan to gather the congregation in groups of thirty-five to be led by officers of the church. The plan encouraged greater communication and fellowship within the congregation. Anderson expended enormous energy to make the plan work, but it had only moderate results through the years.

Fourth Presbyterian, like the country, turned inward during the 1930s.[19] It became less vibrant in its outreach and leaned on the heroes of the past for its inspiration. In the October 1938 *Fourth Church* three individuals were chosen as exemplars of Fourth Presbyterian laypeople. Two of them were men that Stone had converted and nurtured in leadership. The first was Arnim Ecke, a doctor, whom Stone convinced to be on the invitation committee. Within four years of his conversion Ecke personally led a hundred individuals to Christ; before his death in the early 1930s he converted many more (*Fourth Church,* October 1938). Stone used Ecke, more than any other individual, as a model of an evangelical Christian. Dick Ferrell was second. Ferrell, from a blue-collar background, had come to Chicago as a young man to fight professionally. He attended an evening service at Fourth Presbyterian, listened to Stone, and immediately wired his manager and said, "The fight all off—in future will fight for Jesus only" (quoted in *Fourth Church,* October 1938). Ferrell went on to become a missionary to the lumberjacks of the Pacific Northwest.

The last individual, R. B. Smith, was from Anderson's ministry. A successful businessman and an elder on the session, he was described as a "Christian gentleman," devout in his personal devotions, and faithful to his duties as an officer. Smith delighted in visiting those who had come to the city recently. At the end of each visit he invited the person to attend the Fourth Presbyterian Church. Smith's example looked rather pale in comparison with Ecke's and Ferrell's.

Anderson was not as effective as Stone in persuading others to follow his vision. At the same time, the theological controversy in the Presbyterian Church

U.S.A. in 1920s and the economic downturn of the 1930s significantly reordered many Americans' priorities. The Protestant church during this period lost some of its power in the culture. Nevertheless, men and women carried on Christian missions throughout the world from Fourth Presbyterian. Sam Higginbottom, another close associate of Stone, pursued mission work from the church. Focusing on agricultural development, he went to India to set up the Indian Agricultural Institute to teach better dairy farming. He introduced more efficient farming tools and provided instruction on how to make more efficient use of arable lands. Higginbottom and his wife also took over the care of a leper colony. For thirty-three years, beginning in 1903, Higginbottom and his wife cared for what began as a struggling group of fifty lepers. He recalled that through the improvement of clinical practices almost 98 percent of the children born from mothers infected by the disease had no trace of leprosy later in life. Higginbottom said, "Neither the leper asylum nor the Agriculture Institute were forms of work that I had contemplated when I went to India, and if I had followed my own inclination I would have refused to do either one, but God, as it were, drew me into them, and as I look back at the thirty-five years of it, I am glad that He gave me sense enough to accept His plan for my life rather than my own" (quoted in *Fourth Church*, October 1938).[20]

Men and women from Fourth Presbyterian continued to take up roles that were not in keeping with Gold Coast expectations. They served those in need throughout the world. Their examples reflect the power of Christian symbolic boundaries to transform loyalties and move individuals into divergent occupations. Anderson, in the midst of much social upheaval, continued to challenge his congregation to embrace these alternatives.

Gold Coast Boundaries Persist

The advertising in *Fourth Church* during the 1930s catches the ethos of the Gold Coast—a world in many ways unaffected by the depression. In these ads the Gold Coast clientele were upbraided for accepting anything less than the best: "It is folly to consider cheap stuff advertised as just as good" (*Fourth Church*, June 1933). This tag line came from an ad for the Martha Weathered Shop in the Drake Hotel. The year was 1933, the nadir of the economic depression. Social boundaries were to be kept regardless of the sacrifice it would take to maintain one's sense of distinction and the quality of one's appearance.

The advertisements also had racial, ethnic, and gender boundaries in mind. A tag line in a Martha Weathered ad used a racial stereotype: "To wear the finer things because they're rare and you'll feel wonderful. Not like some galley slave" (*Fourth Church,* January 1937). In the following month's advertisement for Martha Weathered the ad was a short story about a mother and daughter's appeal to the father: "If he takes them fishing, and buys each a dress, then they'll brag about how big a fish he caught" (*Fourth Church,* February 1938).

These messages convey the power of specific cultural assumptions that shaped the Gold Coast and the church. The values demanded distinctions in dress and appearance and accurately described the power and priority of males to make decisions for the family. The advertisements conveyed the status signals and the behavior that dictated the tastes and values of this upper-middle-class group.

Similar signals of class are less obvious but more profoundly reflected by the choice of colleges and universities for this Protestant establishment congregation. The *Fourth Church,* in October 1938 and January 1955, provided comprehensive listings of the colleges and universities that students of Fourth Presbyterian members would be attending. In both 1938 and 1955 a third of the college students went to Ivy League schools or to other elite universities. Two or three of the students in each of the years attended a Presbyterian-sponsored college. The elite did not choose to go to denominationally affiliated schools.

We Took Care of Our Own

Fourth Presbyterian stood by those in its congregation who suffered during the depression. The church took immense pride in the fact that it found jobs for more than twenty-five individuals during the 1930s and that it spent more than $41,000 on the poor and their families during this difficult decade. It became a badge of honor, often repeated, that the church supported two hundred of its own families during the depression, even though Fourth Presbyterian's budget was cut in half during that period.[21] The pastors volunteered a 10 percent cut in pay in 1935. At the same time, however, the church did not tap its endowment funds. The endowment stood at $469,000 in 1932, but by 1938 it had nearly doubled, to $800,000.

The church took care of its own. It cared for Fourth Presbyterian families in need and nurtured its investment capital for the future. Fourth Presbyterian also reached beyond its own borders. In a 1939 sermon Anderson, who loved statistics, listed the numerous neighborhood houses that the Presbyterian churches in the city supported. These houses functioned as social service agencies. Fourth Presbyterian contributed to the Association House, the Erie Neighborhood House, and the Peniel Neighborhood House. The agencies served the needs of the poor and unemployed. Anderson recalled that in 1938 more than a million people came through the doors of these institutions for help. Anderson, as he was wont to do, used a military metaphor to describe the Presbyterian churches in a December 11, 1938, sermon entitled "The Wrestle for the City's Soul": "We are a regiment in Chicago, 50,000 strong, fighting for the soul of the city. We carry the responsibility for one-third of all the neighborhood houses in the city" (*Fourth Church*, February 1939).

Fourth Presbyterian's ministries to the homeless, hungry, and unemployed proceeded with little or no public fanfare. Indeed, colleagues criticized Anderson for the lack of ministries of social service and advocacy for the poor at the church. He bristled at the charge. He defended his church by stressing the importance of helping individuals rather than lobbying to transform structures: "We have participated in ecclesiastical assemblies which have passed ringing sets of resolutions on social matters, but we have been persuaded that the more effective way of correcting the abuses which these resolutions condemn is to deal with persons and their problems. There seems to be no way to form or to reform society except through transformed lives" (*Fourth Church*, March 1936).

This individualistic refrain resonated throughout the decades of Fourth Presbyterian's ministry to the Gold Coast, the city, and the world. It lacked a sociological perspective; it refused to take into account the power of systems to injure individuals. Anderson confirmed the prerogatives of his class by assuming that those in power should remain so. At the same time, he consistently called this Protestant establishment church to assume responsibility for those less fortunate. Moreover, he confronted members' moral failings and challenged their ethical laxity at every point. He thus continued to ply the tension inherent within a vision of the Protestant ethic that supported the privilege of a dominant social class while demanding it adhere to Puritan moral standards.

No Supreme State over All

Anderson was neither a pacifist nor a militarist. He knew firsthand the horrors of war from his experience as a chaplain in World War I in France and supported Woodrow Wilson and his proposal for the League of Nations after the armistice. Throughout his tenure at Fourth Presbyterian Anderson advocated for an international tribunal that could adjudicate injustices. Like many others, Anderson feared the advancing nationalism of the early 1930s, a fear made concrete by the rise of Hitler and the power of nazism. Traveling in England and France in 1936, he witnessed the popularity of national socialism. He spoke out in a July 1, 1934, sermon, "Church and State—1934," about how he saw the church as a force for liberty to rally against the coercive nature of the state:

> Against a supreme State over all, the sons of freedom ought surely to revolt. But will they? Is there a love of freedom today? Will men again die for it, if needs be? Here let us differentiate between license and liberty. How men confuse them! Some men are demanding today not liberty to live their lives, but license to destroy others. But liberty is vastly different. We take it for granted that men wish liberty. Do they? The terrible indictment against slavery is that it makes a man content to be a slave. (*Fourth Church*, July 1934)

Anderson criticized his own government, which he thought had been given too much power with Roosevelt's New Deal. He seconded the judgment of one of his heroes, the Presbyterian layman Robert Speer, who as secretary of the Board of Foreign Missions advocated for military disarmament: "Not a war has ever been prevented by armaments. Armaments are only the invitation to war. Preparation for war is no prevention of war, it is an invitation to war. And [I've] almost come to believe, standing under the meaning of the cross, that if we cannot secure disarmament by agreement, it ought to be the glorious privilege of some nation to set the example all alone" (quoted in *Fourth Church*, May 1935).

As the 1930s came to a close, most American Protestants believed that the United States should stay out of the war. This changed with the threat to England and the fall of France (R. M. Miller, 1958:344). In time many in the Protestant camp fell in line behind Reinhold Niebuhr's neoorthodox judgment that pacifism was naive. That is, it underestimated the power of evil and in the end capitulated to the forces of tyranny. By 1940 Anderson himself warned his congregation against minimizing the power of evil. With the bombing of Pearl Harbor, he prepared his congregation to stand behind the government. Even so, he publicly supported the right of individuals to claim conscientious-objector status.

Anderson confronted national public opinion most directly in his decision to allow a group of Japanese Americans to worship at Fourth Presbyterian. In May 1942 Albert W. Palmer, president of the Chicago Theological Seminary, requested that Anderson and his elders allow a group of Japanese Americans to worship at Fourth Presbyterian. The Japanese Americans had been harassed by the police at their former place of worship. In the fall of 1942 they began to meet in the Fourth Presbyterian chapel early on Sunday afternoons. Anderson reportedly often stood by the door at these worship services. This unpopular decision was underscored as the nation soured on Japanese Americans living in the United States, embodied by the Japanese internment camps on the West Coast.

A current Fourth Presbyterian elder, a woman who had become a member of the church in the 1920s, painted a vivid picture of Anderson's initiative to give sanctuary to the Japanese Americans:

> This little group of Japanese were denied the use of a storefront church. At that point they were enemy aliens. Anderson was very sensitive to people who were hurting. He got the officers together and convinced them to take up the cause of these Japanese Christians. I'm not sure that would have been an easy enterprise. He was a dominant person in a different way. He was so convinced that this was the Christian thing to do, that we must help our Christian brothers in need. By the next Sunday the Japanese Christians were allowed to worship in Westminster Chapel. They worshipped at 2:00 P.M. Most people didn't have any idea that they were worshipping in the church at all. It was done quietly with few people knowing about it; it wasn't talked about a great deal. I would frequently stop in there and worship with them. I didn't understand a bit of Japanese. I would say there were around thirty-five to fifty people. (Interview, March 30, 1994)

No record of resistance to this decision by Anderson and the elders of the church exists. Neither Anderson's son nor his daughter remembered that this caused hardship on their father. Both of them said that it was a point of great pride, on their father's part, that Fourth Presbyterian stood behind the Japanese American Christians. Anderson nurtured this group of Japanese Americans throughout the war, and in January 1947 the Presbyterian Church U.S.A. accepted the membership of the Church of Christ Japanese. The Reverend Masaya Hibino, a pastor of the church, came to the memorial service for Anderson at Fourth Presbyterian in November 1979 and spoke of Anderson's courage:

> During World War II, Japan was fighting against the United States. Because of this, Japanese living in Chicago at that time were looked upon with suspicion to the extent they were not allowed to meet together even to worship the Lord Jesus Christ. In those days it was not popular for the American to be friends of Japanese. Even some professing Christians in those days withdrew themselves and disassociated themselves from Japanese Christians. They [Japanese Christians] felt lonely and friendless. In such a time as that Dr. Anderson was a true Christian friend. He faced opposition but he stood firm to his Christian conviction. (Anderson's memorial service, November 11, 1978)

The Power of Patriarchy

Despite his position on Japanese Americans, Anderson shared his contemporaries' prejudices against women. He condemned the women's movement, and, as a confidant said of him, "He would ridicule women who were rising in the church as more interested in what dresses they were wearing than in what the issue was" (Interview, August 13, 1994). His son said in his eulogy about his father that no women made it into his inner circle. An elder who worked closely with Anderson put it this way: "To put women on the board was discussed. I don't think Dr. Anderson was comfortable with it because he felt that women had their place. He compartmentalized everything: women were women and men were men, and women would respect men more if they each had their roles. There was men's work, and then there was women's work" (Interview, April 19, 1994).

The highest role that a woman held during Anderson's pastorate was the paid position of deaconess. It was a challenging position because the deaconess served the deacons' board, which up until 1958 was made up of forty-eight men. Viola G. Baker held the position during the 1930s. She administered Fourth Presbyterian's ministry to the neighborhood houses and to the families of the congregation. Mae Ross Taylor took Baker's place and continued as the church's deaconess into the early 1950s.

Taylor not took on the deaconess role but also became a vocal advocate in the church struggle over the ordination of women. She confidently expressed her opinion on the issue to the wider body of the Presbyterian Church U.S.A. Following the war the debate over women's ordination gained attention. Taylor wrote an article in *The Presbyterian,* a conservative denominational journal. John MacKay, the conservative president of Princeton Theological Seminary, and Anderson sat on the board of directors of *The Presbyterian.* She entitled it "Why I Do Not Want to Be Ordained." Taylor dismissed the arguments that women were either intellectually incapable or emotionally unstable. For Taylor the case for the ordination of women revolved around how they could best serve the kingdom of God: "I do not wish to be ordained, not because I feel a lack in womanhood, or an inferiority in relationship to men, but through experience I feel women can do a greater work for the kingdom outside rather than inside the ministry" (Taylor, 1947:8).

Taylor asserted that the church needed pastors who could be shepherds to their people. Women, especially married women, did not have the time to fulfill these tasks because it would take away from their responsibilities at home. For Taylor the only reason for the ordination of women was the shortage of men: "Do we need more ministers? Then we women, who have the privilege and responsibility of teaching and training youth, need to examine how adequately we are fulfilling this trust" (Taylor, 1947:8). An editor introduced the article with a note about the defeat of the overture for the ordination of women at the recent 159th meeting of the church's General Assembly. Taylor's article was written before the vote and, according to Taylor, with Anderson's "approval but not in anyway at his instigation" (Taylor, 1947:8).

There is no doubt that Anderson approved of Taylor's argument and sentiments. For Anderson the position against the ordination of women had little to do with theology and more to do with cultural values. He upheld traditional social boundaries between the sexes; each gender had its role to fulfill in society. Taylor put the onus of responsibility on women to produce and socialize more men for the ministry. Women did not lack skills for ministry, but their primary responsibility was the home. The patriarchal impulse of the Protestant church lingered well into the decades in which the women's movement gained strength. A part of the stability of Fourth Presbyterian, as a Protestant institution, was the continuing patriarchal structures of its leadership, an institution that espoused and defended gender inequality.

Serving the Cause of Righteousness

Frank Loesch served as an elder of Fourth Presbyterian for thirty-one years and as president of the congregation for fourteen years, until his death in 1944. Just as Loesch fought for civic righteousness in the nation and in Chicago in the 1920s and 1930s, so Anderson and the leaders of Fourth Presbyterian continued this battle through the 1940s and 1950s. Numerous resolutions in the session minutes reflect this impulse: one opposed a bill for a national lottery in 1943; another, in 1947, protested the advertisement of alcohol. In 1950 a session resolution decried public apathy toward motion pictures that betrayed civic trust and were "violations of domestic decency" (Session Minutes, March 5, 1950).

Anderson, throughout his pastorate at Fourth Presbyterian, consistently condemned the consumption of alcohol in any amount. In 1955 the session went so far as to debate the membership of anyone connected to the alcohol beverage industry. The session understood that the local church was free to set conditions of membership, and yet the constitution of the church did not proscribe membership to anyone associated with this industry. The only condition of membership was the applicant's sincere commitment to Christ and to the church. The session decided against refusing or recalling membership, but it made its position clear on the issue: "Our Committee is unanimous in its belief that the Church must maintain a strong position of opposition towards the evils brought about by the alcohol beverage industry which contribute to the sorrow and misery of society. We believe, therefore, that the only stand we can and should take as a Session, and church, towards the evils of this industry is to condemn them" (Session Minutes, February 11, 1955).

Anderson and the leadership of Fourth Presbyterian also condemned the distribution of indecent literature and even the production of a Santa Claus parade on Thanksgiving weekend along North Michigan Avenue. They claimed that each of these evils was a part of the general "secularization of society" and of the holidays in particular.

The evil Anderson was referring to went deeper than alcohol, indecent literature, and parades. For Anderson corruption threatened the heart of the government. Elected as moderator of the General Assembly of the Presbyterian Church U.S.A. in June 1951, Anderson was at the height of his power and influence. He spent much of his year in office traveling the country preaching against moral corruption in high places. In one sermon he asserted that the two greatest threats to the nation were communism, which he felt had lost ground, and political leaders' loss of honesty and morality. In clippings from Anderson's personal folder on his year as moderator, there is one article after another on this theme of political corruption and the importance of "erasing" America's shame. Anderson painted this shame with a wide brush to include all levels of society as well as the church.

Anderson knew the level of political betrayal and bad politics in Chicago. Martin Kennelly, one of Chicago's reform mayors, followed Edward Kelly into office in 1947. Kennelly, a Democrat, proclaimed himself the one who would clean up the city government and crack down on organized crime. Like other reform mayors, Kennelly made a weak attempt at reform, which in the end amounted to breaking up small-time African American rackets, or what were called "policy wheels." This inflamed the anger of African Americans in Chicago, particularly William Dawson, the most powerful African American politician in the city. Dawson gained his political power under the Kelly Democratic machine. Dawson was a key figure in encouraging the party to drop Kennelly and nominate Richard J. Daley for mayor in 1955. Daley was nominated and won election that same year. He came into office and immediately displaced Dawson and his political leadership.

Police corruption and the influence of organized crime were simply a part of Chicago politics throughout this era. Regardless of whether the mayor was a reformer the Mafia prospered. In February 1952 an acting Republican committeeman of the Thirty-first Ward was murdered. The city council immediately put together the Emergency Committee on Crime. Over the following ten months investigations into police and city corruption uncovered a dozen major areas of criminal activity. Organized crime had insinuated itself into alcohol distribution, labor unions, the police department, municipal courts, and any number of city departments, including licensing, streets, electricity, and city purchasing (Kohn, 1953:3–4).

The official summary, called *The Kohn Report,* a 120-page document detailed the political corruption of a city. The report called for the resignation of the chief of police, Timothy O'Connor. O'Connor attempted to hinder the investigation at every point. The report also outlined the process in which the investigation was scuttled by the city council, which had called for the probe. It was in response to this perversion of justice by city officials that Anderson, with the session's approval, took the bold action of reading a prepared statement from the pulpit on July 27, 1952. It was delivered to the mayor and the city council:

> This is a statement which I regret has to be made from a Christian pulpit. It appears that another crime investigation is being brought to naught by the officials of this city. One would suppose that the leaders and citizens of Chicago would not only welcome the investigation but would encourage it. There is a growing feeling in Chicago that the leaders of this city, fine as some of them are, have become a moral facade behind which wicked, greedy and irresponsible men operate. In your name, I appeal to the Mayor, whom I count a friend, to take such leadership as to remove this feeling and restore confidence. As Christian citizens, you will act as your enlightened conscience dictates. (Session Minutes, July 27, 1952)

Anderson refused to stop with this declaration. In a sermon summarized in an article in the *Chicago Daily News* on March 2, 1953, Anderson excoriated the mayor by name and called for the resignation of the church's neighborhood aldermen for their collusion in illegal gambling. He questioned the legitimacy of local government. Anderson noted that from 1925 through 1952 there had been 666 gang murders and that only 13 of them had resulted in prosecution. He said that many Chicagoans did not report crimes because they feared for their safety. Anderson exclaimed, "I turned in to the police a house of male prostitution, a nest of homosexuals. The police betrayed my confidence, and I was threatened by the owner. Nevertheless, let us make such reports. If we fear for our families, let us act as groups, through our churches."

Anderson's forthright and plainspoken declarations from the pulpit of Fourth Presbyterian did not change the course of city government, but they did get the attention of the city council. In May of 1953 the city council received a petition that questioned the right of the clergy to address themselves on the civic issues of the day. Anderson and the session responded in forceful terms, outlining that it was their responsibility in the Reformed tradition to work for civic righteousness:

It [the church] can accept the role many would assign to it that the sole responsibility of the Church is to get souls from earth to heaven. The Church becomes merely a heavenly elevator and is not concerned with the world in which it was instructed by its Lord to be light and salt. Our Lord taught us to pray Thy kingdom come, Thy will be done ON EARTH as it is in heaven. Or by lawful means and in a respectful manner the Church can speak out as the conscience of the city and for the welfare of the city. The second choice is in line with the Prophets of the Old Testament and the Apostles of the early Church. It is in keeping with our historic Reformed Faith. To do any other than this is for the church to betray her Lord. To be silent is for the Church to betray the city. (Session Minutes, May 1953)

Nonetheless, Anderson was losing the cultural battle in the displacement of Puritan values and behavior. Moreover, his Republican party was further weakened by the demographic shifts in Chicago's population in the 1950s. At the beginning of the 1950s Republican aldermen had sixteen of the city council's fifty seats. Chicago's population decreased minimally during the 1950s, but there was a significant change in the racial and ethnic makeup of the population. In 1950 African Americans were 13 percent of the population; by 1960 they were 23 percent (Grimshaw, 1992:97). With this transformation Chicago became a one-party town. Anderson's political power was undercut, and his only tool for change was the power of public opinion to pressure the city. In spite of Anderson's passionate attacks on local government corruption, public opinion most often ignored his pleas.

Chicago's Democratic machine helped Daley win 74 percent of the vote in the 1959 mayoral race. The reality of police corruption did not seem to matter. Ben Adamowski, a Daley political opponent, was elected as a Republican to the state's attorney's office in 1957. Adamowski mounted a public crusade against corruption that in the end targeted Daley himself. This failed to affect the election outcome in 1959. The investigation continued, however, and in 1960 the tide turned for the forces of reform and in favor of Anderson's fight for civic justice. That same year it became public knowledge that some Chicago police not only fixed traffic tickets but also were a part of a burglary ring (Royko, 1971:116–17). This scandal got the attention of the public. Daley, using his considerable public relations skills, scapegoated the police chief, Timothy O'Connor. O'Connor, who had been appointed by Kennelly as a reform chief, was fired.

In February 1960 Fourth Presbyterian came out with an official document on the police corruption case that detailed the problem and the solution. The police were under the sway of political interests. The police department needed a new independent leader from outside the system. Daley, in conjunction with a committee to investigate the corruption, chose Orlando W. Wilson, a criminologist from the University of California, to head the investigation. Wilson chaired the committee, and by mid-February of 1960 Daley asked him to become the new chief of police. Anderson reported later that he had recommended that Wilson be considered for the job. Anderson had known Wilson as the police chief and as an earnest Christian in Wichita, the site of Anderson's first pastorate in the 1920s. Wilson accepted the position and went on to reform the Chicago police department in the early 1960s; corruption remained but at a much diminished level.

Throughout this era Anderson represented one side of what William J. Grimshaw has called "Chicago's classic political fissure, poor against rich, Catholic against Protestant" (Grimshaw, 1992:18). Anderson represented the wealthy Protestant Gold Coast. He did this in the archetypal terms of the Protestant ethic and in the spirit of civic duty, honesty, righteousness, and hard work. Anderson supported the social boundaries of his Protestant elite. To purify these boundaries, political and structural power needed the antidote of honesty and integrity. In the world of the Protestant ethic everyone who worked hard and demonstrated moral sobriety had the opportunity to succeed. This ideal came up against the intransigence of racism, classism, and power politics that paid dividends to those who could manipulate the system, a system that victimized people regardless of their work ethic. Nonetheless, in part because of Anderson's and the Fourth Presbyterian Church's leadership, local government was held accountable and changes were made.

Anderson made no compromise with the more intemperate aspects of his upper-middle-class status group or, for that matter, with the interests of ethnic minorities who dominated the political life of Chicago at midcentury. He was passionately committed to the good of the city and its moral life as defined by his Puritan ethos. This meant challenging his congregation and the political powers of the city and winning the battle for civic honesty and good government; Anderson refused to back down when it came to confrontation. This political activism, however, derailed with the arrival of the civil rights movement.

The Church and Civil Rights

Anderson's forays into the political arena were the direct consequences of his Reformed Protestant tradition that valued civic righteousness and demanded faithful service to the city. Nonetheless, Anderson criticized and derided the social activism that was brewing in the United Presbyterian Church in the late

1950s. Eugene Carson Blake, a Presbyterian minister, symbolized this movement. Blake was president of the National Council of Churches in the 1950s,
the stated clerk for the United Presbyterian Church U.S.A. in the early 1960s,
and the general secretary of the World Council of Churches from 1966 to 1972.
Blake's strong support of the civil rights movement culminated in his arrest
in an effort to desegregate a park in Baltimore in 1963 (Reifsnyder, 1992:265).

Anderson, along with other more conservative Presbyterians, condemned
Blake for "prostituting the ministry" to social causes (Harrison Ray Anderson
Jr. Interview, August 13, 1994). Anderson stood against any actions that were
not strictly a function of the church's ministry. During Anderson's era church
members attempted to integrate Fourth Presbyterian, but, according to his son,
"he resented this because it was cause-oriented rather than inspired by the
gospel" (Harrison Ray Anderson Jr. Interview, August 13, 1994). Anderson's
judgment on the civil rights movement was incongruous. If the righteousness
of a cause was determined by whether its source was the gospel, the civil rights
movement was legitimate since African American clergy and churches inspired
and led the movement. Nonetheless, Anderson made no attempt to include
African Americans in the life of Fourth Presbyterian. Anderson was not alone
in his short-sighted perspective; many in the Protestant establishment failed
to respond to the civil rights movement.

Anderson's and Fourth Presbyterian's lack of leadership in civil rights and
in other attempts to improve the situation of African Americans in Chicago
was a manifestation of their collaboration in the segregation of African Americans in the city and nation. Blacks were not welcome on North Michigan Avenue. Fourth Presbyterian and the Protestant church joined with other powerful social and cultural forces to exclude African Americans from social,
political, and economic opportunities. The church failed to resist the social inequality rampant in the city of Chicago.

SYMBOLIC BOUNDARIES OF A RIGHTEOUS PASTOR

The Style of a Protestant Pastor

Anderson was a man of piety and a pastor to his congregation. He spoke of
his frequent visits with businessmen in their offices. Unannounced, he would
stay a few minutes, pray, and then leave. He venerated successful professionals and sought to bring to them his own earnest piety. In doing so he maintained the peculiar tension within the worldly asceticism of the Protestant
ethic: holding together a devout religious life and a passion for success in the
world. He nurtured the religiosity of these Protestant businessmen by press-

ing his faith on them in the midst of their professional lives and challenging them in the stewardship of their rewards.

Anderson excelled in administration. He was said to be an autocratic, though not inflexible, leader. He sacrificed his own salary raises for the sake of the church and its budget. He made it public that he gave 10 percent of his income to the church. He published his pledge of $4,000 to the capital campaign for the construction of the Westminster House. His determination and perseverance were legendary in the Presbyterian Church.[22] This strength translated into motivation that inspired others around him. In his thirty-three years of ministry at Fourth Presbyterian, fifty-one students, men and women, went into full-time Christian service.

Anderson was not as dynamic a speaker as his predecessor, John Timothy Stone, or his successor, Elam Davies, but he was considered a strong preacher, who focused on the exposition of the Bible. As one of his assistant ministers explained, "Anderson was strong in the pulpit. He was well organized. He came on with a kind of closed-fist strength. There was a minimum of ambiguity. If he struggled, it was deeper down. You had a sense that the man was not simple at root. The simplicity was in the way he lived and in the way he thought of the world, which was purchased at a certain amount of repression" (Interview, October 12, 1994). Anderson was married to the church. This single-mindedness had negative effects on his family. He was not a man of great affection; according to his children, he rarely expressed his feelings to them. This stoic style was consistent with his Protestant and Puritan heritage.

Anderson's Theological Boundaries

Like his predecessor, Anderson was a theological moderate. He, along with many likeminded colleagues, sidestepped the modernist-fundamentalist controversy of the 1920s. Anderson had no strong ideological ax to grind. He did not take Scripture literally and was open to the historical interpretation of the Bible. Unlike Stone, Anderson did not enjoy the same intimate relationships with the evangelicals in his congregation. He was not close to Henry Crowell, as Stone was, even though Crowell remained an elder on the session during the first decade or so of Anderson's pastorate.

Crowell was chairman of Quaker Oats and president of the Moody Bible Institute throughout this period. A profoundly conservative Christian, Crowell quit membership and the session of Fourth Presbyterian in 1943 because of Anderson's decision to second the nomination of Henry Sloane Coffin for moderator of the General Assembly in 1943. For Crowell Coffin was a modernist and had compromised the authority of Scripture and the faith itself. Crowell's decision to leave Fourth Presbyterian was painful to him and difficult for Anderson. Crowell, in a letter to Anderson, said, "The appeal of Modernism appears to be gaining strength as revealed by the General Assembly at its last meeting and it leaves the Presbyterian denomination standing on dangerous ground, for there is a vast difference between conservatism and Modernism in the interpretation of Scripture and in being loyal and true to the well defined standards left us by Jesus Christ, our risen Lord" (quoted in Day, 1946:285–86). Crowell believed in the inerrancy of Scripture, Christ's atonement for sin, and the need for personal conversion to Christ. That Anderson diverged from this ideological stance put him squarely in the camp of moderate Protestants, who continued to try to hold the liberal and conservative wings of the Presbyterian Church together. For Crowell this position was apostasy; for Anderson it was the Presbyterian way.

In a June 11, 1961, sermon, "The Limitations of the Christian Ministry," Anderson spoke of the internecine conflicts that he had withstood during his tenure at Fourth Presbyterian (*Fourth Church,* July 1961). He described a group that desired to make this an "exclusive church of well-to-do, cultured people." This was before the depression. Anderson later staved off attempts to make the church more liberal and attempts to make it more conservative: "I came to see that in Jesus Christ right and left lost their divisiveness and were joined at the center of the cross. In a crisis at that time twenty-nine of the thirty elders of the session stood with their pastor. It was Christ who had died, not the leader of a party. This session has stood around me like a wall of fire" (*Fourth Church,* July 1961)

As a theological moderate, however, Anderson remained an evangelical. Fourth Presbyterian supported the Restoration Fund of the Presbyterian Church U.S.A. with a pledge of $100,000 to help restore missions in Europe and Asia in the late 1940s and the 1950s. Fourth Presbyterian stood behind the "new life movement" of the Presbyterian Church U.S.A. that pushed for new church development and membership in the postwar years. This movement had results, with 700,000 new communicants in the church by 1950 (Coalter, Mulder, and Weeks, 1992:149).[23] Anderson, throughout his pastorate at Fourth Presbyterian, pressed the importance of evangelism. He was pointed and provocative in an address on evangelism entitled "Revelation and Response," presented at the General Assembly in Pittsburgh, Pennsylvania, on May 26, 1958. He began rhetorically with the question "When was the last time one of you personally led someone to Jesus Christ?" He returned to this question in various forms throughout his speech, highlighting the long history of exemplars in evangelical history who had preached the gospel of Jesus Christ for conversion. These figures ranged from the Wesley brothers and George Whitefield of England, the Tennents of Pennsylvania, Jonathan Edwards of Northampton, and David Brainerd from Yale to John Anderson, one of Anderson's ancestors, who was a missionary to the Indians in the Ohio Valley in the early nineteenth century. Anderson scolded his fellow ministers for their hesitancy and their lack of evangelical action. Anderson asked the question again, "Why don't we proclaim the message? Is it because of evangelistic methods? Are our cluttered methods approved of God if they produce no fruit? Said Mr. Moody to one of his critics, 'At least, I like my way of doing it better than your way of not doing it.' No one is forced to follow false methods. Use your own, but choose and act!" (*Fourth Church*, July 1958).[24]

Anderson pressed his evangelical message. That he could use D. L. Moody, the American revivalist and founder of the Moody Bible Institute, as a model further underscored the fluidity of his theological boundaries. For most Presbyterians Moody had become a symbol of the fundamentalist camp, an object of derision to liberals. Many Presbyterian ministers had come to believe that the gospel was about social justice, not evangelism. Anderson challenged his colleagues and his congregation toward goals that were no longer taken for granted.

A Theology of Human Depravity

On the subject of sin there was no theological ambiguity for Anderson. He believed in the depravity of human nature. Christianity and a personal commitment to Jesus Christ were the only antidote to this tragic condition. After his experiences in the war and his dealings with organized crime and political corruption in Chicago, he had no illusions about the innocence of human nature. First and foremost for his Christian worldview was the recognition of sin and the need for repentance. It is therefore not surprising that one of his theological models was Augustine. On February 9, 1941, in his sermon "Augustine—Apostle of Grace," Anderson viewed the world and the nation through the lens of Augustine's judgment on Rome:

> Because of a people grown soft through ease and immorality; because of slavery on one side and great wealth on the other and a middle-class between being taxed to death in order to pay for incessant wars; because of laziness and the dole and an unwillingness to defend their nation; because of people who lived for the passing show of the circus and the gladiatorial contest. "The Roman world was laughing when it died," and it was stupidly unaware of the forces from the north which

were waiting and ready for the spoils of a nation grown fat and soft. These were Augustine's times. Did you think I made a mistake and said our times? Similar they are; but Augustine's times they were. (*Fourth Church,* March 1941)

Anderson accepted this apocalyptic view of the nation. His historical hermeneutic was determined by the moral vitality of a people. It was clear to him that the depression and the world wars were God's judgment on the sins of the nation and the world. As he outlined in his July 6, 1941, sermon, "This Nation under God," the sins of the nation were "cheating, crime, liquor and the so-called new morality which is simply fornication and adultery, accepted in certain smart circles" (*Fourth Church,* October 1941). In the same sermon Anderson interpreted the economic collapse of the nation and the tragedies of the world wars as failures of moral principle and personal integrity: "Our times have been brought upon us by a deep deed of betrayal of God and each other. We have each turned to his own way, his own selfish way, German, English, French, American way, and the night is on us all. We are under God's judgment and these judgments are right."

Anderson's symbolic boundaries were molded by an individualistic and moralistic religious tradition.[25] This standard American understanding of the world kept him from seeing the complexity involved in social structures that created ambiguity and defied the moralistic judgments of right and wrong. Nonetheless, Anderson was not unaware of the interpretations of those who took a more sociological perspective on societal dilemmas. In his April 30, 1944, sermon, "Not Radical Enough," he adamantly attacked social activists who diagnosed problems as social and structural:

To keep on talking about social ends and ignore repentance, conversion, and faith in Jesus Christ seems to me to be not only the height of folly, but a betrayal of the very ends that good men desire. As the first was a denial of the incarnation; so this, it seems to one man at least, is the denial of the atonement. It is a human proposal to save man and society without God. Will it work? Was the Cross of Christ an error? Can any of our deep problems—war, race, class, home—be resolved without Him? Isn't He the first and last of every solution? (*Fourth Church,* May 1944)

Anderson was squarely in the camp of the neoorthodox who condemned liberals for underestimating the depth of human sin and its destructive capabilities. For Anderson the life, death, and resurrection of Christ was a necessary saving act for humanity. It was the fundamental prism through which the world, the nation, and each individual was judged. Anderson's theological perspective assumed that all had sinned—even the people of his Gold Coast congregation. Even if all needed God's grace, the ideal of moral purity motivated his civic activism. Good and evil could be differentiated and thus named. Anderson therefore did not hesitate to make judgments on nations and people. He had a well-charted list of sins that made individuals impure and corrupt. Uncompromising in his judgments, he risked himself and his reputation by confronting those who trespassed on these moral rules.

Rationalization of Wealth

Anderson did not question the wealth of his members. At the height of the depression, the culture of business had lost its gilded edge. Business and businesspeople were no longer valorized, and, particularly after 1932, the decline in their reputation was, as some have described, "cataclysmic" (Lundén, 1988:181). In spite of this cultural shift Anderson built a symbolic defense of those with wealth. He fought against the prevalent assumption that the wealthy were necessarily morally bankrupt. After reviewing the biblical warnings on the danger of wealth in his January 1, 1933, sermon, "New Life in Christ," Anderson reminded his congregants, "But here is the fine word of it all. Even the rich man can enter in. The rich man must become the poor man, poor in spirit—conscious of his need, else he will never need nor enter Christ" (*Fourth Church*, January 1933).

In his June 29, 1938, sermon, "A Christian and His Money," Anderson was even more forceful in his comments on money, challenging those who criticized successful businesspeople in the United States. Anderson constructed a "sociodicy" of wealth that assumed it was a consequence of God's blessing and thus a resource for underwriting the mission of the first church and the mission of the church in contemporary society:

> Because a man has succeeded in honest business it does not make him a scoundrel, and it's time to call a different tune in America. Money isn't evil or good, per se; it's what you do with it and what it does with you. It entered into the betrayal of our Savior, I know. It also supported Him in the days of His flesh, and it anointed Him for His death, and furnished His tomb. It is the love of money that has in it all sorts of evil roots. The man who makes it and saves it and gives it in Christian ways is to be commended. (*Fourth Church*, September 1938)

For Anderson those who had succeeded in their business life were to be commended, particularly as they came to understand their responsibility to support the work of ministry. Anderson defended the honest earning of wealth, but he passionately denounced capital debt as a strategy for wealth production. He consistently criticized the federal government in the 1940s and 1950s for the spiraling debt it incurred.

As has been noted, Anderson was caught up in the dilemma of the Weberian worldly ascetic. One should work diligently at one's vocation, but one must be careful not to fall into the trap of some who are rich: a self-satisfaction that diminishes one's need for God. A summary of Anderson's views on money and religion could parallel John Wesley's classic dictum that, in Max Weber's words, "those who gain all they can and save all they can should also give all they can, so that they will grow in grace and lay up a treasure in heaven" (Weber, 1958:176). This, no doubt, epitomized Anderson's perspective on his Gold Coast congregation: "Wealth is . . . bad ethically only in so far as it is a temptation to idleness and sinful enjoyment of life, and its acquisition is bad only when it is with the purpose of later living merrily and without care" (Weber, 1958:163).

Anderson reprimanded any sort of frivolous enjoyment, particularly when it involved alcohol. For Anderson work was a sacred calling, whether in the church or in business. Recreation, especially for the working class, was a license for moral corruption. Anderson preached with passion on the importance of repentance and a new life in Christ. He could challenge and scold his congregation and nation for moral indiscretion and corruption, and he made no excuse for behavior that strayed from the Puritan values of his midwestern heritage. In this way he was a latter-day Puritan prophet.

CONCLUSION

Fourth Presbyterian remained a powerful Protestant church throughout Anderson's pastorate. Anderson fulfilled his calling to conserve what he found when he came to Fourth Presbyterian. At the same time, Anderson challenged, in conjunction with his church's leadership, the moral and political corruption of the city of Chicago. He attacked civic degradation with a ferocious sense of righteousness. Anderson courageously defended the virtues and values of the Reformed tradition to the end. He believed in the role of the church in preserving civic order. Fourth Presbyterian remained a stable religious institution in the midst of social upheaval and the cultural indifference to religion that arose in American culture in the 1930s. The Gold Coast and the city of Chicago felt the pressure of Anderson's rhetoric of judgment. Corruption would not be tolerated in the demand for civic righteousness.

Anderson put all his power into maintaining the cultural Protestantism of the early century, yet the Protestant cultural center would not hold. Social forces were beginning to fragment the putative center of the culture. The social movements of minorities and women, along with changes in the moral ethos of the country, erupted in the midst of America's Protestant cultural landscape. The Protestant emphasis on individual effort and the promise of success fell on the deaf ears of the working classes, which knew instinctively that their opportunities were few no matter what their efforts. Social structures privileged certain groups of citizens; success was not merely God's blessing but a constructed element of the cultural, social, and economic life of the city. The Protestant worldview fractured partly because its explanations hid the reality of the oppression of ethnic minority groups and those on the underside of the economic, social, and political establishment.

In focusing on civic order, Anderson and Fourth Presbyterian's leaders failed to confront the racial and class divisions in Chicago. H. Richard Niebuhr was correct—Anderson and his Protestant leadership were more concerned about personal and social moral corruption than about the evils of injustice and inequality. Fourth Presbyterian did not confront the injustices toward African Americans in the construction of the second ghetto. The exclusive social boundaries of the church resembled those of the city government and other ethnic minorities. Anderson and Fourth Presbyterian embodied the spirit of the Protestant ethic in its powerful ability to create wealth and in its unwillingness to deal with issues of social inequality.

In the end the defeat of this Protestant ethic was a fait accompli with the social changes of the 1960s. No amount of willpower and moralistic preaching could defend or hold back the desires of a generation. The 1960s brought with them dramatic cultural upheaval, and only someone of quite different strengths could maneuver Fourth Presbyterian through this passageway— Elam Davies.

NOTES

1. In the nearly hundred extant sermons by Anderson, not one explicitly mentions eternal life as the purpose of Christian evangelism. This same stance on other-worldliness continued with Anderson's successors, Elam Davies and John Buchanan.

2. A newspaper article reporting on Fourth Presbyterian in 1961 said that the church had "no Negroes" in its membership (Dave Meade, "A Stranger Goes to Church," *Chicago Daily News*, February 10, 1961).

3. This world included bootlegging and the sale and distribution of alcohol. During the 1920s there were nearly 20,000 speakeasies in Chicago alone. In 1927, according to conservative estimates, more than 1,300 gangs, made up of 25,000 members, were active and competing with one another. During the era more than 500 gang murders were committed, most of which went unsolved (Bergreen, 1994:78).

4. "Big Bill" Thompson, Chicago's mayor, colluded with organized crime in Chicago, particularly Al Capone. Thompson's mayoral reign was interrupted in the middle of the 1920s by William E. Dever, a Democratic reform major. Capone contributed $260,000 to Thompson's campaign when he defeated Dever in 1927 (Bergreen, 1994:221).

5. Loesch met with Capone at the Lexington Hotel in Chicago. He described how Capone sat behind a desk surrounded by six bodyguards. Pictures of Washington, Lincoln, and Mayor Thompson hung on the walls. Loesch said that he was not there to investigate Capone's illegal dealings; he simply wanted a favor from Capone (Bergreen, 1994:294).

6. The most celebrated foreclosure was on the Medinah Club building. Even in its prime it only had a 32 percent occupancy rate. As the depression struck, membership restrictions were dropped. Nonetheless, it went into receivership in 1932. In a trial in 1942 its debt ran over half a million dollars in bad mortgages and as much in unpaid taxes (Stamper, 1991:206).

7. Roosevelt's resuscitation of the economy faltered throughout the 1930s. The National Recovery Administration (NRA) and the Works Progress Administration (WPA) only began to have effects late in the 1930s with a decrease in unemployment (Leuchtenburg, 1963:69). The coming of World War II was fundamental to the economy's full recovery. Nonetheless, even in 1941 six million people remained without work. High unemployment did not subside entirely until 1943. The economy was fully engaged only at the height of war (Leuchtenburg, 1963:346–47).

8. Midwesterners constituted the largest and most powerful group of political advocates for isolation. This group was led by such Protestant establishment men as Jay Hormel, the meat packer, and Robert Wood of Sears, Roebuck. Douglas Stuart, a Yale Law School student and the son of the vice president of Quaker Oats in Chicago, was its chief organizer. They established the America First Committee. Nearly two-thirds of this committee came from Chicago itself (Leuchtenburg, 1963:311).

9. Elizabeth Woods, the longtime director of the CHA and an advocate for fair housing, particularly for African Americans, lost her job in 1953. She was felt to be a liability to further development and partly the cause for ethnic violence that erupted off and on throughout this period. The event that finally brought about her dismissal was her handling of the Trumbull Park incident. The white ethnics of Trumbull Park violently protested CHA's movement of African American families into their neighborhood. White ethnic groups succeeded in keeping public housing out of their neighborhoods, and Woods lost her job.

10. The poverty rate for African Americans in 1948 was 5.9 percent; in 1984 it was 14.4 percent. There were 195 murders in Chicago in 1965, 810 in 1970, and 970 in 1974. More than 50 percent of all arrested for violent crimes were African American. A quarter of African American births in the early 1960s were out of wedlock; by the 1980s the percentage was close to 60 percent. In 1980 nearly half of all African American families were headed by women (Wilson, 1987:20–62).

11. Anderson volunteered to minister at the front lines of the conflict. At one point he was temporarily blinded by mustard gas. After recovering in a hospital, he immediately returned to the front.

12. At the same time, Anderson saw himself as an outdoorsman and small-town clergyman, so much so that he would speak of working at Fourth Presbyterian and in the city of Chicago as a sacrifice and obedience to God. In a personal letter to the session in 1953 he reflected that in his years of ministry he had been called to be the pastor in churches in New York and California, the director of the Board of Foreign Missions, and general secretary of the Board of National Missions. He was also called, twice, to three mission churches in Grand County, Colorado—churches that Fourth Presbyterian helped start. As Anderson wrote, "In some ways the latter intrigued me more than any of the others" (Anderson, Personal Correspondence, October 15, 1953).

13. In Anderson's personal correspondence there are two letters from Billy Graham, the well-known American evangelist. In the first letter in August 1956 Graham commended Anderson on his prayer at the Republican National Convention: "It is one of the finest prayers I have ever heard." In the December 1961 correspondence Graham thanked Anderson for the kind comments about his ministry and Fourth Presbyterian's support of a forthcoming Graham crusade in Chicago in 1962. He then said, "I have heard you preach on several occasions and consider you one of the great preachers of our time."

14. Anderson strongly supported Woodrow Wilson's plan for the League of Nations. He was disappointed that the United States never joined the World Court. The World Court was the popular name of the Permanent Court of International Justice, established in 1920 by the League of Nations. The World Court was dissolved in 1945 and was replaced by the United Nations International Court of Justice.

15. No one could impugn Loesch's dedication, however. The Chicago Crime Commission, an independent watchdog institution, recorded in its *Journal for the Chicago Crime Commission* detailed observations on the behavior and decisions of all judges in Chicago. The work involved enormous research. Loesch and his team of associates were determined to expose corrupt judges and to bring criminals to justice.

16. Mary Douglas in her 1966 classic, *Purity and Danger,* sums up this process of social demarcation: "For I believe that ideas about separating, purifying, demarcating and punishing transgressions have as their main function to impose system on an inherently untidy experience. It is only by exaggerating the difference between within and without, above and below, male and female, with and against, that a semblance of order is created" (M. Douglas, 1966:4).

17. *Fourth Church* reported in April 1936 that the number of Presbyterian missionaries had decreased substantially over the previous twenty years. At that time, there were 1,307 missionaries in the field. The largest number of new missionaries in one year was 161 in 1920; the smallest was 9 in 1935. The average number in the 1930s was 10 per year.

18. Anderson created five goals for Fourth Presbyterian each year. Every year one of the goals was to bring 100 new Christians to church membership by confession of faith.

Throughout Anderson's tenure Fourth Presbyterian averaged 75 new members per year through confession of faith.

19. Fourth Presbyterian recorded one of its largest budgets in 1930. That year its operating budget reached $110,000, while its total benevolence was $125,000. This benevolence total was not achieved again until 1959, when benevolent giving reached $129,000. That same year the operating budget was up to $200,000, however. After 1930 Fourth Presbyterian never again spent more on others than on itself.

20. Sam Higginbottom was a highly regarded member of Fourth Presbyterian; he went on to be elected moderator of the General Assembly of the Presbyterian Church U.S.A. in 1939.

21. The total budget was $220,000 in 1928, including operating funds and benevolence. The budget was pared down to $110,000 in 1935. The church's total benevolence was $110,000 in 1928 and $31,000 in 1935.

22. Anderson worked untiringly to bring together the southern and northern Presbyterian churches. As he said many times, the failure of the two churches to unite was the greatest disappointment of his life. Anderson was fond of reciting the story of how his great-grandfather W. C. Anderson brought to the floor of the General Assembly in 1861 the Gardner Spring Resolution, which committed the Presbyterian Church to the Union cause and led to the formation of the Presbyterian Church in the United States, that is, the southern church.

23. Fourth Presbyterian's membership, however, plateaued at 3,000 members throughout the 1940s and 1950s. Nonetheless, the endowment fund of the church during this time grew from $900,000 in 1944 to more than $2 million in 1961. The population shift of the Protestant establishment to the suburbs had its effect on church membership, but the investment funds of the church continued to grow.

24. This evangelical task became a singular focus of Anderson's last years. Instead of retiring at sixty-five in 1958, Anderson initiated a new project at Fourth Presbyterian, the building of a student center to meet the needs of college and graduate school students in the area. The Westminster House was completed in 1960 at a cost of $1 million. The sum was fully subscribed and even oversubscribed to give the building a permanent maintenance endowment fund. The building was intended for outreach to college students, but when this ministry failed to materialize, the church used the building for children's and youth activities.

25. An excellent example of Anderson's style and method of evangelism can be seen in an autobiographical story of a conversation he had with a national congressman during the Kefauver hearings, which were investigating crime in American cities in 1950–51: "When I was dining with an American Congressman during the Kefauver investigation our conversation revealed a need even deeper than the open lawlessness indicated. 'Doctor,' said the congressman, 'the need for our country is for moral revival.' 'You believe that, do you?' I asked. 'I certainly do,' was the answer. 'Well, congressman, what are you doing personally about it? Do you go to church? Are you a Christian?' Then came the reply which we parsons hear day in and day out. 'My mother

was a great Presbyterian. I am too busy to go to church. I like to spend a lazy Sunday with my newspaper and my cigar, and my slippers, and now and then I turn on the radio and listen to a sermon'" (Anderson, 1955:62–63). This is taken from a sermon called "A Countryman in the Capital," preached at the National Presbyterian Church in Washington, D.C., in January 6, 1952. John Stennis, a senator from Mississippi, was so impressed with the sermon that he had it entered in the Congressional Record (*Fourth Church*, February 1952).

THE PARADOX OF THE
EVANGELICAL LIBERAL CHURCH,
1961–84

> The fact that the new beginning has been made with revelation of God's
> grace does not change the fundamental situation as far as grace and sin
> are concerned. Grace is in God, and sin is in man. The grace of God is not
> a substance, a *mana*-like power, which is mediated to men through hu-
> man acts. Grace is always in God's action; it is God's attribute. It is the
> action of reconciliation that reaches out across the no-man's land of the
> historic war of men against God.
>
> —H. Richard Niebuhr, *Christ and Culture*, 1951

As the Fourth Presbyterian Church of Chicago entered the decade of
the 1960s, the Puritan and ascetic Protestantism of their pastor of thirty-two
years, Harrison Ray Anderson, encountered many obstacles. American culture
was opening to new social trends, symbolized most vividly by changing the
name of the Palmolive Building, a famous icon of the city just kitty-corner to
Fourth Presbyterian, to the Playboy Building. These social changes included
a growing sensitivity to women's rights, an awareness of the diversity of the
U.S. population, and the rising countercultural movement of the baby boomer
generation (Handy, 1984). The cultural authority of Protestantism was attacked
in universities, and alternative cultural outlets competed for attention (E. P.
Morgan, 1991). Nonetheless, even as Protestant mainline churches declined in
numbers during this period, the Protestant establishment maintained its economic hegemony (Coalter, Mulder, and Weeks, 1990; Hoge and Roozen, 1979;
Roozen, 1993).

Fourth Presbyterian remained a stable religious institution in the 1960s and
has retained this vigor. Fourth Presbyterian thrived even though it was an upper-middle-class church in a downtown setting, a type of church that was

particularly vulnerable during this period (Roof and McKinney, 1987:20). Arriving in 1961, Elam Davies negotiated the social change of this time by doing two things at once: he normalized the internal struggles of his upper-middle-class congregation, and he related these to the sociological conflicts of the ethnic minority groups in Chicago. Davies challenged Fourth Presbyterian to transgress its social boundaries without alienating his congregants. Davies and his leadership created a strong institutional identity that legitimated the Protestant establishment culture and demanded that it serve the poor.

Theologically, Davies's deft balancing of Christ and culture came from his own paradoxical perspective on the divine-human relationship. Davies held that all human efforts were finally fruitless but that the radical message of the gospel was that out of defeat came victory. During his leadership there was a relativization of human effort and at the same time an ability to accommodate the church to rapid cultural change that translated into community outreach and the integration of the church across lines of race and class.

CLASS AND RACE ON THE NEAR NORTH SIDE

The Gold Coast

From the beginning of the twentieth century, as Harvey Warren Zorbaugh described in his 1929 classic *The Gold Coast and the Slum*, the Near North Side supported exclusive boundaries of race and class. In the 1910s developers designed the Gold Coast as a retreat for wealthy Chicagoans. Large mansions dotted the lakefront. It grew into a moneyed residential district filled with brownstones and two-story flats that served the middle- and upper-middle-class professionals who worked in the Loop business district, directly to the south. One Fourth Presbyterian member, who joined the church in 1928 and lived on the Near North Side her entire life, said, "Fourth Presbyterian was a neighborhood church up until the 1960s. A person felt safe walking the streets at night. One would often see Pastor Anderson making pastoral calls at the homes" (Interview, March 30, 1994).

The 1960s and 1970s brought dramatic change to the Gold Coast neighborhood. High-rise luxury apartments replaced the mansions to the north and filled the Streeterville district, an area directly southeast of the church. In 1969 the hundred-story John Hancock Building went up across from Fourth Presbyterian. Over the next fifteen years the Ritz-Carlton, the Westin Hotel, and the Water Tower Mall completed the transformation of this area. Taller buildings surrounded Fourth Presbyterian. They dwarfed the church that once dominated the neighborhood architecturally. During this period Fourth Presbyterian became a downtown church by default. The church was enveloped by high rises with security doors, hotels with limousines coming to and fro, and malls with upper-class stores marketing to a high-status clientele.

As a recent study shows, this explosion of wealth on the Gold Coast paralleled an equally dramatic decline in the living standards of the African American community. By the 1960s African Americans dominated the public housing project known as Cabrini-Green (deVise, 1993). Cabrini-Green, situated only one mile to the west of Fourth Presbyterian, became a primary focus of Fourth Presbyterian's mission outreach.

Public Housing: The Case of Cabrini-Green

The history of Cabrini-Green vividly portrays the destructive results of the segregation of African Americans into public housing. In the 1940s and early 1950s the Frances Cabrini Homes were an exemplar of multiracial and mixed-income housing on the Near North Side of Chicago. The construction of this housing complex in the 1940s came as a result of the city's use of a combination of grants to build housing for low-income families. Two-story townhouses took the place of the rickety firetraps that had been called "Little Hell." When the Cabrini homes opened, 586 families moved into them. Seventy-five percent were white, the rest African American; this proportion reflected the city's racial composition at that time. This stable period lasted more than ten years (G. H. Morgan, 1993).

Various white backlash movements interrupted this stability. In 1953 a riot broke out when an African American family moved into Trumbull Park Public Housing, designated for whites only (Hirsch, 1983:233). White violence "paid off" in political terms; Trumbull Park was able to exclude most African Americans from their neighborhood. Moreover, the city's move to segregate African Americans picked up speed.

In 1955 Richard J. Daley became mayor of Chicago. A year later ground was broken on the first high rises just north of the original Cabrini townhouses. The high rises were named for William Green, a labor organizer, and the area was renamed Cabrini-Green. As one former resident of the Cabrini townhouses explained, "Because the Frances Cabrini Homes of our day had about as much in common with today's Cabrini-Green as Mayberry did with Dodge City, it never merited any new coverage. It's as if this entire era never existed" (quoted in G. H. Morgan, 1993:20).[1]

The liberal impulses of the postwar years were quickly transformed into racial segregation. Arnold R. Hirsch summed up the consequences of the urban renewal movement: "The gains for blacks were largely symbolic, and the government concern that seemed so promising was ephemeral. Indeed, the process of urban reconstruction in the postwar era was characterized as much by the absence of black input as it was by the overwhelming force of local institutions and the marginal influence of white ethnics. The emergence of the second ghetto was grave testimony to the persistence of black powerlessness in Chicago" (Hirsch, 1983:245).

The urban renewal movement was testimony not only to African American powerlessness but also to white dominance of economic and political capital. The social inequality, however, was created not only by upper-middle-class Protestants but also by working-class Catholics. Working-class Catholics were affected most directly by the placement of housing projects in their neighborhoods. A spatial map of the fifteen poorest neighborhoods in Chicago in the 1980s starkly outlines a zone of racial segregation, the result of thirty years of racial and class exclusion (deVise, 1993). As Hirsch pointed out, this strategy of discrimination also exposed how government colluded in the structures of segregation:

> Previously, white hostility had been expressed primarily through *private* means— violence, voluntary agreements among realtors, and restrictive covenants were the most powerful forces determining the pattern of black settlement. Before the Depression, government involvement was generally limited to the spotty judicial enforcement of privately drawn restriction agreements. With the emergence of redevelopment, renewal, and public housing, however, government took an active hand not merely in reinforcing prevailing patterns of segregation but also in lending them a permanence never seen before. The implication of government in the second ghetto was so pervasive, so deep, that it virtually constituted a new form of de jure segregation. (Hirsch, 1983:254)

The history of public housing in Chicago illustrates the power of symbolic boundaries to shape structures of oppression against what appear to be good intentions. These "good" intentions were quickly overwhelmed by political and economic interests in Chicago in the 1960s and 1970s. Daley and the Democratic machine, which represented working-class Chicagoans—once themselves powerless—had the most to lose when other minority groups began to increase their economic and political power. Daley and his supporters were powerful partners in the production of the second ghetto.

The social system that created public housing was thus complex and variegated. It was produced by multiple groups colluding to protect their interests. Protestant elites wanted to secure economic growth by putting distance between the slum and the Loop business district. Ethnic groups worked to establish their own identity and a sense of community. They feared the imposition of African Americans into the fabric of their community life. White ethnics denied this process of segregation; Mayor Daley asserted in 1957 and 1963 that "there are no ghettos in Chicago" (quoted in Royko, 1971:133–34).

Protestant business interests sought to create zones of economic opportunity in downtown Chicago. Segregating the poor produced space for upper-middle-class markets. Protestants were not the only agent in the construction of the second ghetto, but neither did they resist its growth. The congregation of Fourth Presbyterian made no attempt to challenge the racial segregation that was so much a part of the public housing venture. To be sure, its laypeople gained from the expansion of the Loop business district. In oblique ways, therefore, Fourth Presbyterian cooperated in the building of public housing—a social experiment that would create chaos and disintegration in African American communities for the next half-century.

The Dominant Social Class

Fourth Presbyterian's Gothic architecture had, from its inception in 1914, an air of class distinction. While its architecture is anachronistic, particularly as it contrasts with the massive modern buildings that went up all around it during the 1960s and 1970s, it presents a powerful visage. Throughout the Davies period the beauty of the church and the style of Davies's preaching filled the 1,400 seats of the sanctuary each Sunday; one-third of the 1,400 congregants were said to be visitors.

The 1960s and 1970s brought enormous changes to the Lower Gold Coast. Fourth Presbyterian was virtually surrounded by wealth. The changes in the neighborhood's social boundaries diminished Fourth Presbyterian in size, architecture, and cultural influence. This Protestant church, which had once embodied the power of the establishment, no longer dominated its neighborhood or the city. The buildings that surrounded the church overshadowed the Protestant cultural agenda and honored the economic sphere with larger monuments of its own.

An establishment does not go away easily, however, and the influence of Fourth Presbyterian continued to be reflected by the leaders of the church during Davies's tenure. In 1967 the thirty elders of the session were pictured with short biographical descriptions in the church's newsletter.[2] Out of the thirty elders listed, a third were either lawyers or medical doctors, and the other twenty were executives or managers of major financial or manufacturing firms in the Chicagoland area. In the second half of the 1970s short biographies about longtime prominent members of Fourth Presbyterian's leadership were written in the church's newsletter. It was a "Who's Who" of prominent, mostly male figures in the Chicago area. These leaders of the church, elders on the session or the board of trustees, came from high positions in the financial, political, and cultural spheres of the city and nation.

William McCormick Blair, president of Fourth Presbyterian from 1960 until his death in 1982 at ninety-eight years of age, was an exemplar of this Protestant establishment tradition. Blair's great uncle was Cyrus Hall McCormick, an industrial giant of early Chicago and a man who was active in Fourth Presbyterian's founding in 1871. Blair married Helen Bowen, the daughter of one of Chicago's most prominent civic leaders, Louise de Koven Bowen. Louise Bowen was a friend of Jane Addams and was instrumental in the founding of Hull-House. In the 1930s Blair founded his own investment banking firm, which he made a success. Two of his children went into the business; another son became an ambassador to the Philippines and to Denmark and was director of the John F. Kennedy Center for the Performing Arts in Washington, D.C. Blair was also a president and trustee of the Art Institute and was extensively involved in the Field Museum and the University of Chicago. In 1971 he gave to Fourth Presbyterian the refurbishment of its chapel—a gift of $100,000. The ornate 150-seat chapel was renamed Blair Chapel.

Davies nurtured these prominent Protestant establishment figures. A representative sample illustrates the kind of individuals that were leaders of Fourth Presbyterian during the period. Luther I. Replogle was founder of the Replogle Globe Company, ambassador to Iceland from 1969 to 1972, and a president of the trustees for Princeton Theological Seminary (Princeton's president flew to Chicago for Replogle's memorial service in 1981 at Fourth Presbyterian). Helen Beiser, a distinguished child psychiatrist in Chicago, was made president of the American Academy of Child Psychiatry in 1981. Paul Randolph served more than thirty years as an elected representative to the Illinois General Assembly, representing the Near North Side. Edward C. Logelin, Midwest vice president of United States Steel Corporation, won multiple civic awards in Chicago and was close to becoming the moderator of the General Assembly for the United Presbyterian Church in 1971. Marlin W. Johnson was a special agent in charge of the Chicago FBI office until 1971. Judge John S. Hastings was chief judge of the U.S. Court of Appeals for the Seventh Circuit (Indiana, Illinois, and Wisconsin) until his retirement in 1969.

All of these men and women were part of the session, deacons, or board of trustees almost continuously during Davies's tenure. Two of the men were memorialized in the pages of *Fourth Focus,* Fourth Presbyterian's newsletter. The eulogies provide insight into the quality and dispositions that Davies and the congregation admired and wanted reproduced. Replogle, who gave $100,000 in 1974 for the start-up money for Fourth Presbyterian's Lorene Replogle Counseling Center, was known for two traits, according to Davies: self-improvement and joy. The first involved a "tireless" energy for what Davies referred to as "self-realization." Second, Replogle's faith had brought him a joy that "brings the serenity which lies deep under the turbulent waters of experience. . . ." Davies concluded his eulogy by saying, "He died in quiet surrender to God's encompassing love. He had reached his goal, but still it was the upward call of God in Christ Jesus—not to a sentimental surrender to achievement, but improvement" (*Fourth Focus,* September 1981).

The themes of success, hard work, strength in purpose, and improvement even at the end of life are clear. These classic themes of the Protestant work ethic—delayed gratification and discipline—ring throughout the pages of the biographies of longtime Fourth Presbyterian leaders. They describe not just successful men and women but characters who achieved their success with dignity and distinction. These Protestant figures modeled the symbolic and cultural boundaries of men and women of this church. These were individuals reared to possess the power of position in the context of service to the community and the church. They modeled the tradition of noblesse oblige through their generosity.

William McCormick Blair's memorial service in 1982 again is emblematic of the Protestant establishment in its most vivid incarnation. Davies portrayed Blair as a man who was a success in the world but who served his community and church with "humility" and a sense of "dignity." Davies painted a picture of a man of privilege who served others: a man of "restrained dignity, a gentleman of the old school, an elegant man." Davies summed up Blair's character in this fashion: "I think I've got it in one word, *humility.* No! Not self-deprecation, not contrived self-effacement, but that which always makes this virtue sterling. It is the capacity to make others all important, giving them special value, making them feel regal. The New Testament calls it 'losing yourself for the sake of others.'" (*Fourth Focus,* June 1982). It is remarkable that in 1982 this kind of laudative remark could be said without self-consciousness. In the midst of times that did not support these character traits or praise establishment figures, these men continued to lead and be honored at Fourth Presbyterian. Fourth Presbyterian served as a type of time capsule for the establishment, around which cultural shifts were taking place. It was an institution where the social and symbolic boundaries of position and power were respected, reinforced, and reproduced. These elite figures supported traditional social boundaries and enjoyed the recognition of their generosity to the church, but they maintained a "sober" and "subdued" sense of their social and cultural power. This is not to say that the leadership and laypeople of Fourth Presbyterian did nothing to adapt to the social change of their time or that they were unaffected by the 1960s and 1970s.

THE CHALLENGE OF CHANGE FROM WITHIN

Adapting to New Times

Harrison Ray Anderson had been an example of stability and continuity. Records show that during the entire period from 1928 to the end of Davies's tenure in 1984, church membership at Fourth Presbyterian hovered near three thousand. During Anderson's period Fourth Presbyterian was in a neighborhood of upper-middle-class homeowners, people who enjoyed the neighborhood's close proximity to the waterfront to the east and the Loop business district to the south.

When Anderson retired in 1961, Davies was called by a Fourth Presbyterian search committee. Davies came to the church from a ten-year pastorate in Bethlehem, Pennsylvania. He had built a large new church there, doubled the size of the congregation, and ministered to the executives of the Bethlehem Steel Company, which the search committee regarded as especially advantageous because Davies would be accustomed to dealing with powerful men.

An immigrant from Wales, Davies had come to the country with his wife in 1951. His Welsh accent remained with him throughout his tenure at Fourth Presbyterian. His dramatic style and accent drew many to the church during this period. When Davies got off the plane at O'Hare Airport in Chicago at the beginning of his pastorate at Fourth Presbyterian, he was escorted into a press room for a news conference. A reporter asked him, "Reverend, what makes you think that ten years from now there will even be a church where you are going? All the important people have died out. They are no longer around. It doesn't have the influence it used to have." Davies responded by saying, "The church is not a community of people who are well-heeled; the church is the place where members are drawn together by the influence of the Holy Spirit. So long as the Spirit works through that church, the church will be there not only ten years from now but for many years to come" (Davies Interview, December 10, 1993).

One of Davies's main rhetorical strategies was to push the focus off himself or Fourth Presbyterian and onto a theological explanation for the vitality of the church's ministry.[3] An associate, who was a part of the leadership during Davies's tenure, said that Davies was always concerned that the focus was too much on Fourth Presbyterian itself and not enough on what the church was doing for the community.

A strategy of reframing was consistent with Davies's ministerial vision of the church. Davies repeatedly asserted that the church exists primarily for those "outside it—for the least, the lost and the last in society" ((Davies Interview, December 10, 1993). One of the leaders from that period said she told Davies after hearing him say this one too many times, "There are other people in the world than the poor; they have rights too" (Interview, June 22, 1994). Davies attempted, at least in the first years of his ministry, to reframe the social and symbolic boundaries of Fourth Presbyterian as a religious institution. The first challenge to Fourth Presbyterian in the 1960s thus came from Davies himself.

Davies as Change Maker

From the inception of Fourth Presbyterian the church had used a pew rental system to raise revenue. The system allowed families who rented pews to arrive five minutes before the eleven o'clock Sunday morning service and assume specific seats. No one else was allowed into the sanctuary or into rented pews before that time. Crowds of people would have to wait in the narthex and outside the front door until five minutes before the beginning of the service. Upon the release of the pews the crowd would come rushing into the sanctuary.

Davies, describing the pew selection process, reported, "Persons would be seated appropriate to their profession and proportional to their income. An elder would say, 'Wouldn't it be nice to seat you with your colleagues?' The purpose was that people would associate with their kind—with their set" (Davies Interview, December 10, 1993). The social registry that was a part of the Gold Coast social set of the time was mirrored in Fourth Presbyterian's attempt to nurture the social elite in its own context. Davies's response to this was typical of his style: "I came from the Welsh valleys. My stock comes from miners. I have coal dust in my veins. When I looked out and saw what was going on, I nearly collapsed. This cannot be—this is not the church" (Davies Interview, December 10, 1993). Davies's remarks were often exaggerated for effect. He frequently referred to his working-class origins, although his background was middle class and he was educated at Cambridge University; his mother's father had, however, been a coal miner.

Davies took two years to evaluate the pew rental system.[4] The politics of

Fourth Presbyterian and his own sense of caution kept him from moving faster. Since the 1920s pew rentals had consistently produced income for the church, from $20,000 to $50,000 each year. This was nearly a third of the annual budget. But in 1963 Davies, who had stayed in William McCormick Blair's home when he first arrived in Chicago, told Blair that it was time to discard the pew rental system. In his typical dramatic fashion Davies told the story of how he ended the pew rental system:

> He [Blair] called some of the most prominent people in the church down to lunch at one of the Chicago clubs down in the Loop. He gave lunch with drinks, so everybody was happy. Mr. Blair said let everyone say what they thought of the pew rental system, and everyone of them was for it to continue. And then I spoke and I spoke against it. I knew that I was up against the power structure. This would be a symbol of change. Mr. Blair then spoke and said that "Dr. Davies came to me and told me just what you just heard, so I checked around the city of Chicago to see what was going on in other churches." Mr. Blair called the head of Sears, who was a part of a big church downtown and said, "Do you have a pew rental system in your church?" And the Sears man said, "Hell, Bill, that went out at the end of the last century." Mr. Blair said, "From now on Mrs. Blair and I are canceling our rental on our pew. And we shall give our money to the church. Now would anyone like to change their minds?" And every one of them did change. What happened at the Chicago club had huge reverberations in the church on Michigan Avenue. (Davies Interview, December 10, 1993)[5]

This is a paradigmatic story about Davies because it foreshadows how he worked within Fourth Presbyterian in a dramatic and yet subtle way to change the church and adapt it to the new social movements of the era. Davies first acknowledged those at the center of power, convincing them of the necessity of change and using them as a lightning rod for the transition. Davies mastered the strategy of having church leaders adopt his vision. His style, unlike the aggressiveness of some 1960s social activists, was only obliquely confrontational, which usually enabled him to get what he wanted.

Davies did, however, offend some powerful people in the church leadership. Davies related several incidents in which elders left the church's boards because of his actions or the sermons he preached. Several leaders from that period recounted his willingness to cut people out of leadership positions if he felt that they were against him or were dividing the church. One former church officer said that what made Davies effective was his outsider status: "He felt no great loyalty to certain families in the congregation. Criticisms never got to him. He was accessible in some ways, but there was a barrier there that very few people got inside" (Interview, April 19, 1994). At the same, Davies did have close connections with the Blairs and the Replogles, relationships that eventually brought great benefits to Fourth Presbyterian during Davies's tenure.

The Advent of Neighborhood Ministries

During the early 1960s Davies and the church leadership began outreach to the children and teenagers on the Near North Side. The Culture Center was instituted on Tuesday nights for underprivileged children and youth. This program served the African American children of Cabrini-Green.[6] The Teen Center on Friday nights benefited Hispanic youth in the area. Both programs were well attended, each averaging more than a hundred youth every week. Davies and his lay leadership broke new ground in Fourth Presbyterian's ministry. Up to that point ministries to the poor had always taken place through the auspices of neighborhood social service agencies. For the first time racial-ethnic and lower-class individuals had access to Fourth Presbyterian's property. Again, Davies garnered the support of powerful leaders in his congregation. One of the elders, Edward Logelin, the United States Steel executive, spearheaded the Friday night Teen Center.

During this time Davies collaborated with John Fry, the minister from the First Presbyterian Church in Woodlawn. Fry later became embroiled with police over his attempt to mitigate gang violence by storing the guns from gangs in his church. Fry was working with gang leaders in his area to get them to put away their weapons and work in more peaceful ways for social justice (Fry, 1973). Davies remained loyal to Fry. In 1968 Davies went to Washington, D.C., and spoke to the McClelland Committee in defense of Fry's actions and ministry. Davies reported that he explained to the committee about the ministries taking place at Fourth Presbyterian:

> "Senators, you should come around our church on Friday nights. We have programs for Hispanic youth. We have Chicago police frisk them on their way into church to take their guns from them. If you look under the bushes at night you'll find guns and knives and Molotov cocktails." A senator said "I don't believe it. What would your trustees say about this?" "I don't know what they would say, but that is what is taking place." I was able to show that both of us [Fry and Davies] were doing the same things, in different ways, but we were doing the same things to help the cause. (Davies Interview, December 10, 1993)

Davies faced strong resistance, including death threats, to the social outreach programs from members of Fourth Presbyterian and from businesspeople in the neighborhood. Business owners feared their businesses would suffer because of the presence of minority youth. Speaking in his dramatic way, Davies described the reaction from some of the Fourth Presbyterian members: "'You know what he's doing—he's throwing open the doors to the niggers. He's allowing the riffraff into the church. He's driving out those who are the upper cut.' The battle was on" (Davies Interview, December 10, 1993).

Administratively, Fourth Presbyterian's session formed a committee on city ministry early in the 1960s. In the summer of 1964 it joined forces with an ecumenical community group called Committee on Community Organization (COCO). The purpose of this organization was to address issues on the Near North Side, such as to "improve law enforcement, fight juvenile delinquency, combat dilapidated housing, and work for a more responsible citizenship" (*Fourth Church*, July 1964). A Fourth Presbyterian elder was chairman of COCO. The organization's agenda reflected Fourth Presbyterian's ethos and its maintenance of Protestant mainline values: hard work, clean living, responsibility, and the upkeep of private property.

Gender Boundaries in Question

Davies promoted women leaders in the church. In 1964 Davies hired Fourth Presbyterian's first woman minister, Leslie Anbari. She was among the first thirty women ordained in the Presbyterian Church U.S.A. The Presbyterian Church U.S.A. first ordained women to the ministry in 1957. Anbari, the third woman ordained by the Presbytery of Chicago, was one of the first women to be called to a city church. Upon Anbari's resignation in 1966, Davies heralded her as "a shining example of the ordination of women" (*Fourth Church*, September 1966). Davies, however, did not hire another ordained woman for his staff until 1981.

From the early days of the church, laywomen at Fourth Presbyterian resisted women in leadership positions. Three women in lay leadership from the 1960s reported in interviews that Anbari was disliked by the women of Fourth Presbyterian. One church officer, who was the first of two women on the session in 1972, had no use for the feminist movement and felt that Anbari "pushed too hard on social issues" (Interview, June 22, 1994). She also felt that Davies was unenthusiastic about having women in leadership positions. Davies, however, defended himself when I asked about women and Fourth Presbyterian: "I wished we would have pushed harder, but you cannot push on every front. I did push for the woman associate pastor. I could not afford to have a gender revolution on my hands. I had opposition down the line" (Davies Interview, January 18, 1994).

The opposition to women in positions of authority came from both genders. The men of Fourth Presbyterian opposed women in leadership from the beginning. The only advocacy for women in leadership came from Davies, with the hiring of Anbari, or from a few outspoken women in the congregation. Most women objected to women in leadership or were indifferent on the issue. One woman, who was a lay leader, said that the reason Anderson and Davies had a tough time getting women on the boards was because none were "qualified," and she added, "I think they were right in their estimation" (Interview, March 30, 1994).

In 1921 the Presbyterian Church U.S.A. had allowed women to become elders, but it was not until 1972 that a woman became an elder in Fourth Presbyterian. This occurred only after a resolution passed at a session meeting in which the nominating committee was "urged to include women on the slate of candidates from which ruling elders and trustees will be elected" (Session Minutes, 1972:557). From the 1920s Fourth Presbyterian employed a woman deaconess to be in charge of women's ministry. Davies continued this practice for most of his tenure at Fourth Presbyterian.

This patriarchal impulse at Fourth Presbyterian preserved the Protestant elite tradition throughout the first half of the twentieth century. Excluding women from positions of power maintained the clublike atmosphere of Fourth Presbyterian's leadership through the 1960s. The exclusion of women enabled a male Protestant cadre to extend its sense of authority in spite of counter-cultural forces demanding that men and women share power. A part of Fourth Presbyterian's stability was its refusal to change its core ruling structures, particularly during the 1960s. The defeat of Edward Logelin for moderator of the General Assembly in 1971 signaled real change in the wider Presbyterian Church and at Fourth Presbyterian. He lost to the first woman moderator in the Presbyterian Church's history.

Boundaries within Women's Organizations

Class boundaries infused the women's organizations of Fourth Presbyterian during this time. The Women's Federation, composed of married women, met during the day, and the Business Women's Club and the Missionary Society, organized for single working women, gathered during the evening. These groups enjoyed a long tradition in the church, beginning in the nineteenth century. One single professional woman who had been involved in Fourth Presbyterian from 1928 put it this way: "The daytime women were in the image of 'Lady Bountiful'; they made sure that everyone got a Thanksgiving basket or toys for the children. They were ladies who wanted to give the appearance of being generous but were really not that benevolent. They tickled their consciences. Single women never saw the married women. There was never that much of an opportunity to get together. There wasn't any tension between the two groups" (Interview, March 30, 1994).

This rather stinging comment is typical of those made by the women I interviewed who were church members during this period. All of them openly commented on the rigid boundaries between the married women, who were well-to-do, and the single professional women, who were living in the city and making their own way. Both of these groups noted the male-dominated leadership, but there was no explicit, widespread resistance to it:

> The leadership was male-dominated. There were no women officers, until one became a deacon [in 1958]. The first woman minister was in the image of the deaconess [in 1964]. She never preached. I think Fourth Presbyterian was unique in having a woman as the head of the women's ministry. The church was not against women being involved but just so they kept their place. This was very acceptable to women. In fact it was women who opposed having women officers. "Women will wear flower hats." This was not the right image. These were the women who would stay at home. Most of the women were at home all day. Fourth Presbyterian was their social outlet and their charity outlet. That's what the Women's Federation was. (Interview, April 12, 1994)

Some women in the congregation, however, spoke out for women in leadership. One church member from that time explained that beginning in the late 1960s several women at the annual meetings demanded representation on the session. As I noted, this finally came in 1972.

Davies made some progress on women in leadership. In general, however, Davies and Fourth Presbyterian took their time in the changes they made. External challenges, however, began to impose themselves on these conservative impulses, and social boundaries had to be defended and finally negotiated.

THE CHALLENGE OF CHANGE FROM WITHOUT

The Vigorous Moderate

Davies had no use for leaders representing the social gospel during the 1960s. He ignored the pronouncements of the National Council of Churches and the Presbyterian General Assembly. Social activists, Davies recalled, asserted that "the day is over that we go out and evangelize other peoples. What we need to do is evangelize General Motors, General Electric, IBM; we need to get into the power structures." Davies witnessed firsthand the power structures at

Bethlehem Steel: "I knew that you couldn't evangelize structures, you can only evangelize people who change the structure. It has been the evangelical emphasis all along. As against the easy-talking social change theorists" (Davies Interview, December 10, 1993). Davies, in his interview with me and throughout his sermons, criticized those who spoke of structural transformation. He thought it was so much abstraction and a waste of energy. Davies, as he said of himself, was a pragmatist.

Davies spoke of how during the 1960s few intellectuals respected the work that Fourth Presbyterian had done through its outreach ministries. Fourth Presbyterian started ministries to older adults (the Older Adult Center was opened in 1964), Hispanic teens, Cabrini-Green youth, as well as Cook County Hospital and Prison. Many suggested that Davies give the Fourth Presbyterian endowment to the poor.[7] Davies resisted the Left and took a position that criticized both sides of the political spectrum, liberal and conservative. Davies embodied the "vigorous moderate" (Baltzell, 1964:25). He supported the maintenance of class privilege while demanding recognition and support of those outside these class boundaries.

This same nonideological position of compassion from a position of privilege summarized the work of Fourth Presbyterian's session during the 1960s. Fourth Presbyterian served its neighborhood through its outreach ministries but for the most part ignored the major political causes. The session did approve taking an offering for an Emergency Fund for Freedom in 1964 and 1965 to support the civil rights movement in the South, but in the spring of 1965 the session responded to the action of the Presbytery of Chicago, which was supporting clergy and laypeople who were going to Selma, Alabama, by issuing a statement of policy on the Presbytery's position: the session "was not prepared to endorse the action of the Presbytery," although "it honored the right of any individual minister or layman who acts in response to the dictates of conscience either affirmatively or negatively in the Civil Rights struggle." The session added that if any minister did participate he would not be "censured." The session, however, refused responsibility for injury and declared that if any employee of the church went, this should not be seen as an endorsement by Fourth Presbyterian (Session Minutes, March 28, 1965:232).

This tepid support was followed by a slightly elevated concern for the racial tensions that came to the surface in Chicago. In April of 1965 the session discussed an Illinois House bill regarding sanctions against property discrimination. The session debated whether Fourth Presbyterian should invite real estate agents and other influential people in real estate to discuss segregated housing patterns and their Christian responsibility. The session minutes never disclosed any action that was taken on either point.

During the summer of 1965 Chicago experienced the first race riot of the era. Mayor Daley maintained, as he did consistently throughout the unrest of the 1960s, that it was the result of "hooliganism and lawlessness" (quoted in Royko, 1971:147). This concern for law and order and the responsibility of citizenship mirrored many of the pronouncements by the Fourth Presbyterian leadership during this period.

The Civil Rights Movement: Boundaries Maintained

In the early months of 1966 a special committee of Fourth Presbyterian reported back to the session that twentieth-century Christians should "speak up collectively on such political, social and economic issues as Civil Rights, dishonesty in government, morals and social customs, economic and spiritual poverty and irresponsible labor practices" (Session Minutes, March 1966:281). Some concern for unjust social structures was expressed, but the overwhelming weight was on the maintenance of law and order. Another statement cautioned that any political or social concern should avoid "opposition to specific individuals or agencies or political parties" (Session Minutes, March 1966:281). A special committee of the session studied the potential for racial unrest in the neighborhood and issued a report that dismissed any such possibility.

These studies coincided with the arrival of Martin Luther King Jr. in Chicago during the spring and summer of 1966. King had come to work for better housing for African Americans and for the integration of the public schools. King led marches through both African American and white neighborhoods during the summer of 1966. It was in one of those neighborhoods that King was hit on the head with a brick. As Mike Royko reported, "The bump was headlined around the world" (Royko, 1971:156). King began mounting pressure on Daley's administration, threatening that he would march three times a day until his demands were met. Daley finally gave in, and a summit was called. As Royko recalled, "Daley came up with the programs that King demanded, papers were signed, King went away triumphant, but in the end nothing changed for African Americans in the city" (Royko, 1971:158).

Fourth Presbyterian made no comment on the unrest. An elder for Fourth Presbyterian during the mid-1960s, who lived at LaSalle Street on the Near North Side at the time of Martin Luther King Jr.'s marches, described the events this way: "We stood up on our roofs at the time Martin Luther King came through on one of his marches, and they came down Division Street. The police stopped them, and they turned down Sedgewick and went south. They burned many houses and destroyed several grocery stores. Norman Swenson [a long-time Fourth Presbyterian business administrator] said, 'Why do they burn these buildings down when we go out and encourage companies to build in their neighborhoods?'" (Interview, April 19, 1994). This question was typical of the white community at that time, which had little understanding of the real oppression of the black community in Chicago.[8]

In a related matter the session did mention the police raid on John Fry's First Presbyterian Church in Woodlawn. The session was concerned about Fourth Presbyterian's Teen Center on Friday nights. It formed a committee to study the possible dangers of the center's presence on Fourth Presbyterian's campus. In the fall of 1966 the task force approved the continuance of the program with Hispanic youth. This program thrived for several years but disappeared at the end of the 1960s when the neighborhood from which these youth had come succumbed to an urban renewal program.

In 1967 the session took a series of positions that upheld the social boundaries of Fourth Presbyterian. The session approved advocacy for gun control and pushed the legislature to support this action—a law and order issue to be sure. The session refused to allow the sanctuary to be used by Clergy and Laymen Concerned about Vietnam, an antiwar group. The chairman of the Committee on Community Organization, who was an elder in Fourth Presbyterian, resigned and encouraged the session to end the funding of COCO. These actions did not, however, signal a withdrawal of help to the poor; the church continued to experiment with ways to reach out to the West Side of Chicago.

The King Assassination: A Call to Action

Martin Luther King Jr. was assassinated on April 4, 1968. This murder finally stimulated Fourth Presbyterian into action. On April 17 the same elder who had resigned from the COCO board called the session to three forms of response. One was for the session to get behind a program called Operation Abandon Middle Wall. It was a plan to develop leadership in conjunction with leaders from the West Side of Chicago to help that area. The second pushed Fourth Presbyterian to "immediately secure an office within the ghetto limits, where a paid staff under the leadership of a black director would be the point of referral between the church and neighborhood—referral in a dual sense, both from within and without. There is need for us to become acquainted firsthand with the problems to be dealt with not as those who are 'going in' to solve them, but as those who are willing to be there to work with others already engaged in the tasks." The third was to have the session finance committee approve funds for this project (Session Minutes, April 1968:392).

At the same time, Davies made appeals to corporations to raise money to finance the Cabrini Summer Project. Davies raised nearly $100,000 to finance programs for youth in the Cabrini-Green neighborhoods during the next several summers. A board was formed, and it was composed exclusively of African Americans from the neighborhood. This project eventually became the Fourth Presbyterian Summer Day Program that has continued to serve more than a hundred youth from Cabrini-Green at Fourth Presbyterian in a more intensive form of tutoring. In conjunction with these programs approximately a hundred youth from Cabrini-Green were sent to Presbyterian summer camps for a week in the late 1960s and early 1970s.

In the December 1968 session minutes the board rescinded the recommendation to create an office in the ghetto and employ a black staff person. Other strategies were to be pursued. These strategies included the funding of a day care center in an African American church on the West Side. They also involved the organization of the Chicago-Orleans Housing Corporation. This became the Atrium Village housing complex at Division and Wells streets, an area directly between Cabrini-Green and the Gold Coast. The plan called for affordable housing for low- and middle-income families. The $10.5 million project broke ground on April 17, 1977, and was completed two years later. The residence included a nine-story building with 205 units and another 102 units in eight three-story apartment buildings. A racial and economic quota system was maintained to ensure a racially and economically integrated residence. An ecumenical group sponsored the project that included five churches in the neighborhood, led by Fourth Presbyterian. This housing project responded to the housing needs of the lower-income neighbors on the Near North Side. Moreover, it linked the Gold Coast and Cabrini-Green in a new way.

By the late 1960s Fourth Presbyterian had changed in response to Davies's leadership and the social movements of the time. The church continued to uphold the law and order boundaries of the Protestant mainline, yet it also reached beyond status quo social boundaries by creating ministries to the people of the West Side. Davies and his leadership creatively sought to bridge social boundaries of race and class. From Davies's time onward Fourth Presbyterian's social boundaries expanded and included a greater diversity of groups.

THE CHARISMATIC LEADER

Davies's Style of Leadership

In Elam Davies Fourth Presbyterian had a star preacher. In 1966 Davies gave the "World Famous Preachers" lectures in Australia; in 1976 he preached at the General Assembly of the Presbyterian Church of Wales; in its December 31, 1979, issue *Time* magazine featured Davies as one of the "seven star preachers" from across the nation; and the *Chicago Tribune Magazine* celebrated him on its August 16, 1981, cover as one of the "ten spellbinding preachers" from among preachers across the Chicagoland area.

Davies was, from the beginning of his tenure at Fourth Presbyterian, a celebrated preacher of the gospel. In the summer of 1964 alone he preached to the synod of California, at the Presbyterian women's quadrennial meeting at Purdue, and for three Sundays at the Fifth Avenue Presbyterian Church in New York. He also addressed chaplains and enlisted men at the U.S. Army base in Berchtesgaden, Germany. During that period, besides preaching on Sunday at Fourth Presbyterian, he regularly prepared two other preaching and speaking engagements each week. He was sought after by forums throughout the world.

For a man who was larger than life in the pulpit, he was a relatively small and fragile person. Many associates of Davies, when talking about him, refer to his fragility and his continual concern over his health. He was a shy and introverted man. Leaders of Fourth Presbyterian who knew both Anderson and Davies spoke of Anderson as a robust and outgoing man who continually dropped in on church meetings unannounced; the average parishioner saw little of Davies outside the sanctuary.

Davies served on no community boards. He had limited involvement in the General Assembly of the Presbyterian Church. He had no ambition to become moderator, as had his two predecessors at Fourth Presbyterian and his successor, John Buchanan. He focused on preaching and on leadership within the neighborhood of the Near North Side. He felt strongly that denominational officials overlooked the congregation and its power to serve its community.

Davies nurtured a small group of loyal leaders at Fourth Presbyterian, including the business administrator, the director of music, and several leaders on the session and board of trustees. Few lay leaders felt close to Davies. Indeed his associates had difficulty naming any intimates. The loneliness of his style was not lost on Davies: "A thing I find most irksome is being constantly expected to conform to the clerical image in people's minds. Life is very lonely for a minister and his family if they are kept on a pedestal. We are all human beings, with human limitations, inhibitions, weaknesses and natural human reactions. Sometimes when I am a guest at dinner I want to say, 'All talk of religion is out!'" (*Fourth Church,* June 1964). This isolation was in part his own making.

Though a loner Davies was an able administrator, counselor, and politician. He had the ability to accomplish an enormous amount through a quiet but intense way of working through other people. Several individuals used the word *autocratic* to describe his administrative leadership.[9] One mentioned that session meetings merely rubber-stamped Davies's initiatives. At the same time, his lay leaders demanded definitive leadership. They embodied in themselves an autocratic style and were accustomed to making decisions and getting their way. They expected this kind of leadership from their pastor, and Davies delivered.

Davies's Political Strategies

Davies's political style bypassed ordinary channels of political process and went straight to the source. Fourth Presbyterian remained a significant player in Chicago's political world. Davies thus had some leverage and influence with those in the city and state governments. When he had trouble with neighbors who resisted Fourth Presbyterian's outreach to the youth of Cabrini-Green, he took care of business directly. Davies explained, "We had access right to the heart of the city council, right to the mayor. I took a group of Cabrini-Green people down to see the mayor" (Davies Interview, January 18, 1994).

This direct appeal in political conflict was reflected in the way Davies dealt with the Native Americans who came to Fourth Presbyterian for asylum twice in 1971. The first incident occurred in March of that year. Forty Native Americans occupied the Fourth Presbyterian dining room basement area. Davies convinced their leader, Michael Chosa, to leave the church "peaceably and quietly" with his group after a discussion of their demands. The demands involved mortgage loans, a grant for an American Indian school, and help for several in the group whose apartment had been without heat and electricity for a month. Davies set up a meeting with the head of the Chicago Presbytery to negotiate a deal for a loan. Davies and the session also secured a special offering from Fourth Presbyterian for the American Indians of Chicago.

In July Native Americans, again led by Chosa, occupied a Belmont Harbor missile site for two weeks to dramatize the plight of their people. A violent confrontation occurred on July 1 when city workers, while pulling down the fence around the site, began fighting with the Native Americans. When the police arrived, more conflict occurred. Twelve Native Americans were arrested, and several were hurt. The rest of the group walked south, apparently to go to city hall, but detoured to Fourth Presbyterian. Norman Swenson, the business administrator, allowed them asylum in Fourth Presbyterian and asked the police to stay out. Chosa explained that he went to Fourth Presbyterian because "a lot of power comes out of this church. The vice president of US Steel is a member here" (Ingersoll, 1971:28). In fact, Edward Logelin, a United States Steel vice president, mediated the conflict between Chosa and Governor Richard Ogilvie. The governor's Office of Human Resources responded to Chosa's demand. By this time the Native Americans had lost all faith in Daley and city hall and refused to talk with them. Davies summarized his dealings with the mayor on the event this way: "After the Indian affair, the mayor lost faith in us." Davies added, "The mayor was a tyrant" (Davies Interview, January 18, 1994).

Davies took risks with his connections, and he had enough power to leverage his demands with political officials. Nonetheless, Davies always exercised his political power from behind the scenes. His strategy was far from democratic, but it was effective in that he produced the results he wanted with little or no conflict with those opposed to him.

Davies the Counselor

Davies's introversion and sensitivity to human conflict marked him as a sought-after counselor. About a third of his time was spent in individual counseling with congregants (Davies Interview, January 18, 1994). Several church members said when they asked to see Davies, they were asked whether it was an administrative concern or a personal one. If it was administrative, he would give them fifteen minutes; if it was personal, he would give the person whatever time was necessary, sometimes up to two hours. Davies clearly distinguished political and personal boundaries. In political conflicts he was hard and stubborn until he got his way. In the personal concerns of others he was empathic and open.

As an example of his ability to reach out to diverse individuals, Davies described his contact with and ministry to a group of streetwalkers, women who worked Michigan Avenue. Apparently they turned to Davies in their distress. He said they came to his last sermon at Fourth Presbyterian, and all ten of them sat together in one of the front pews (Davies Interview, January 18, 1994). Even as Davies nurtured his Protestant elite social boundaries, a part of him felt at home with those on the underside of society.

Davies spoke in the most glowing terms of his friendship with Karl Menninger, the well-known American psychoanalyst and founder of the Menninger

Foundation. Menninger frequently attended the Fourth Presbyterian worship services. He led several adult education events at the church during the late 1960s, attracting on average five hundred people each night. Menninger admired Davies, and Menninger understood Davies's ability to be sensitive to the psychological needs of his congregants. Davies described one event in which Menninger came down the center aisle of the sanctuary at Fourth Presbyterian after one of Davies's sermons and nearly bellowed:

> "Davies! I have something to tell you. Do you realize the privilege you have Sunday by Sunday to stand up there and preach? Let me tell you. When I was a young psychiatrist I would see five or so patients a day and around thirty a week. Every Sunday, you have hundreds of people who come in here. We need to hear what can help us in moments of anxiety, we need to hear what can help us in our moments of despair, we need a few words of comfort in times of sorrow, and now and again we need a bit of hell!" (Davies Interview, January 18, 1994)

Davies's Oratorical Style

From nearly every quarter Davies received high reviews for his oratorical style. The overused phrase is that he was the "Richard Burton of the pulpit." Davies pointed out that it was Burton who modeled himself after the great Welsh preachers of the day, as Davies himself had. Davies's voice continued to hold onto its Welsh lilt throughout his preaching career. His voice could rise and come close to a shout and then lower and become a whisper in an instant. Davies was known for his ability to rouse the emotions of the congregation with the modulation of voice and tonality. As one church officer described, "Davies could preach the same sermon each Sunday and it wouldn't matter, because he was so good" (Interview, October 12, 1994).

In his charismatic leadership style Davies would demand attention with his constant "Listen, men and women!" Rhetorically, he would guide his listeners through his sermons, so all would know that a point was coming or the conclusion had arrived. He could persuade with a moving story or the lift of his voice, but he could also entertain. He had a quick wit and a sense of humor, often poking fun at himself. As one church officer said, "I'll never forget the first time he spoke at Fourth Presbyterian. The sanctuary had standing room only. Davies was this little man standing in the pulpit with his tabs [Geneva tabs, a part of traditional Presbyterian clergywear] poking out of his collar, much smaller and less impressive than Anderson, and he said, 'Now I have to admit I am a bit nervous, but not nearly as nervous as the committee who has invited me.' Davies could roll you in the aisles" (Interview, June 22, 1994).

Davies was also famous for his ability to preach without a manuscript. He would go into the pulpit with a three-by-five card and usually never look at it. Davies said that he wrote his sermon out, without illustrations, but that he spent little time in sermon preparation. He would come up with a title on Wednesday, give it to the secretary, but still not have much of an idea until Friday, and then he would use Saturday to prepare the sermon. This lack of preparation also led to sermons that had to be cut short because time had run out. Davies would often say at the end of the sermon, "I will finish this next week," and spontaneously a series in two parts would be created.

Davies described his feeling before going into the pulpit this way: "I felt terrified going into the pulpit. Just as I was about to get into the pulpit, however, I felt like a racehorse just wanting to get out of the gates. And once I was in the pulpit I just forgot myself." Davies described his philosophy of preaching as, using the Phillips Brooks's line, "truth mediated through personality. Not personality speaking the truth. Now there is a big difference." Davies often took the focus off himself. Davies did not like it when people called his sermons dramatic performances. For him his preaching was not dramatic but "fervent." Davies, in response to my question about what the essence of preaching was, put it this way:

> Preaching is like the Old Testament story of Elijah at Mount Carmel. God is the one that sends down the fire. The altar was completely soaked with water. Fire came down. This was not proof of how great a prophet Elijah was but how great God was. The fire doesn't always come down. The fire will never come down if the preacher is focused on being a great performer. Preaching is the fire coming down on all the preparation that one has done, that one has set aside so that the truth can come through. (Davies Interview, January 18, 1994)

His preaching was also intellectually compelling. As one church officer, a child psychiatrist, said, "I found it fascinating that he could both interest me intellectually and arouse me emotionally; he was an absolute genius at that" (Interview, June 22, 1994).

A Type of Charismatic Leadership

Davies was a typical charismatic leader.[10] He was treated as a unique man with exceptional oratorical and personal gifts. These "powers" were said to lift him up above ordinary leaders; he described his own experience of preaching as transcendent and empowered by the Holy Spirit. Davies consistently deflected others' admiration away from his own character traits, but he no doubt used his personality to persuade, move, and convince others of the truth of what he asserted.

As Max Weber pointed out, charismatic leadership finds bureaucratic process repellent: "There is no hierarchy; the leader merely intervenes in general or in individual cases" (Weber, 1978:243). Time and again church officers describe Davies's autocratic behavior and his penchant to ignore bureaucratic rules. One longtime employee of Fourth Presbyterian reported that Davies said to him that as senior minister of Fourth Presbyterian he had "plenipotentiary power." He could hire whom he wanted without the approval of his leadership boards. Of course, this type of power is completely antithetical to the Reformed tradition, which is highly bureaucratic in its modern incarnation. Nonetheless, Davies's leadership style was effective.

Charismatic leaders abhor rules and administrative processes, particularly in the acquisition of funds.[11] Both contemporary clergy and laypeople noted Davies's tendency to ignore regular stewardship campaigns. Several times during his pastorate, notes of financial stress were recorded in the session minutes, and he would respond with calls for calm and flexibility. Several church officers said that at these times Davies would simply call one of his benefactors for a financial favor. I have already outlined three substantial gifts that subsidized Davies's vision to create the Blair Chapel, to inaugurate a Fourth Presbyterian-sponsored counseling center, and to finance the Summer Day Program for Cabrini-Green. Moreover, an account for ministerial discretion was discovered at the end of his ministry. Davies used this fund to balance the budget or to help a congregant in need. The fund was close to $100,000.

During a time of social anomie Fourth Presbyterian turned to a charismatic leader. Charismatic leadership is fundamentally "revolutionary," according to Weber, and thus is willing and able to change with the times (Weber, 1978:244). Davies inherited Fourth Presbyterian from Anderson, a bureaucratic leader, and was able to use his own style to attract many to the church while most mainline churches, particularly in urban areas, were losing members. Although Davies's leadership was not revolutionary, he was an agent for change, helping Fourth Presbyterian adjust to the rapid social and cultural transformations of the era.

DAVIES'S PREACHING: INSIDE OUT

An Evangelical Liberal

Davies repeatedly said, "I preach from struggle and not from solution," which gets to the heart of the pastoral side of his preaching. As Menninger alluded to, Davies was attuned to the internal struggles and dispositions of his congregants' lives. He would say in different ways that he knew his listeners not only because he would counsel with them but also because he was listening to his own struggles: "I figured that at least two or three people had experienced what I had gone through" (Davies Interview, January 18, 1994). His authority as a leader came in part because of his empathy with the struggles of his congregants.

In a number of sermons Davies tells the story of being reared in a fiercely evangelical atmosphere in Wales. In his childhood he had struggled with the passionate demands of forceful preachers calling him and others to complete dedication to the gospel. It was preaching that was accompanied by carrot and stick. Salvation was for those who conformed to God's will, and damnation awaited those who failed. For Davies the gospel had been distorted and had become a burden, certainly to him and to those who listened to this evangelical preaching. When he constructed his own theological perspective, he did so in relation to this difficult theological background. His questions were existential: How does the gospel relate to the internal conflicts and struggles that all moderns face? As he would often note, his time was one in which dealing with anxiety had become fashionable. He responded to these internal struggles with a message that admitted that human beings are flawed and that faith does not require perfection before it can be tried. "Men and women," he declared in a September 13, 1964, sermon entitled "On the Danger of Doing People Good," "what melts your heart and mine, what bends our stubborn wills, what overcomes at last our proud spirits is not the news that God is waiting to receive us when we have straightened out, or been made over, or when we have uttered the right shibboleths, but that He accepts with a grace that is limitless, and with a love which is unbelievable."

Though Davies was a fervent evangelical preacher, a liberal Protestant discourse lurked beneath much of his preaching. He preached against all forms of self-righteousness, whether against those claiming a special knowledge about God, a certitude about God's will, or even right judgment about matters of justice in the world. Davies chided those who claimed that they knew themselves or God fully because, to him, each of us is a mystery to himself or herself, and God is the greatest mystery. For Davies Christians believe that their faith in Christ, in whom God's grace is sufficient, is more important than understanding the mystery. Davies's theology came out of the neoorthodox tradition of evangelical Christianity, which was unwilling to define God in absolute terms but was evangelical about faith in Christ, which gave life hope in the midst of uncertainty.

In a July 16, 1967, sermon called "All or Nothing Christianity," Davies attacked forms of Christianity that demanded complete submission to God before God would accept the individual. To make this point, Davies would often use himself as an example of personal vulnerability: "But I want to tell you something, men and women, . . . there are shelves and corners behind the facade of my personality and the door of communication with it that I even have not suspected or know anything about." Davies was well aware of the psychoanalytic convention that behind every certitude there are compartments of doubt that are never fully known to the individual. Despite these hidden parts, for Davies God's grace was sufficient.

A Therapeutic Gospel

Davies, as he enabled his congregants to negotiate their own internal boundaries, performed a double task. First, he promised that God's grace was near despite the areas of darkness and mystery in the self. Second, he asserted that God's presence extended even to the darkest edges of social reality. There were therefore no psychological or sociological boundaries to God's grace.

In one of Davies's most eloquent sermons, "On Finding God Where You Least Expect Him," delivered on September 27, 1964, he outlined the ways that Jesus is captured by "romanticized history, by contemporary religion, and by our own piousness." He then pointed out that the New Testament says that the "place you find God is in the whole of life, among the spiritual and among the sensual, in the midst of the beauty and the bawdiness of existence." The hermeneutical key for this universal Christ is that God is the one who, in Christ, suffered on a cross and experienced the full pleasure and pain of human existence. No place, however peripheral or depraved, is therefore too far for God in Christ to go:

> Christ is in the world where the victimized are struggling for recognition, where the frustrated and perverted sex-obsessed are looking for meaning. He is in the world of dirty politics and vicious polemics, in the world of gang warfare and juvenile delinquency, of dope addiction and drunkenness, of broken homes and battered lives, and He is in the world nailed to a cross, and where He is nailed to a cross God is—loving and reconciling! Reconciling! Never forget that!

In Davies's first and only book, published in 1964, he wrote about the reasons for going to church: "It is a deliberate setting of oneself side by side with people who spiritually are poor, maimed, blind and halt, and confessing by our presence that we are one of them, one of the least, last, lost, met by God in the company of our fellow needy" (Davies, 1964:57). This is the most explicit mention that Davies makes of the connection between the psychological sense that one is needy and lost and the feeling that because of this one is no different from those in the city who are sociologically the least, the lost, and the last.

Sociologically, this analogical connection is relatively meaningless, since the reality is that Davies ministered to upper-middle-class Protestants, people who, for the most part, had never experienced social or political deprivation. Their lives were filled with privilege and a sense of status. No doubt Davies knew the sociological facts of his congregants' lives, but he also knew their psychological despair and their confusion in the face of changing times. Davies used these internal struggles to turn the congregation toward the neighborhoods to the west, where the sociologically needy lived and died. He normalized the tension of his upper-middle-class congregation by theologically rationalizing their troubled conscience and at the same time challenging them to reach out to those excluded by class stratification and racial segregation.

Under Anderson, Fourth Presbyterian conserved its social boundaries and demanded moral conformity to conservative and traditional cultural values. Social inequality was assumed. Outreach meant taking care of one's own. Social witness equaled moral admonition. Davies's leadership, his preaching and outreach programs, opened the social boundaries of Fourth Presbyterian; social inequality, though confirmed, was challenged and judged. This transformation of a Protestant mainline church, while not dramatic, was evident. Membership and money remained stable, and congregants recognized their participation in the boundaries of class and race so intransigent in Chicago.

DAVIES'S PREACHING: OUTSIDE IN

Boundaries of Law and Order

While Davies was tenaciously straightforward about the internal struggles of his congregants' lives, he was often contradictory in his observations about the social boundaries of his Protestant church. He was consistent, however, in his critique of the political Left and Right. Davies attacked the certitude, self-righteousness, and unconditional demands of conservative evangelicals, but he was no less passionate in questioning the declarations and actions of social activists during the 1960s, as can be seen in his October 8, 1967, sermon, "The Dilemma of Conflicting Loyalties":

> A young Milwaukee priest disrupts his whole city by a series of marches into segregated neighborhoods. I cannot but admire his unflagging zeal, his courage and his utter indifference to his own personal safety, but I wish I could be as sure as he is that he is obeying God rather than men in taking this approach to the problem. Perhaps he is, who knows? What surprises me is the serene confidence dis-

played by such protesters when they claim that they are wholly obeying God's higher law, while those who disagree with them are on the side of men, or worse perhaps on the side of the devil.

Davies could sound the note of law and order without flinching. He stood against civil disobedience; he was not certain that it was God's will. He also questioned the loyalty and patriotism of those protesting the Vietnam War.[12] He could sound as conservative as Richard Nixon, who asserted that war protesters empowered the enemy. In a January 17, 1971, sermon entitled "The Kind of Religion That Counts in the End," he attacked by name the Berrigan brothers, the Jesuit priests who led many acts of civil disobedience during this period.

Davies was speaking the mind of the congregation when in his September 3, 1968, sermon, "What Has Happened to the Religious Idea of Judgment," he recalled his impressions of the violence and protest during the Democratic National Convention in Chicago. Davies explained in his sermon that he was present to observe the rioting at Balbo and Michigan Avenue during the Democratic National Convention. The violence and hateful calls of the student radicals outraged him: "What could have been said if the Mayor of this city had ordered these men out, and left the town to the radicals who wanted to take it over? If the hippies and the yippies want a night out at the expense of order, then they must expect the kind of swift judgment which follows. I deplore it when the protection becomes brutal, but we are always going to take this risk or chance anarchy."

Underscoring Davies's preference for order, this sermon followed the assassination of Martin Luther King Jr. in early April of 1968 and the riots that occurred in Chicago in the West Side ghettos. It was during these riots that Mayor Daley gave the ominous "Shoot to kill" order (Royko, 1971:168). Davies upheld law and order against the violence perpetrated by protesters against the status quo; moreover, he supported the coercion of the state in maintaining civic order at almost any cost.

Confronting the Status Quo

On April 7, 1968, the Sunday following the murder of Martin Luther King Jr., Davies preached one of his most provocative sermons, "The Protest of a Modern Palm Sunday"—a stinging call to repentance and responsibility that compared King, in a figurative way, with the person of Jesus Christ. In an eloquent sermon, masterfully constructed, Davies wove together the Palm Sunday theme that Christ was celebrated by the very people who would soon kill him and the implication that Davies and the congregation had colluded in King's murder. The message offended members of his congregation. Davies himself reported that two of his elders stood up during the sermon and walked out. One was an FBI agent, who later took Davies out in a limousine and explained the private side of King's alleged sexual dalliances. This made no impression on Davies.

In the sermon on King, Davies began with a question: "What I am saying is that there is sufficient in common between the parade of the first and the present Palm Sunday to make us stop and ask, Whose side are we on? The palm wavers or the cold-water throwers?" Davies drew out the comparison that Jesus' walk into Jerusalem brought out the "orthodox good people, those like you and me, who set so much store by order and decency." He subtly drew a deeper comparison between King and Jesus: that Jesus' demands were not sentimental but political—"To set at liberty those who are oppressed. . . ." Through rhetorical repetition he confronted the congregation with the question: On whose side would they be? "Of course, we don't all hate in the same way. Some of us are very refined about it." Davies implicated his sophisticated audience in the violence that would destroy any who would disrupt social boundaries of power and prestige: he and the congregation do not do the actual violence, but by a passive attitude, others, less refined, do the job for them.

Davies then painted a picture of political, economic, racial, and social oppression and asked the question, "Why are we so stupid as to think that we can get away with oppression or injustice, or plain indifference? You don't have to wait for America to be attacked by the enemies without. It will fall, unless we wake up, by the hand of enemies within."

The sermon climaxed when he told members of the congregation to be careful about what they wished—that is, that Jesus would come again—because he is not the meek and mild Savior pictured by the Sunday school drawings but the fierce Christ who upends the money-changer tables in the temple, the Christ who questions all barriers based on race or class: "But if we ask him to enter in, let's not expect him to come accommodatively. That's not how he entered the temple on the first Palm Sunday, any more than Dr. King entered the sacred precincts of the Memphis establishment last week. Let us never forget that there is a strong element of militancy about nonviolence, especially when it assails our prejudices and our cherished privileges. God grant that we may know the day of our visitation."

It is difficult to put the law-and-order Davies together with the Davies who preached the sermon about Martin Luther King Jr. Yet this tension and Davies's

ability to speak with conviction from different perspectives made him a powerful if a contradictory preacher. Davies's propensity to pivot between prophetic judgment and the sanctioning of the status quo signaled a key structural tension in this Protestant religious institution—the knowledge that its
status was judged by its religious tradition even as it carried the responsibility
of its enormous resources.[13] This was Christ and culture in paradox. That is,
Christ judges the world and the church, each has failed, and yet the result is
not indifference and apathy but the pursuit of justice despite one's inherent
failings. Davies spoke the truth as he saw it, but he was not a consistent ideo-
logue for the Right or Left. Davies judged events individually and spoke to each
situation, depending on the context and event.

This differentiation of judgment relative to events is exemplified in how
Davies addressed the Robert F. Kennedy shooting in a sermon entitled, "Some
Reflections on the Nation's Need," given on June 9, 1968. In this carefully
crafted piece Davies responded to the national hysteria over what was called
at the time "a sick country, a disintegrating democracy": "Some have tried to
cover a whole nation with a shameful sense of guilt over the ghastly demise of
the promising young senator from New York. I want to say as unequivocally
as I can this morning that if we succumb to this sense of guilt, it will be a false
one." Davies was reflecting on a passage from Joel 2:12: "'Yet even now,' says
the Lord, 'return to me with all your heart . . . and rend your hearts and not
your garments.'" For Davies the wails of shame in the United States were false.
Why should Americans claim guilt for the deed of a killer from a foreign country? Davies thought that this "garment tearing" over the Kennedy assassination missed the point.

Davies quoted James Reston, the *New York Times* editorialist, who reflected
that the whole world seemed to be slipping into a state of anarchy and violence: "This is not merely rejection of the view that life is essentially decent,
rational and peaceful. . . ." Davies skewered this ethnocentrism, asserting that
life is neither essentially rational nor decent for most of the world: "The revolution which is convulsing the world today is not an American export. It arises
indigenously in every quarter of the globe and we are part of it, like it or not."

At the end Davies separated false from true guilt. He looked straight into
the heart of his Protestant mainline church and declared, "I think we need a
change of heart about some of the lobbying procedures of big business in this
land. . . . I think we need a change of heart over the distribution of wealth in
this country so that we shall resist the unbelievable nonsense of trying to land
a man on the moon when those around us on earth are deprived and dispos-

sessed, so that in the name of the compassion of Jesus Christ, we shall fight the trend whereby those who have, have more and those who have not, have less." Davies was unblinking in this unsentimental attack on inflexible social boundaries of class. He called his elite church to do more than give guilt-ridden lip service to the violence in the country. The congregants needed to change their hearts and act anew in the face of unequal capital distribution.

Attacking the Idols

As Menninger said, Davies was willing, when he felt called, to give his congregants "hell." Davies, reflecting on the 1980 presidential elections in an October 12, 1980, sermon called "When Revival Is Threatened by Rhetoric," commented on the superficial use of religion on both ends of the political spectrum. He defended the evangelicals for their newfound voice in the public arena. He found the liberal Protestants hypocritical for asserting the division of church and state after they had complained all along that the evangelicals spoke only of heaven and not of issues of peace and justice.

Davies, however, challenged both sides by saying, "The greatest threat to truth is not untruth but half-truth; the most powerful assault on righteousness is not by open evil but by counterfeit goodness." For him religion is trivialized when one worries about who is truly "saved" or focuses on sexual immorality as the locus of evil in the nation. For Davies God's "Holy Divine Wrath" would be aimed at one thing alone: all forms of idolatry. Davies then listed eight forms of idolatry, naming after each the god worshipped and the attitude practiced by the idol's followers:

Idolatry	God	Attitude
The idolatry of privilege	The god of exclusiveness	"I'll keep mine."
The idolatry of power	The god of tyranny	"Blow them off the face of the map."
The idolatry of pride	The god of hubris	"We're number one!"
The idolatry of prejudice	The god of racism	"One color under God."
The idolatry of possession	The god of heartlessness	"Let them eat cake."
The idolatry of piousness	The god of lovelessness	"I thank Thee that I am not as others are."
The idolatry of passion	The god of lust	"What is right is what makes you feel good"
The idolatry of personhood	The god of narcissism	"I love me, me, ME!"

In this succinct categorization of modern idols Davies brought home the point that all modern obsessions bear a darker side, a side that refuses an easy identification of righteousness with any one point of view. God judges all attempts at the absolutizing the "relative," so well explicated by H. Richard Niebuhr in *The Meaning of Revelation* (Niebuhr, 1941:16–26). Davies pushed at the edge of Fourth Presbyterian's social boundaries, contesting the congregation's complacence. He challenged his congregants to aim their sights above the comfort of their privilege toward the least, the lost, and the lonely. Davies helped his congregants identify the places in their own lives where their sense of limits permitted them to relate to those who knew no privilege. In the end Davies failed to destroy the social boundaries of privilege, class, and race, but he did make these lines of demarcation less rigid and more permeable.

CONCLUSION

During the critical decades of the 1960s and 1970s Fourth Presbyterian negotiated the social changes of the era in creative ways. Davies, who had the heart of an evangelical, had the head of a neoorthodox and liberal Protestant. Davies maintained a profound sense of God's grace. Christ was known through the beauty and depravity of the world. God also judged the self-righteousness of the Left and the Right and called his followers to give from their abundance and serve the poor. The ethic of noblesse oblige summoned the congregation to serve those with less. Davies thus secured the hearts of his congregants and turned them toward others. He normalized their internal chaos caused by the social change of the 1960s and related this inner conflict to the social discord occurring across the nation, particularly in the ghettos of Chicago. In subtle ways he and his lay leaders built bridges over class and race as none of their predecessors had been able to do. Christ dwelt not only in the church but in all people, regardless of their status or color. Church and culture were fundamentally corrupt yet redeemed by God in Christ. This theological boundary work translated into a church willing to reach out to those with less.

Davies nurtured his elite Protestant congregation and confirmed the privilege of its social class and thus inequality, but through his charismatic leadership style and subtle symbolic persuasion, he enabled the congregation and its leadership to make connections with other classes and races. Fourth Presbyterian turned its face from the Gold Coast to the West Side. The transition was a quiet one, preserving privilege but demanding that the congregation recognize the least in society. The church remained an upper-middle-class Protestant church, yet the doors had begun to open.

NOTES

1. In 1995 the Chicago Housing Authority, spurred to action by the drug trafficking and the gang activity in the Cabrini-Green housing projects, put in motion the plan to raze each of the tallest high rises. The plan was to replace these buildings with low-rise, mixed-income units. Residents of Cabrini-Green voiced suspicion over plans for replacing high rises with mixed-income housing. Historically, this meant replacing those who were poor with those who had economic and social capital (Spielman, 1993:24).

2. Fourth Presbyterian's bimonthly newsletter, *The Fourth Church*, was discontinued in 1961. In 1964 it reverted to its earlier name *Fourth Church* and continued as a quarterly newsletter through 1970. From 1971 to 1991 a bimonthly newsletter was produced called *Fourth Focus*. From 1991 to 1995 it was the *Fourth Newsletter;* in 1995 it was renamed the *Fourth Press.*

3. This strategy was consistent with Davies's lack of interest in the maintenance of Fourth Presbyterian's archives during his tenure. His sermon tapes and manuscripts were collected after his tenure by his successor's leadership team, which sought to preserve the historical record.

4. The movement to change the pew rental system was partly initiated by the younger people in the congregation, who threatened a sit-in if the pew rental system was not discontinued (Scroggs, 1990:503).

5. On January 17, 1964, the session of Fourth Presbyterian passed the resolution to dissolve the pew rental system over time. From that date on no more pews were rented. Moreover, the rented pews were opened to the general public fifteen minutes before the eleven o'clock worship service began.

6. Late in the 1960s this program became the present tutoring program. Throughout the 1990s it annually served more than five hundred children and youth, mostly from the Cabrini-Green and Henry Horner housing projects, who were bused each week to Fourth Presbyterian to be individually tutored.

7. In 1961 the Fourth Presbyterian endowment stood at $2.2 million. In 1994 the endowment was over $16.0 million. John Timothy Stone created the endowment fund in 1926 to ensure the preservation of the church in the city.

8. Studs Terkel's *Division Street: America*, a compilation of Chicagoans' views on social issues from the mid-1960s, catches this typical reaction: "'Martin Luther King scares me because he's done destructive things in peaceful ways. I've talked to many white people who despise him. In the white race, he stirs up resentment. They feel he's going too far, upsetting our society as we know it. And I think nuns and priests who have been demonstrating are being taken in. The type of peace they're advocating is going to cause havoc and destruction'" (Terkel, 1993:54).

9. An elder who served on the session in the late 1970s and early 1980s said that Fourth Presbyterian's assistant ministers were not invited to come to the monthly session meeting. Davies wanted only a handful of individuals involved in the leadership of the church.

10. I am using Max Weber's definition of *charisma:* "The term 'charisma' will be applied to a certain quality of an individual personality by virtue of which he is considered extraordinary and treated as endowed with supernatural, superhuman, or at least specifically exceptional powers or qualities" (Weber, 1978:240).

11. As Max Weber pointed out, "What is despised, so long as the genuinely charismatic type is adhered to, is traditional or rational everyday economizing, the attainment of a regular income by continuous economic activity devoted to this end. Support by gifts, either on a grand scale involving donation, endowment, bribery and honoraria, or by begging, constitute the voluntary type of support" (Weber, 1978:244–45).

12. Protests against the Vietnam War were not just an academic question for Davies and the church. During the 1968 Democratic National Convention in Chicago antiwar protesters disrupted worship services (Scroggs, 1994:502).

13. As Pierre Bourdieu asserts, the multiple logics that are contradictory within an institutional setting give the social institution and context its magnetism (Bourdieu and Wacquant, 1992:17).

5

THE LAY LIBERAL PROTESTANT CHURCH, 1985–98

> Our findings show that belief is the single best predictor of church participation, but it is orthodox Christian belief, and not the tenets of lay liberalism, that impels people to be involved in church. . . . Lay liberalism, and the individualism and the tolerance of diversity that it celebrates, make civility and cooperation in human relations possible in a pluralistic society, but they also make for weak churches. They are particularly suited to a membership that is fully engaged in such a society, largely because they easily coincide with science and university-based intellectualism.
> —Dan R. Hoge, Benton Johnson, and Donald A. Luidens, *Vanishing Boundaries: The Religion of Mainline Protestant Baby Boomers,* 1994

IN THE SPRING OF 1998 Fourth Presbyterian had completed the renovation of its sanctuary and the reconstruction of its church buildings. A capital campaign begun in 1994 had raised more than $14 million from nearly five hundred donors. This was the outcome of a long-range planning committee that had been formed in 1986, a year after John Buchanan's arrival. By 1998 not only had the church finished a large capital campaign, but its membership was more than 4,000, the largest in its history. Moreover, the endowment of $16 million in 1994 was nearing $28 million because of investment income and bequests.[1]

Fourth Presbyterian, unlike many downtown Protestant establishment churches, maintained institutional stability throughout the twentieth century. It accomplished this task in the face of changes in American culture and its local social setting. In the 1920s it was an evangelical church intent on evangelizing the Protestant ruling class. In the 1940s and 1950s it was a church that advocated for civic righteousness in the city and nation. In the 1960s and 1970s it opened its previously closed social boundaries of race and class. Under Buchanan's leadership, the church has continued its deft balance between its accommodation to the Gold Coast and its mission to reach out to the city.

Buchanan has furthered this institutional vitality with a liberal Protestant theological vision, in spite of reports proclaiming the death of mainline, liberal Protestantism (Finke and Stark, 1992; Roof and McKinney, 1987). Explanations for this decline are legion (Bruce, 1992; Hoge, Johnson, and Luidens, 1993; Kelley, 1972). Notwithstanding such documentation and dire predictions, many continue to be attracted to Fourth Presbyterian, a liberal Protestant church.

Under Buchanan's leadership Fourth Presbyterian has become a "lay liberal" church. Buchanan is both a product of this ethos and a creator of its momentum. Lay liberalism is a nondogmatic belief system about religion. It is a form of "golden rule" Christianity that believes in doing good for others and seeks a worship experience that has a sense of mystery and transcendence but is tolerant of other religions and their truth claims (Ammerman, 1997a:196–216). This ideological framework has a middle- and upper-middle-class social ethos, one that is in tension with itself over issues of class and status. Status markers remain important, but the celebration of these identity signals is less socially acceptable.[2] Buchanan and his leadership nurture this lay liberal ethos and at the same time tap the tension over the class issue by both confirming and challenging the status quo.[3]

Buchanan, unlike his predecessors who struggled with exclusive social boundaries and rigid class hierarchies, has had to negotiate symbolic boundaries, particularly theological language, that have become porous. Some have argued that this liberal perspective, which creates a new fluidity in theological symbol systems, has undercut institutional identity (Hoge, Johnson, and Luidens, 1994:181). Nonetheless, it is precisely Buchanan's vision of theological lay liberalism that has built a distinctive church ethos. This identity has as its core the vision of Christ transforming culture. This transformation is not a symbolic conversion of others to faith but a drive for justice at all levels of society. It moves into the liberal impulse for tolerance, inclusion, and the rights of the individual. The contemporary incarnation of Fourth Presbyterian manifests the fullest accommodation of the church to modern liberal trends in culture, including a call to resist the consumerist nature of modern life and to challenge social inequality by working toward a level playing field so that all can have the opportunity to succeed.

THE NEAR NORTH SIDE IN THE 1990S

North Michigan Avenue

By 1996 Fourth Presbyterian was literally surrounded by wealth—the upscale European boutique Escada was on one side and Henri Bendel on the other;

the John Hancock Building loomed across the street; the Water Tower Mall kept sentinel on the southeast corner; and the Westin Hotel was on the northeast corner. It was not always this way. When Stone argued for the church to move to Michigan Avenue in 1912, the street was unpaved. There was a tavern to the north and rooming houses and factories to the west. The decision to move to North Michigan Avenue, however, was prescient. The wealth and power of Chicago relocated north during the twentieth century. The Gold Coast by the 1990 census was the richest area in metropolitan Chicago (deVise, 1993).

North Michigan Avenue became known as the Magnificent Mile in 1947. Fourth Presbyterian arrived before this economic rise and thus witnessed the spectacular growth of the district over the second half of the twentieth century. The architectural extravagance of the area makes Fourth Presbyterian's classic architecture look antiquated. A John Hancock worker asked a minister of the church in 1994, "Why haven't they torn down that old church building? It sits on such valuable real estate!" In the 1990s the Magnificent Mile was a "Who's Who" of shops and stores appealing to an upper-middle-class consumer market. Nike Town was built in 1992, and its style and taste are emblematic of the contemporary scene:

> Not far from Michael Jordan's downtown restaurant, over on North Michigan Avenue, a 68,000-square-foot expanse of pure retail theater called Nike Town was drawing some 12,000 visitors every day. The store looks much more like an athletic shoe and sports museum than a store—with a basketball court, white statues of Michael Jordan and other Nike athletes, giant tanks full of tropical fish, and vivid Nike imagery built into every wall and even the floors. As soon as Nike Town opened during the summer of 1992, it passed the Lincoln Park Zoo, the Shedd Aquarium, and the world-renowned Art Institute to become the single most popular tourist attraction in the Chicago area, a Nike place in a Nike city. (Katz, 1994:11)

The striking popularity of such stores as Nike Town exemplifies the power of the message in the famous Nike tag line, "Just do it." This symbolic signal runs parallel to the ethos of the baby boomer generation that admires athletes and celebrities like Michael Jordan. This generation is well ensconced at Fourth Presbyterian, where the median age of the congregation was forty-six in the 1990s. It also resonates on a deeper level with the message that action and style dominate content and reflection in contemporary American marketing. This ethic of activity and élan is consonant with the Protestant ethic, although it has shed its ascetic and Puritan mores over the last thirty years.[4] Happiness is the goal of activity. Indeed, the activity itself and the style of the performance are keys to the pleasure that the activity brings. At least this is the image that Nike, along with others, produced in its advertising (Katz, 1994).

The cultural milieu of the Gold Coast affects and challenges Fourth Presbyterian to compete in the market with a style and appeal that resembles and is a legitimate alternative to the commodities modern marketers produced. From Stone's pastorate through Buchanan's, Fourth Presbyterian has balanced an appeal to class with the challenge to meet the needs of the poor. This same peculiar structural tension pervades the cultural milieu of North Michigan Avenue.

Companies like Nike use a marketing scheme that includes a total experience of space and product. The product is set in an environment that is as appealing as the commodities for sale are. This turn in advertising expresses the tastes and desires of a privileged consumer group, though without any explicit appeal to class. Nike's advertising displays lithe athletes pursuing their activities in an aura of individualized monastic dedication—though they happen to wear Nike clothing and equipment. The focus of the marketing campaign is the middle- and upper-middle-class American baby boomer generation. One consumes the product with a taste for autonomy and singularity, yet in reality one is incorporated into a homogenized social climate. The market frame capitalizes on a privatized sensibility of privilege that expresses a consciousness of distinction without an explicit design to create group hierarchies of status and class.

The mix between the markers of rank and the sensibility of individuality thus permeates the Gold Coast and influences Fourth Presbyterian. Fourth Presbyterian must create a structural and social ethos that appeals to status, but it also counters this with a message that the playing field is level and that all have a chance for the good life. This mix of status and individual opportunity runs throughout the symbolic message and the rhetoric of social outreach. One may not be able to change the system, but each individual should have a chance. In the face of this message of individual opportunity is the reality of social inequality that is ubiquitous in the Near North Side.

The Lower Gold Coast and Cabrini-Green

Fourth Presbyterian borders the Lower Gold Coast, where the per capita income was $82,169 in 1989 dollars.[5] This was a 65 percent increase in per capita income since 1980. In 1990 more than 60 percent of the population of 6,693 were college graduates, compared with approximately 25 percent in the total U.S. population. This portrait mirrored each of the ten richest areas in Chicago, all along the North Lakefront. For these ten areas, per capita income grew by 53 percent between 1980 and 1990, while the income of the ten poorest areas in the metropolitan area of Chicago dropped by 30 percent.[6] The average income among the richest ten was twenty-seven times that of the poorest ten in 1990. As Pierre deVise explains, "Another way to express these disparities is to consider that a weekly paycheck in the Lower Gold Coast and a biweekly paycheck in the city's ten richest areas must be stretched the whole year in the poorest areas" (deVise, 1993:2).

Social boundaries of status and class were starkly framed in the comparison of the Lower Gold Coast and Cabrini-Green in the 1990 census. In 1989 dollars the Lower Gold Coast earned more than thirty times the per capita income of Cabrini-Green, $2,379. Cabrini-Green's per capita income, along with that of all of the other public housing areas, decreased by approximately 30 percent from 1980 to 1990. Not surprisingly, the population in the Chicago Public Housing declined by 30 percent over the same ten year period and by 55 percent since 1960. Cabrini-Green, by itself, lost 43 percent of its population in the 1980s alone. The population numbers for the ten wealthiest areas in Chicago had an increase of 5 percent over the 1980s. The population of the ten poorest areas showed a dramatic decrease of 30 percent.[7]

The problem of the income gap between rich and poor and the racial divide of white and black is summarized by deVise: "All 15 poverty areas are the result of conscious public planning to concentrate and insulate public housing population. These neighborhood-sized projects condemn most of the residents to live, breathe, reproduce, sicken and die in institutionalized poverty, crime and dependency" (deVise, 1993:4). The causes for this segregation, whether intentional or not, are multiple, and the ways in which the Protestant elite participated in the creation of the second ghetto were documented in the chapters on Anderson and Davies. In any event, the results of public housing have been devastating to the people who inhabit these projects.[8]

The Lived Experience of Cabrini-Green

In 1994 Fourth Presbyterian began a program at Cabrini-Green called Center for Whole Life. Families dropped in for child care and for resources to help them care for themselves. The theory was that healthy families make healthy children. It was an effort to broaden the care given children in the tutoring program and to establish a more holistic approach to community empowerment. The director of the Center for Whole Life was an African American woman. The center focused not on providing social services but using the center as an arena where Fourth Presbyterian could be present and involved in the community of Cabrini-Green instead of simply providing services from the outside. The church discovered, however, that the sociological realities of

Cabrini-Green were more bleak and frustrating than expected. In the year following the opening of the center Fourth Presbyterian and the center's leadership confronted the reality that their ministry and mission at Cabrini-Green functioned under the auspices of the gangs that ruled the buildings and controlled the lives of the residents.[9] Moreover, in February of 1995 a murder took place in broad daylight outside the building in which the center was housed, something that had not occurred since a truce was called in 1993, following the 1992 murder of Dantrell Davis, a seven-year old who was shot in the head while walking hand in hand with his mother to school. The employees at the center were concerned for their lives. Buchanan and church leadership decided to remain at Cabrini-Green despite the threat of violence.

The lived experience of life at Cabrini-Green is difficult to comprehend from the outside. An African American who grew up in Cabrini-Green in the 1970s furnished a window into the social realities of life in the projects—realities that mirrored the projects of the 1990s. The book, *The Horror of Cabrini-Green,* is an autobiographical, though novelized, account of the story of a young man's struggle to survive the chaos of Cabrini-Green. It is a nightmarish narrative that portrays the violence, police abuse, parental powerlessness, teenage revenge, and murder in the projects. It is the story of Bosco, a young man who becomes involved in a gang and watches as his friends are brutally murdered one by one. Bosco is transformed into a man who is able to murder in cold blood and treat women solely as objects of pleasure. As he says, "It was pretty nice around here when we first moved in because the buildings were brand new. . . . Why, there was even a few whites living around here then. After a while it turned all black and started going down fast" (Conn, 1975:11). At the end of the novel Bosco's only escape from the reality of early death is to join the United States Army; the last scene has him boarding the bus for basic training. The realities of Cabrini-Green were as far from the lifestyle of the Gold Coast as one can imagine. Indeed, it was often the case that young adults of Cabrini-Green had never been to the shore of Lake Michigan, a journey of only one mile but a far country for most Cabrini-Green residents.

None of Buchanan's predecessors challenged the growth of the second ghetto, partly because of their acceptance of social inequality and partly because of a sense of their own powerlessness. The creation of the second ghetto in Chicago was a collaboration of political, social, and economic groups, including ethnic communities. Despite Martin Luther King Jr.'s best effort to change the segregation of African Americans in Chicago in 1966, little progress had been made. The walls of segregation have been enormously forceful in shaping the beliefs and behaviors of many in Chicago.

The sense of powerlessness reverberated in the rhetoric of Fourth Presbyterian in the 1990s. The intransigent distinctions of class and race pricked the conscience of congregants and the leadership. The leadership expressed frustration about how to respond to Cabrini-Green without patronizing or alienating the population. Throughout 1994 and 1995 focus groups and interviewees consistently voiced this concern. The leadership of Fourth Presbyterian was eager to "level the playing field" and to engage this lower-economic group. Education was the main tool in this task. The intention was to use education to lift individuals into economic opportunity, a desire of not only whites but also African Americans. During the 1993 and 1994 school year 470 children from Cabrini-Green traveled to Fourth Presbyterian to receive individual tutoring by Fourth Presbyterian volunteer tutors. As the director of the program said, "If families at Cabrini-Green did not trust that Fourth Presbyterian was helping their children educationally, not one child would be coming to the program" (Interview, December 13, 1993). To further underscore this fruitful collaboration, the number of children being tutored in 1998 had increased to 530, with 80 on a waiting list.

Not only was education a concern but so were increased gang activities and rising crime rates. A poll taken of whites in Chicago in 1993 revealed their fear over deterioration in the city because of crime and their hopes to leave the city.[10] These fears, however, were the concern of not just whites in the city but also African Americans, who are the ones most affected by violence, crime-ridden housing projects, and poor educational opportunities. In 1993 Cabrini-Green actually had a waiting list because it was perceived as the safest public housing project in the city and had many social service agencies.[11]

In the 1990s Fourth Presbyterian's congregants and leadership struggled with the stark division of class and race. These issues pressed on their sense of justice and fair play. They desired the benefits of privilege that were a part of the Gold Coast cultural milieu, yet they sought to respond to those without privilege through outreach and advocacy programs. The negotiation of this tension made Fourth Presbyterian a magnet for those concerned about these issues.

LAY LIBERAL CHRISTIANITY

Architecture and Style

Fourth Presbyterian is an upper-middle-class church in a powerful economic and social setting. The church's Gothic architecture though traditional is striking, particularly when viewed next to the massive modern buildings all around it. The difference provides a visual contrast between tradition and modernity, nostalgia and progress, faith and function, stability and motion. The mission statement of the church, developed in 1992, states, "We are a light in the city."[12] It conveys a bold attempt on the church's part to recapture a prominence that was architecturally lost by the towering buildings that have come to surround it. The church buildings were originally designed by Ralph Adams Cram, who was the leader of the school of architecture known as Gothic Revival. Adams designed Princeton University Chapel as well as the Cathedral of St. John the Divine in New York City. The Fourth Presbyterian sanctuary is a free adaptation of English Gothic tradition. It is cruciform in shape, built with gray limestone. It has a gabled roof, belfry, and spire. Along Michigan Avenue there is a courtyard. In the middle of the courtyard is a fountain designed by Howard Van Doren Shaw. The courtyard opens to Michigan Avenue and attracts many into the gardens and to the beauty of the building and fountain. The building draws hundreds of visitors to the church on Sundays. In 1998 the head usher estimated that one-third of the 1,800 or so congregants who attended the church on a given Sunday were visitors (Interview, February 1998).

To come into Fourth Presbyterian, particularly following the completion of its $14 million refurbishment in 1998, is to enter a world of precision, formality, and beauty. The interior space is an impressive one. The massive pillars and soaring arches amplify Fourth Presbyterian's interior height and depth. Capping the pillars in the nave are fourteen life-size angels representing the musicians described in Psalm 150. The seats and carvings in the chancel area, along with the lectern, are all oak. To the right of the communion table is the pulpit; it is raised so that the preacher can be seen and heard from all parts of the sanctuary. Above the chancel area are the organ and choir. The 1995 rebuilding of the organ makes the 126-rank (6,603 pipes) Aeolian-Skinner organ the largest organ in Chicago and one of the largest in the Midwest.

Stained-glass windows surround the sanctuary. In the front is a chancel window made in medieval fashion of heavy slabs of glass, intentionally subdued in brilliance. In the center is the risen Christ, declaring, "And I, if I be lifted up, will draw all men unto Me." Around the Christ are the worshipping angels of heaven. Below are three groups. The first represents various races: a missionary with an open Bible, a man from India, an Asian, and a kneeling Ethiopian. The second depicts the social classes: worker, soldier, king, and beggar. In symbolic terms it is the Christian ideal of permeable boundaries of class and race. The rear rose window is ornate and made spectacular by its eastern location. It shows the prophets of Hebrew Scripture, the apostles, and the flame of the Spirit's fire. At the top is Christ as a triumphant lamb, leading the church to victory. All the windows were designed by Charles J. Connick of Boston.

The ambiance of the sanctuary makes those who occupy the boardroom comfortable and at home. Stone's vision was that those who lived on the Gold Coast would identify with their surroundings instantly and that those in the rooming houses, who were seeking to come up the ladder, would find in Fourth Presbyterian and its environs the socializing ethos of promise and possibility. This same aesthetic pull is just as magnetic to those with power and those seeking power at the turn of the century as it was in 1914.

Fourth Presbyterian's worship service is a visceral reminder of embodied structures of traditional cultural and moral tastes. The rationality and order of modernity are infused in each of the efficiently orchestrated worship services. In 1986 an 8:30 A.M. worship service was added to the 11:00 A.M. and 6:30 P.M. services. Buchanan created a task force in 1986 to review the Sunday worship services. From Stone through Davies the liturgical order had followed the "Puritan" order of worship, which had the Scripture readings, prayers, and offering before the sermon. The sermon was at the end and was the climax of the service. The committee, with Buchanan's strong leadership, recommended that the order of worship be changed so the sermon would come in the middle, with the prayers and offering to follow. Although the church had rarely used a prayer of confession, Buchanan pushed for its inclusion each Sunday. This new order of worship is called a "Reformed" worship service, suggested originally by John Calvin, the seventeenth-century founder of the Reformed Presbyterian Church.

Buchanan and his fellow clergy perform the worship with practiced precision and skill. The clergy wear the traditional black Presbyterian robes, with collar and Geneva tabs. This signals a traditional Reformed ecclesiology, though the patriarchal clergy leadership of the tradition is interrupted with three women associate ministers, one an African American;[13] each leads worship on a regular basis and preaches on occasion.[14] The service lasts approximately sixty-five minutes. The hymnody is in the Reformed tradition. The choir is small and paid; congregational singing is strong.

One is met at the door with a friendly greeting from the ushers. The ushers wear dark clothing to maintain a sense of formality and decorum. In the 1980s women began to serve as ushers. They were expected to wear dark attire as well. When ushers proceed to the chancel with the offering plates, they walk in synchronized pairs, denoting order and control. In the fall of 1993 the session acted, at the request of Buchanan, to dispense with the morning coats that the ushers had worn for over a hundred years. There was little negative response to this action.

The majority of the congregation dresses formally. Men wear suits or sport coats; many are in ties. Women wear dresses or professional attire. They represent a group that is accomplished, sophisticated in taste, and not apt to waste time with mediocrity. They respond to a lay liberal message that represents God as a mystery, encourages charity toward those less fortunate, and embodies an ethos of order and control.

Boundaries of Lay Liberal Christianity

The demographic data of my 1994 church survey of the Fourth Presbyterian congregation confirmed that the members were similar to the general population of the Lower Gold Coast in income, education, and cultural values. The median income range for Fourth Presbyterian members in 1994 dollars was $50,000 to $74,999. Eighty-nine percent of the Fourth Presbyterian members were college graduates, and 46 percent had a graduate degree.[15] Only 2 percent in the survey had a minority racial-ethnic background. Despite the public rhetoric of congregational diversity, Fourth Presbyterian, at least ethnically, was a homogeneous social group in the 1990s. The congregation reflected the income status, education, and ethnicity of the Gold Coast's upper-middle-class population.

The 1994 membership was satisfied with the church as an institution. Most congregants would have attended a similar church if Fourth Presbyterian had not existed. The reasons for the initial involvement of members in the church were its preaching, location, and style of worship. Because of the lay liberalism of its preaching, the form and aesthetics of its ritual practice, its place-name status, and its serving as an outlet for charitable resources and action, the Fourth Presbyterian was a magnet for those who inhabited the Gold Coast social setting and embodied the interests of a middle- and upper-middle-class white culture.

Fourth Presbyterian's congregational religiosity in terms of personal piety was high. The majority of congregants reported praying two to three times a week or more. Reflecting its lay liberal perspective, the majority expressed traditional but nondogmatic Christian beliefs. They believed in Christ as Savior, the Bible as the word of God, and the existence of eternal life, but they expressed a high degree of tolerance for other kinds of religious perspectives and values. Although they held the Bible as the inspired word of God, they thought it should not be taken literally. Most agreed that Jesus Christ is Savior but that he is also a religious leader, like Buddha or Mohammed. The survey reflected a group with highly porous theological boundaries and a worldly approach to issues of faith and religion.

The congregation had only a moderate stake in a specific Christian Reformed belief system. Seventy-eight percent of the congregants came from a mainline Protestant religious background. They were neither recent converts, who were evangelically fervent, nor people who had rejected a more conservative Christian tradition and were reacting against a religious system. Distinctive denominational doctrines were not central motivating factors in attendance at Fourth Presbyterian.

Members' beliefs were not well defined, yet congregants demanded that Buchanan's preaching be well integrated with the rational discourse of modernity. One congregant, a former elder and a member of the committee that called Buchanan, reported, "Fourth Presbyterian does not force you to leave your mind behind" (Interview, June 22, 1994). When speaking about religious belief, they wanted a religion that was usable in a complex and competitive social environment. Absolutes, whether in the religious or moral realm, were anathema. They wanted a message that challenged, comforted, and helped make their lives less stressful.

The symbolic boundaries for Fourth Presbyterian members are often defined more by what they do not believe than by what they do believe. The boundaries between a liberal and a conservative or evangelical approach to faith are tightly controlled. From the pulpit and from congregants the message is clear—we are *not* fundamentalists. This lay liberal Christianity is used to mark social and symbolic boundaries. For instance, one never hears congregational members assert their differences with Cabrini-Green residents on financial or social grounds, but they do make it clear that the fundamentalist and literalist interpretations of religion are beneath their intelligence. A prominent member of the church put it this way: "I won't park my mind outside the church door. My faith is more intellectual than emotional; I can't accept the rigidity of conservative Christianity" (Interview, January 22, 1995). If anything, religious beliefs and the expressed superiority of liberal education form boundaries of separation. Lay liberalism is partly a function of an ideological and class perspective that excludes specific religious belief systems.

This symbolic boundary maintenance over theological issues does not lend itself to a simple two-sided cultural war analysis. As Rhys Williams outlined, surveys show a fourfold distinction rather than the two-sided cultural war (Williams, 1997:1038–39). Two sets of attitudes set the frame of the conflict, one pertaining to economic and political power and the other to personal morality and cultural symbols. One can be liberal on the one side yet conservative on the other (or vice versa) or liberal or conservative on both. In the case of Fourth Presbyterian there was a trend in the 1990s toward a libertarian perspective on personal morality and a similar perspective on justice issues, thus generally supporting individual choices on moral questions and disapproving of increased governmental involvement in social justice issues. Conservative Christians are generally morality collectivists and justice libertarians, that is, traditional on personal morality and cultural values and laissez-faire on economic matters. African Americans more often than not are conservative on personal morality and communal on governmental regulation of economics (Williams, 1997:1038–39). This partly explains why there are few conservative Christian or African American members of the congregation. As will be seen, Buchanan is able to accommodate the progressive view on personal morality, but he often sounds like a Great Society Democrat on sociopolitical issues; if he runs into tension, it is along the justice axis. His symbolic rhetoric is subtle, though, and he therefore usually avoids creating overt conflict.

The choice to become a member of Fourth Presbyterian involves the congruence of location, style, aesthetics, status, and socioeconomic boundaries. The location, architecture, and style of worship act as guides for a selective status group. The lay liberal symbolic worldview filters Christian claims through a lens that stresses tolerance and the value of diversity, although this belief system excludes conservative Christianity as a legitimate option. The high valuation of remaining open to options precludes a full commitment to specific Christian claims, denominational principles, or even the church.[16]

The free-rider problem at Fourth Presbyterian was a constant irritant to fundraisers and clergy throughout the twentieth century. In the 1990s only 50 percent of the membership contributed financially to the church. Half as many contributed to the 1994 capital campaign. More than two thousand congregants had little or no financial or personal investment in the church. At the same time, because of the liberal ethos of the cultural setting, calls for deeper commitment are circumspect; the pastor and leadership recognize that congregants have multiple priorities in their giving. There is also caution about any coercion on the part of the leadership. The liberal emphasis on choice prevents a demanding approach, both because it would undoubtedly fail and because the pastor and his lay leaders do not feel comfortable in this mode. This deliberateness is typical of middle- and upper-middle-class social dispositions; it resonates with distance in form and style. A committed membership thus involves this dilemma: to attract a sophisticated and highly educated group, demands must be made in ways that can be comprehended rationally; emotion will not settle the issue. Attachment to the institution is therefore not intense. In other words, the lay liberal approach tends to undercut strong commitment, which means that a majority of members are only peripherally involved.[17]

A similar nondogmatic perspective was expressed in the congregation's social and political viewpoints in the church survey. Most shared a liberal democratic tradition of affirming personal rights and a conservative and critical perspective on governmental involvement in the public sphere. They generally supported equal rights for women and homosexuals and the right to choose abortion, but few advocated an increase in welfare or affirmative action for minorities. That individual rights were valued and social structural change was dismissed reflects a group that believes in individual freedoms but not in the redistribution of capital.

The liberal democratic expansion of individual rights that has led to greater freedom for women has affected the distribution of power between the sexes and particularly the way women interpret their professional and personal lives. When the results of male and female responses were compared, the most striking finding was the homogenization of gender ideology across income, religio-moral, and political perspectives.[18] On the basis of the results from the survey, it is possible to assert that in the 1990s social and environmental factors were more important than gender in social and symbolic boundary making. This isomorphic process is a part of the lay liberal ethos and is assumed in most relationships. This is borne out in the professional role trajectories of male and females. From the survey women were as committed to their professional careers as men were; indeed, the two genders looked almost identical in their career ambitions.

Women outnumbered men two to one in the membership. Men had a slightly higher level of education and income, but women reported that they pledged financially more frequently than males. Men and women were similar, however, in the range of what they contributed. They did differ on some questions concerning religious belief. Women were less orthodox in belief in that they were more willing to claim that other religious traditions were as legitimate as Christianity.[19] However, men and women were equally strong in emphasizing the political rights of individuals.

The evidence suggests that not only are social and cultural factors more powerful than gender in the construction of social identity and career trajectory but also Fourth Presbyterian self-selects for high-status individuals, particularly women. That is, individuals who are successful and seek to be so in their professions are drawn to the church. Education, income, and professional occupation are all markers by which one is identified as a part of the group.

The most significant differences in the church membership were reflected in the comparison of economic classes.[20] The low- to middle-income group, those earning less than $49,000, made up 38 percent of the congregation. The upper-income group, those earning $50,000 or more, were 62 percent of church congregants. Lower-income individuals contributed less financially in gross terms than did those in the higher-income group. When the percentages of giving were compared, however, the lower-income group gave nearly 2 percent of family income to the church, whereas the higher-income group gave only slightly more than one-half of 1 percent. Those in the lower-income group were more subjectively affected by the church in terms of the self and their spiritual, social, and political lives. They were more invested in the church both in their proportional financial pledges and in their emotional lives. Moreover, they prayed more often and tended to believe more strongly that one should integrate personal faith and professional life.

The two groups were both nondogmatic in their religious beliefs and political and social viewpoints. Each embraced the lay liberal agenda, and each could be identified as "golden rule" Christians. The church's symbolic boundaries powerfully shape and select out a specific type of individual relative to religious belief and political persuasion. Nonetheless, institutional loyalty does decrease with greater income. Higher income earners were less involved, gave proportionally less money, and were less affected by the church.

The social and symbolic boundaries of this lay liberal congregation describe a group that affirms upper-middle-class privilege but does not celebrate class and social differentiation. That is, distinctions of privilege based on economic and cultural status signals are downplayed. If distinctions occur, it is most likely in the areas of education and religion. Conservative Christianity is not tolerated and is marginalized. Social identity thus is not so much a function of class and status but is marked by more individualized standards of religious and aesthetic tastes. This is also a result of the democratization of the leadership of Fourth Presbyterian. For the greater part of the twentieth century Fourth Presbyterian was a Protestant elite church, led by a Protestant ruling class. In the 1980s and 1990s the egalitarian spirit of liberal culture was infused in the church by a pastoral and lay leadership that led in this direction. Since the 1960s there has been a marked movement toward a democratization of ruling structures at Fourth Presbyterian.

A Transmuted Protestant Establishment

A comparison of the ruling elders of Fourth Presbyterian from the 1960s and 1990s dramatically highlights the cultural and religious changes that have taken place during this thirty-year period. In the 1960s all the elders were men; in 1994 the session was evenly divided between men and women. In 1967 the session of thirty elders was made up of a dozen lawyers and doctors and the rest senior executives with major firms in the Midwest; in 1994, while the majority were professionals, half were consultants of one kind or another, and there were no senior executives with large firms.[21] The session of 1994 included three attorneys, five who worked in corporations, fourteen who were self-employed, and eight who were retired or were homemakers. This is not to say that the elders of the 1990s were people of modest financial resources; most either had well-paying jobs or had substantial wealth through other means. This group, however, was distinct from the elders of 1967. The 1967 elders had control of major industries in the Midwest and had leverage with the city government. The 1994 group represented middle- and upper-middle-class lay liberal Protestants, less powerful than their ruling-class forebears but still a part of a Gold Coast high-status group. It is therefore no surprise that class distinctions are muted among the lay leaders of Fourth Presbyterian.

At the same time, people of substantial power and influence are a part of Fourth Presbyterian's leadership. Ann Petersen, an attorney, was the senior lawyer for the secretary of the U.S. Air Force until she returned to Chicago in 1994. Petersen became the chair of the mission committee at Fourth Presbyterian and was intensely involved in social outreach in Chicago and the development of advocacy for social concerns in the city and state. In February 1995 the mission committee wrote a letter to the session setting out its strategy for advocacy for ethical concerns that included the condemnation of casino gambling in Chicago, the improvement of public education in the city, and concern for violence against children.[22]

Elmer Johnson, a partner in the law firm of Kirkland and Ellis in Chicago, chaired the capital campaign for restoring the sanctuary and church buildings in the early 1990s. Johnson was executive vice president of General Motors during the 1980s. He came back to Chicago in 1988 and joined Fourth Presbyterian. Johnson is emblematic of the lay liberal in that in his career as an attorney he established himself as a major force in business ethics in the city of Chicago. He studied with James Gustafson, the ethicist from the University of Chicago Divinity School in the 1970s, and wrote on the ethical impact of the automobile industry. Johnson, the former chairman of the Center for Ethics and Corporate Policy in Chicago, wrote a letter to the officers of Fourth Presbyterian in 1992 encouraging them to give to the capital campaign: "The most profound ills in our society are spiritual, not economic. We have witnessed over the last decade the excesses of a highly individualistic, commercial culture. The Church is now surrounded by visible reminders of these excesses. . . . Given this setting, it would be a tragedy if we failed to reinvest in our Church to keep its beacon bright: a beacon that proclaims the equal dignity and value of all persons before God . . ." (Johnson, Letter to Session, October 2, 1992).

Nonetheless, Fourth Presbyterian no longer embodies the Protestant ruling class of the past. The Protestant elite have been transmuted into a democratized leadership that includes women and is more diverse. This transformation has not meant a diminution in the vitality of the church as a religious institution. Indeed, as was noted earlier, church revenues increased substantially from 1986 to 1994. Since 1986 member giving rose by well over 80 percent, from $600,000 in 1986 to more than $1.9 million in 1998. The total church budget was $3.7 million in 1998. More than 35 percent of that budget went for mission concerns that were local, national, and international.[23] Almost a third of the church's total revenue was raised by investment income from the nearly $28 million endowment fund.

Buchanan has led the church in pushing for greater participation in stewardship and has sought wider representation on the church boards in terms of gender, class, and race. Buchanan has taken seriously the rotation process for Presbyterian boards that stipulates that no one can serve as an elder, deacon, or trustee for more than two successive three-year terms. Stone, Anderson, and Davies gave lip service to the rotation process, but Buchanan is the first to implement the policy.

The leadership of Fourth Presbyterian is more representational; the autocratic style of leadership of the past is finished. The creation of social identity and cultural capital has to do less with stratification than with privatized standards of personal evaluation. The lay liberal ethos is less attentive to status symbols and looks to more internal gauges of value. The concept of privatization in the construction of social identity is therefore useful in an analytic understanding of this lay liberal congregation.

Privatization as Sociological Concept

The privatization of religion as a response to the rationalization of modern life has been predicted for many years (Luckmann, 1967). The most recent updates use personal autonomy as a tool for understanding the privatization process (Hammond, 1992). Sociologically, the impulse toward privatization increases with greater financial capital. As prosperity increases, privatization grows, and choice becomes a central metaphor, particularly for the middle and upper-middle class (Bellah et al., 1985). Most Fourth Presbyterian congregants tended toward a strong sense of personal autonomy in the church survey.[24] As personal autonomy increased, the religious belief system became less defined doctrinally.[25] The congregation excluded more inflexible and demanding forms of belief, which led to a greater toleration of ambiguity. The liberal Protestant epistemological ambivalence toward absolutist claims is important in attracting this Gold Coast group to the church.

It is important to note, however, that with the onset of privatization, social boundaries relative to class and race have become less rigid and more permeable. As the congregation has experienced an increased consciousness of personal autonomy, sensitivity to racial and class discrimination has also expanded. Culturally, religious affiliation has declined as a marker of status and class identity. Concomitantly, Buchanan's symbolic rhetoric has moved the church away from concentration on the internal dynamics of belief and salvation and has focused on issues of social justice as the locus of theological saliency. The turn away from class structuralization is thus shaped by both cultural forces and the symbolic boundaries of Fourth Presbyterian's leadership.

In this way the privatization process is more effectively described as a strategy of compartmentalization. That is, individual congregants are not so much privatistic, in the sense of feeling a strong sense of individually articulated faith, as they are compartmentalized. They use diverse institutional logics with relative ease, moving between one social context and another. Even as most members tend toward a compartmentalized life, they are uncomfortable with this lack of personal integration in their public and private lives.[26] The disjunction between a strategy of compartmentalization and a conscious desire for their personal and professional lives to make complementary demands on them is a felt contradiction.

This strong desire to integrate one's church and business life was a consistent theme in the written responses to the question about how congregants combine their personal and professional lives. One church member gave a representative description: "There is a seamless relationship between church and business life, because I try to do unto others as I would have them do unto me, in every area of my life." In response to the question of church and business life, congregants used the words *balance* and *perspective* fifteen times as a way of describing how they used their faith and the church to relate their business and church lives. Along these lines, ten individuals commented on the importance of their church life as a way of relieving the "stress" from their professional lives. Several members' comments detailed the difficulty of integrating personal faith and their professional lives. One respondent said, "My faith is a part of who I am and, therefore, is a part of all of my activities and actions. As a businesswoman sometimes the goodness of my Christianity gets lost in tough decision-making situations, but I always rely on my faith to get me through in the end."

Fourth Presbyterian congregants tend toward personal autonomy using a strategy of compartmentalization. They understand the importance of community involvement and the support of the common good. At the same time, there are no calls for the transformation of social structures. The primary agent for affecting society is the self: "I believe the role of the church in my personal life is to guide my understanding about the interrelationship of human beings and their best selves," one congregant wrote. This is a part of the privatization strategy that perceives religion and church life as tools by which individuals maintain their perspective and stability in a highly competitive social world.

To be sure, Fourth Presbyterian and its leadership accommodate to the social boundaries of its powerful status group. Although social inequality is subtly confirmed, it is also significantly challenged. The public rhetoric of Buchanan and the outreach programs of the church articulate and resist the social inequalities of the Near North Side.

CHURCH AND GHETTO: CROSSING BOUNDARIES

Lay Liberal Outreach

To discover how the Fourth Presbyterian Church has bridged social boundaries, I observed and interviewed participants in the tutoring program at the church in January 1994. At that time 470 African Americans from five to eighteen years of age came three nights a week to Fourth Presbyterian to be tutored by church volunteers. On the first night that I observed the program I walked with a group of children down a corridor leading to the church tutoring rooms, and an African American girl, around seven years old, grabbed my hand and began telling me about her day. She was excited about being at the church and spending time with her tutor. We entered Flynn Hall to discover 75 to 100 other children, mostly African American, milling around trying to find their tutors, the majority of whom were white, middle- and upper-middle-class professionals.[27] There were hugs and cries of glee everywhere, as tutors and children greeted one another for their weekly hour-and-a-half session.

This program was twenty-nine years old in 1994 and has expanded significantly over time. In 1994 it was the largest tutoring program on the Near North Side. It is the pride of Fourth Presbyterian, and it is the church's most visible symbol that the Gold Coast and the ghetto can come together and bridge boundaries of class and race. According to demographics and African Americans' perceptions, these boundaries remain very much intact in Chicago.[28] It was therefore a powerful moment when a young African American girl grabbed the hand of a white man, whom she did not know, and felt that Fourth Presbyterian was her home too. On the streets of Chicago or at Cabrini-Green this would not have happened.[29]

At the same time, few families or individuals from Cabrini-Green cross the social boundaries between the Gold Coast and Cabrini-Green except during tutoring. This social distance was the subject of Fourth Presbyterian's Racism Task Force that completed its work in 1992. The report noted that African Americans had to exclude whites to resist the dominant white culture and maintain their own sense of social and cultural identity. The task force interviewed, among others, Clarence Page of the *Chicago Tribune*, who spoke of the importance of African American churches as "unique repositories" for African American culture. The committee also used C. Eric Lincoln and Lawrence H. Mamiya's book, *The Black Church in the African-American Experience*, to understand that African Americans who were involved in their churches should be supported in every way possible. The Racism Task Force thus drew the conclusion that boundaries were important for both sides in the conflict: "These factors suggest that Fourth Presbyterian Church should not actively seek to recruit members of African American churches who are contributing to preservation of traditions and values" (T. Miller and Watson, 1992:8).

As socially sensitive as this report was, in one way it missed the sociological and cultural reality of Cabrini-Green. Reports from individuals who worked closely with Cabrini-Green families and children in the 1990s suggested that few families attend any church at all. Parents were eager to send their children to Fourth Presbyterian to be tutored, but they were not interested in attending the church services. Social boundaries are permeable, but cultural and aesthetic preferences still separate these two neighborhoods. Integral to Fourth Presbyterian's ability to attract its Gold Coast congregation is its distinct means of cultural communication in worship. This style of worship does not persuade many African American families, regardless of class, to attend Fourth Presbyterian. Fourth Presbyterian's cultural aesthetics and symbolic boundaries appeal to a select racial-ethnic group and a specific cultural type: a college-educated, liberal, economically privileged, European American, "golden rule" Christian.

Fourth Presbyterian's outreach programs fit into a type of lay liberal religion. Evangelical religion witnesses the faith to the neighbor, and, upon conversion, the neighbor is invited to become a part of the community. Liberal religion seeks out and serves the neighbor in need, all the while keeping the neighbor at a distance. As R. Stephen Warner pointed out, "Liberal religion is therefore externally directed; benevolence creates a barrier" (Warner, 1988:293). Warner's statement aptly depicts the outreach impulse at Fourth Presbyterian. The needs of neighbors are met, but this happens in a compartmentalized framework. That is, the outreach is designed to help others, not to integrate them into the community. In this way there is respect for the cultural identity of the other and a desire to maintain social distance. Fourth Presbyterian's tutoring program is an ideal form of the lay liberal ethos that gives individuals the opportunity to help others without making the contact too intimate.

Notwithstanding this preference for social distance, the impulse to help others is strong among Fourth Presbyterian members. The 1994 church survey showed that 52 percent of Fourth Presbyterian members were involved in charitable activities.[30] Moreover, 81 percent of congregants at Fourth Presbyterian believed that "to help a person in need is one of my most important values." This desire was not prompted by a sense of self-sacrifice, however.[31] Most congregants felt that they benefited as much from serving others as those who were being served.

The mission statement of Fourth Presbyterian begins, "We are a light in the city reflecting the inclusive love of God. Comforted and challenged by the Gospel of Christ, we strive to be a welcoming, serving community." The mission statement asserts the need for permeable and open boundaries, and an intense amount of outreach to the economically and racially excluded actually comes out of the institution. Fourth Presbyterian serves others through a variety of outreach programs. Many of the community outreach programs were created during Elam Davies's tenure from 1961 to 1984: the Center for Older Adults, the Lorene Replogle Counseling Center, the Elam Davies Social Service Center, and the tutoring program. In the 1990s the tutoring program expanded dramatically, the Center for Whole Life opened, and the church led a campaign to construct a single-room occupancy residence. In the 1990s each program had a budget of more than $100,000. The tutoring program, which became its own not-for-profit corporation in 1992, had a budget of more than $200,000.

In the 1990s the Center for Older Adults had some 400 members. It served older men and women through various educational and health programs. The membership was ecumenical: a third Catholic, a third Jewish, and the rest Fourth Presbyterian members. It was predominantly a middle-class group. The Lorene Replogle Counseling Center in the 1990s averaged more than 5,000 appointments per year, and more than 200 people were involved in various seminar programs each year. Ten percent of the Counseling Center's clients paid little or no fee. Approximately 20 percent of the clients were Fourth Presbyterian members. Eighty percent of the clients were single. The Elam Davies Social Service Center had an average of 1,000 or more drop-ins; it served meals or gave food to 1,000 more and assisted more than 1,000 men, women, and children with clothing, employment, and rents.

Buchanan and Fourth Presbyterian leaders in the summer of 1995 announced that plans for building a single-room occupancy residence had been approved. This was a project that had been in development for several years. Fourth Presbyterian joined with several churches in the city to create Central City Housing Ventures (CCHV)—a development organization. The plan called for a six-story, 170-unit building, with built-in social services to meet the needs of the homeless, low-income wage earners, students on assistance, and older adults, the first newly constructed residence for them in the downtown area in more than forty years. The Second Presbyterian Church, which is part of the CCHV, donated property adjacent to its church, at Eighteenth and Wabash. The Fourth Presbyterian Church pledged $100,000 toward the more than $10 million price tag of the project.

A significant amount of direct service goes out to the community from Fourth Presbyterian, but the tutoring program receives the most public attention. Many individuals are originally attracted to the church by the tutoring program and become members later. As one staff member said, "Tutoring is our best evangelism program." In the two tutoring focus groups not one of the six individuals was a member of Fourth Presbyterian. Nonetheless, the program is often publicized and given wide visibility in the life of the church.[32] Buchanan frequently mentions the tutoring program in his sermons, and the director of tutoring, an African American woman and former Chicago public school teacher, regularly provides mission staff reports and often gives "Minute for Mission" statements at the Sunday morning worship services. The six tutors who participated in the focus groups I led ranged from twenty to fifty years of age. All of these tutors were professionals. Half lived in the suburbs and commuted to tutoring; the commutes averaged more than an hour each way. Half were married, and four of the six were women. In age, occupation, proximity to the church, marital status, and gender, this group mirrored Fourth Presbyterian Church members.[33]

It is evident that the religion of the institutional church had little motivational effect on these tutors. Indeed, the tutors said that they would not participate in the program if they were required to teach Christianity. As mentioned earlier, the tutors were not church members, though some had been members of other churches in the past. These tutors were not, however, unlike respondents in the church survey. Although the tutors did not feel that church attendance was obligatory, they all agreed that Christians have an obligation to care for the poor. Several of the focus group respondents criticized their former churches because they had no social outreach programs in the community. There were, however, several positive comments about Fourth Presbyterian's involvement in community outreach.

Two tutors cited articles by the *Chicago Tribune* columnist Bob Greene for their initial inspiration and involvement.[34] All of the tutors expressed satisfaction in helping others. As one succinctly put it, "I think it is the feeling that you get when you walk away from here. It is different than work where you are just looking at the bottom line. Here you feel like you really did something" (Focus Group, February 1994). Another comment from a respondent about the reason for her involvement is revealing in several ways:

> I think I am doing it in order to learn how to relate to people who are different than I am. I came from a solidly middle-class background. We always had family around. School was really important. It was important to learn how to help other people. Important to learn what is affecting our culture. To find out what is going on in people's lives. I mean to learn more about what is happening over there [Cabrini-Green]. I don't want to sound like it is us against them. I think people put up barriers. We are afraid of those who are different. We must help make it possible for desperately under-privileged people to make it into the middle-class; to help open doors. You can't help people in general unless you help others in specific. (Focus Group, February 1994)

This young woman was from a Catholic middle-class background. She was single, a graduate of an elite business school, and a business entrepreneur. She grew up on the South Side of Chicago, and while in high school she helped tutor at the Robert Taylor Homes, another public housing complex on the South Side. She was a privileged woman passionately interested in, as she said later, helping to "level the playing field." Her language of social boundaries and cultural separation is noteworthy, however, and this was common to both focus groups. Cabrini children are "over there." We must understand those who are "different."

There was nothing pejorative in the comments that assumed social boundaries of "us" and "them." The tutors stated correctly the real cultural and social distance that was felt between the groups, a distance they sought to close through the avenue of education. Along with this sense of separation came fear. One tutor, a white male in his late thirties, said, "Before I started doing tutoring I would literally be in fear of driving anywhere near Division Street. All that would go through my mind was all that I had read and seen through the media of how dangerous the place was. Now I go to his [the tutoring child's] house and pick him up and feel relatively comfortable" (Focus Group, February 1994).

The tutoring program is a cross-cultural experience. Boundaries, both real and imaginary, are broken down. It is individualistic in that it expresses the notion that "you can't help people in general, but you can help individuals." This "help" comes by way of education. Education, as social capital, is the main conduit by which the playing field is leveled. Several focus group respondents commented that education for them and for others is the only way to "get ahead," "to become middle-class." The implicit goal is to obtain and thus reinforce the values and social norms of the white middle-class culture.

This same goal of middle-class socialization is voiced by the leadership of the tutoring program. As one leader of the program commented, "Some of our children don't get jobs because they don't show up on time. Or they have an earring in their ear. Those type of cultural things keep our children from being employed. Knowing how to conduct themselves, knowing how to dress is important" (Interview, January 1994).

The director of tutoring is well aware of these cultural boundaries. She is sensitive to the violence of the Cabrini-Green complex. That is, children are trained to respond to a slight with violence as a form of survival. Parents are disciplinarians to the point of overcorrection—because disobedience, in the context of Cabrini-Green, can mean death. Tutors comment often on the verbal and emotional violence parents inflict on children and children inflict on each other. The explosive nature of this public violence is foreign to white middle-class culture and its desire to protect children from violence. There is little protection for children at Cabrini-Green.[35]

As one of the leaders of the tutoring program explained, there are many reasons why few parents of Cabrini-Green children attend Fourth Presbyterian:

People and families at Cabrini think well of Fourth Presbyterian. Now they may not want to come worship here but this is a good place to send the children. For lots of reasons they don't feel comfortable coming to worship here: they don't eat the same foods; they don't wear the same clothing; they feel out of place themselves. It is more comfortable where they are; they know what the rules are. They are not going to be laughed at for doing the wrong thing. Not that people would do that here, but they don't know that. But even those who are comfortable where they are want a better life for their children. (Interview, January 1994)

Cabrini-Green parents interpret Fourth Presbyterian as a bridge to overcome boundaries of economic deprivation and to open new opportunities for their children. Undoubtedly, the cultural tools and resources that make one feel "at home" are distinctly different for those who attend Fourth Presbyterian and those at Cabrini-Green. Fourth Presbyterian's language of inclusion creates the possibility of openness and mutual aid, while cultural and aesthetic boundaries maintain barriers that continue to separate one community from another.

Outreach as Social Capital

Another leader in the Fourth Presbyterian ministries to Cabrini-Green commented, "Cabrini-Green is our mission field. We depend on them more than they depend on us. Because this mission field is so visible to the rest of Chicago, we get a lot of credibility that a lot of churches simply don't have" (Interview, January 1994). As in the early part of the century when Protestant foreign missions were central to the church's purpose in the world and a major element in its legitimation as a religious organization, at the turn of the century the inner city and places like Cabrini-Green are the objects of mission, particularly for lay liberal Protestants. They are the vehicles through which organizational legitimation is achieved, or what I call the accumulation of social-conscience capital. Legitimation is critical for a religious institution, particularly if it wants to attract the lay liberal. In "golden rule" Christianity, actions are more important than words in the exercise of one's purpose in the world. Thus, if mission is proclaimed and not accomplished, people withdraw. The act of helping the poor is more critical than right doctrine or right belief.

The second section of Fourth Presbyterian's mission statement answers the question of the church's purpose: "At the intersection of faith and life, we share God's grace through worship, preaching, education and ministries of healing, reconciliation and justice." No mention is made of the need to evangelize in the classical sense of proclaiming the gospel. What is traditionally called Evangelism Sunday has been renamed Visitors Sunday at Fourth Presbyterian. The social outreach programs are the evangelism programs since it is only by deed that systems of belief can become legitimate. Individuals, who may otherwise be offended by traditional forms of evangelism, are drawn to the church by the outreach of its programs to communities and individuals in great need. Furthermore, serving others, particularly African Americans, has social status attached to it. One of the tutors in the tutoring focus group stated that "one tutor [a young white professional woman] got a white child. She was really disappointed. To have a black child it would be a good thing to brag about at a cocktail party. Social conscience is very hip to have" (Focus Group, February 1994). The tutoring program is an instrument for establishing social status for individuals. Moreover, it provides a social context for young adults to meet potential companions. A mixture of motivations thus make up the subjective matrix of reasons why tutors are involved in outreach.

A somewhat cynical side was expressed by some of the leaders in the church when speaking about the mission to Cabrini-Green: "We are not giving them a way out of Cabrini. What we are doing is not necessarily education but the bringing down of barriers along lines of race and class. Let's say that 50 percent of the kids extend their schooling two more years. We gain a lot more than they do. They give to us what is not easily found in a city, that is the opportunity to serve others" (Interview, January 1994). The dependence that Fourth Presbyterian has on Cabrini-Green was put in stark terms by another volunteer leader: "Because of Cabrini and because of what we do there, Fourth Presbyterian is able to say we practice what we preach" (Interview, January 1994). Cabrini-Green is, in other words, the strongest defense against the charge of hypocrisy, that is, that Fourth Presbyterian merely expresses the social dominance of the Gold Coast.

At the same time, Cabrini-Green families expend enormous energy to see that their children are able to come to their tutoring sessions each week. As the director of tutoring makes clear, "If Cabrini-Green decided that Fourth Presbyterian was not providing a good service to their children, our tutoring children would be gone in a minute" (Interview, January 1994). The parents and children of Cabrini-Green depend on Fourth Presbyterian for hope that their children will someday move away from the projects. This lay liberal Protestant church not only gains from its social outreach but also instills in young people the belief in a new future for themselves and their families.

THE VOICE OF LAY LIBERALISM

The Critique of Liberal Protestantism

Liberal Protestantism is all but dead in the eyes of many religious researchers (Johnson, 1982). The most recent explanations for this decline have focused on the weakness of the liberal Protestant belief structure and its inability to create vital religious institutions (Hoge, Johnson, and Luidens, 1994; Finke, 1992; Bruce, 1990). This decline began in the 1960s, and it has forced the mainline denominations to rethink their liberal political agenda. Many members of mainline churches did not follow the liberal leadership of the church in the 1960s (Hadden, 1969). Benton Johnson, in his 1982 article "End of Another Era," upbraided liberal Protestantism for its failed politics and its lack of an evangelical message: "By failing to embrace a truly distinctive politics, the churches have allied themselves with a wing of bourgeois thought. And by failing to recover old theological motifs, they have forfeited any claim to be genuinely Christian" (Johnson, 1982:194).

In 1993 Johnson and his fellow researchers continued to critique the inadequacy of theological training for young mainliners (Hoge, Johnson, and Luidens, 1993). In their study of young Presbyterians they found that the stongest predictor of church involvement was beliefs, especially core beliefs and belief that truth is in Christianity (Hoge, Johnson, and Luidens, 1993:252). The problem, in Johnson's terms, is that liberal Protestantism, in the face of modern pluralism, has watered down the specificity and ultimacy of its theology. Since most mainliners do not feel that their belief is the only true way, they lack loyalty to the mainline denominations and have little or no incentive to bring others into the fold. Dean Hoge, Johnson, and David Luidens created a phrase for this kind of relativistic theological perspective, lay liberalism: "This perspective is 'liberal' because its defining characteristic is a rejection of the orthodox teaching that Christianity is the only true religion. Lay liberals have a high regard for Jesus, but they do not affirm that He is God's only son and that salvation is available only through Him. We use the modifier 'lay' because no one we talked to seemed to know about, or speak the language of, any of the formal systems of thought that might be regarded as theologically liberal or post-orthodox" (Hoge, Johnson, and Luidens, 1994:112–13).

If lay liberalism is such a failed ideology, why has Fourth Presbyterian continued to thrive under the leadership of a classic lay liberal? I have argued in this chapter that lay liberalism is the belief of choice for many middle- and upper-middle-class Protestants. What many critics of liberal Protestantism are saying is that only a distinctive, demanding, and exclusivist system of belief ensures a vital religious organization (Kelley, 1972; Finke, 1992; Iannaccone, 1994). Fourth Presbyterian is a church that has adapted to its social setting by employing a lay liberal, low-demand Protestantism that has brought stability and growth to this religious institution. Nancy Ammerman's project of understanding this kind of religious perspective as a religious type is validated by the study of Fourth Presbyterian (Ammerman, 1997a). The symbolic boundaries of Fourth Presbyterian confirm the lay liberal ethos of the church.

Buchanan: Background, Style, and Cultural Assumptions

John Buchanan is the central figure in the construction of this theological vision of lay liberalism. Buchanan was born and reared in Altoona, Pennsylvania, a working-class town. He received his religious training in a small Presbyterian Church. His roots were conservative, but he was affected by the liberal politics of the 1960s. He graduated from the University of Chicago Divinity School, a liberal and neoorthodox theological school that reinforced these liberal leanings. In the early 1960s he served two congregations in Indiana before going to Broad Street Presbyterian Church in Columbus, Ohio, in 1974. While at this church he was recognized in a national magazine as a pastor who had "reversed a decline largely because of [his] ten years of outstanding preaching and quick responses to parishioners' concerns" (Carey, 1984:73). Buchanan's name was chosen from several hundred resumes for the Fourth Presbyterian pastorate. He was installed as Fourth Presbyterian's tenth senior minister on Sunday, September 23, 1985.

Buchanan's style of leadership is much more democratic than that of previous Fourth Presbyterian pastors. He strives to include the staff and laypeople in all decisions. Nonetheless, many laypeople find him intimidating. Though responsive to their needs, Buchanan is a manager, a forceful and strong administrator. It is common for people to comment that he would be an excellent CEO in a large corporation. Buchanan has an activist style that is embodied in his constant search for new initiatives for programs within the church and in his passion for social outreach to the community.

Buchanan's activist and managerial style is reflected in the expansion of the staff that occurred under his leadership in the 1990s. Historically, Stone had managed Fourth Presbyterian with one associate pastor during his tenure; Anderson worked with two associate pastors; Davies had four. In 1998 Buchanan had eight associate pastors on staff. This meant an augmentation of programs at every level of congregational fellowship, education, and outreach. For example, the Academy for Faith and Life, a much-expanded educational program for adult education, began in the fall of 1998.

This same energetic and purposeful manner can be seen in Buchanan's style of preaching.[36] He preaches from a manuscript. For Buchanan the content of the sermon is more important than the form of delivery. The sermon is a rationally argued speech that is often topical, although the exposition of the scriptural text is woven throughout. If one is persuaded, it is by reason, not by personality. Buchanan is intentional about this method of rational discourse. Truth is mediated not by his personality but by the power of rational argumentation.

Buchanan's style of preaching is consistent with his assumptions about the kind of people who form the Fourth Presbyterian congregation. He assumes that they come from a rational and somewhat skeptical perspective:

At this church you have a very interesting mixture of people who are not in any way classical religious folks. I'm assuming that for the vast majority of people that their coming here once a week or once a month is the only thing in their lives that resembles classic religiosity. They pretty much regard themselves as secular. They would fall into [Wade Clark] Roof's category of believers but not joiners. They believe in God, that there is good and evil, but they don't believe at all in institutional religion. (Buchanan Interview, December 15, 1993)

From the church survey we know that Buchanan is accurate in that most Fourth Presbyterian congregants are wary of commitment to an institutional church. This is characteristic of lay liberals. They are hesitant to commit to an institution, yet they want to find an outlet for their charitable giving and a place where they can experience a sense of spirituality and transcendence. Buchanan is less accurate about his congregants' personal religiosity in that the majority of members do pray fairly frequently. Nonetheless, Buchanan's assumptions shape his preaching. The tone and flavor of Buchanan's sermons assume an ideal type secular person—a person who could be described as sophisticated, educated, privileged, and socially elite. In challenging the congregation to understand that God speaks through the ordinary and the common, Buchanan described the congregation this way in a May 3, 1997, sermon, "Christ and the Commonplace": "By us I mean most of us here this morning, by anyone's standards, wealthy, healthy and secure, successful, used to being number one, feeling pretty good about being number one."

Buchanan's sermons are pitched to his listeners to catch their interest. Sermons are topical in that they relate to the issues of the day. Buchanan consistently comments on the latest news, whether it is the Challenger tragedy, the Iran-Contra scandal, violence in Chicago, issues of abortion and sexuality, or the impeachment of President Clinton. He is, however, nondogmatic in his stance toward issues. Positions on abortion, homophobia, social inequity, gun control are all taken—but the positions are framed in oblique terms in order to persuade rather than to dominate his listeners. Buchanan is not as strident in positions on civic issues as Anderson was, but he engages the public life of his congregation more frequently than Davies did.

The best example of Buchanan's approach to controversial social issues is the way he has handled the conflict over homosexuality in the Presbyterian Church (U.S.A.). In 1978 the General Assembly of the United Presbyterian Church U.S.A. voted to deny ordination to gays and lesbians. Despite numerous studies and proposals in the Presbyterian Church (U.S.A.) in the late 1980s and early 1990s, gays and lesbians are still not able to be ordained as ministers of the gospel or as elders and deacons in local Presbyterian churches. Buchanan established the Fourth Presbyterian Task Force on Homosexuality, which did an exhaustive study and presented a report on the topic to the boards of Fourth Presbyterian in the summer of 1995. It came to the tentative conclusion that the biblical judgments against homosexuality were not relevant to today's debate. According to the task force, the "litmus test of the biblically ethical relationship, be it heterosexual or homosexual, is the presence of the commitment of love and care for each other as human beings made in the image of God, and for who Christ died" (Task Force on Homosexuality, Report, June 9, 1995).

The task force's recommendations essentially promoted inclusiveness and the understanding of gays and lesbians and their concerns. The task force did not, however, directly recommend the ordination of gays and lesbians. Instead, it asked that the Presbyterian Church (U.S.A.) reconsider the 1978 ruling. This subtle distinction and diplomacy is emblematic of the way Buchanan has approached difficult social issues. For the most part it has enabled him and his leadership to avoid major conflicts and to push forward an agenda that highlights the inclusive nature of the Christian gospel.

A Radical Narrative of Inclusion

Lay liberals value diversity and inclusiveness but do not seek to let go of their positions of power. Privilege is sought, not to flaunt it but to secure one's future and to make it possible to care for others. Buchanan tapped these inherent tensions within his lay liberal congregation in an October 7, 1990, sermon on Hagar entitled "God's Other Chosen People." Hagar is the woman in the Hebrew Scripture who is the substitute childbearer for Sarah, the barren wife of Abraham. Hagar has a baby by Abraham and calls him Ishmael. Sarah subsequently becomes pregnant with Isaac, and Hagar is summarily dismissed (Genesis 16, 21). Hagar, however, is not forgotten by God: "the angel of God called to Hagar out of heaven and said unto her, 'What aileth thee, Hagar? Fear not . . .'" (Genesis 21:17). Buchanan wove together the "big story" of Abraham, Sarah, and Isaac with the "little story" of Hagar and Ishmael:

> From the beginning God has a special love for the other people, the little people, the different people, the ones who get pushed aside so the big story can proceed. From the beginning God's passion for those who are excluded argues with, judges and confronts the tradition of the chosen people. It is God, not some liberal dogooder, who has to remind even the people of the Bible that the big story cannot exclude the little stories if it is going to be God's story.

Buchanan then used this Scripture to challenge reified social boundaries. He used Hagar as a trope to confront exclusiveness on the part of those in power in the church, in the nation, and in the world. He implied that the inclusiveness of God's special concern for little people—God's other people—is the narrative that should be lifted up in the "Church of Jesus Christ, the Holy Catholic Church, the Presbyterian Church (U.S.A.), the Fourth Presbyterian Church of Chicago—a place where God's argument with religious and racial and economic and social exclusiveness is remembered and revered." Buchanan had the Hagar story stand for "exploited minorities, the gap between the Western world and the Muslim, a gap which in the heat and conflict around the Persian Gulf, treads close to racism. . . . Let her [Hagar] stand for pregnant teenagers, for the permanent underclass, for persons with AIDS, for homeless men and women in Chicago."

Buchanan used this figurative symbol of Hagar as a literary strategy to include excluded narratives of those whose speech has been suppressed. This radical narrative of inclusiveness is a double-edged sword, however, in that it opens the social boundaries but gives a weak epistemological structure to the beliefs of those who are a part of the group. That is, when all are included, how are community boundaries maintained? They are maintained because Buchanan knows to whom he is speaking; even as he challenges his congregation, he also honors them in their privilege.

Lay Liberalism and Noblesse Oblige

Buchanan's symbolic matrix and his assumptions about those who visit the congregation act as guides to listeners for whether they are included. This symbolic world echoes the social and cultural boundaries of the Gold Coast. The inclusion of those who are privileged is clear; that these people are called to serve those who have less is also unequivocal. For instance, in an April 18, 1988, sermon, "All in the Family," Buchanan excoriated the congregation on the state of African American families and the price that "we," as a nation and as the dominant culture, are paying for the history of oppression and slavery that "we" perpetrated upon this group:

> One hundred years of segregation, humiliation and legal discrimination was a focused assault on the institution of marriage and the personhood of black men, particularly. We legalized the removal of pride, autonomy and power of men, then have the audacity to wonder what happened to the family. And a quarter of a century under a welfare system that further encourages the demise of family and marriage has virtually completed the tragic assault. Twenty percent of the white

babies and sixty percent of the black babies born this year will enter life without the stability of married parents.

Even as Buchanan took the perspective of the socially dominant and painted their guilt in this sermon, he assumed a barrier between the dominant, those who are able to afford to pay taxes, and those who are dominated, for whom care is needed. He laid responsibility on the dominant in a direct but gentle manner:

> We are paying and will pay an enormous price for racism and for the demise of the family in the subculture of poverty. The tragedy is that we know at least part of the resolution, but our ideological zeal prevents us from implementing it. (Or is it simply selfishness?) We know that providing pre-natal care, pediatric health care, nutritional assistance, guidance counseling, day care—saves money, lots of money. We know that we are the only nation in the Western world without public support of daycare centers. We know that public schools are, for many youngsters, the only structure, the only hope and we don't want to support them if it will cost us more money.

Buchanan wove throughout this painful portrayal of this subculture the costs not only to the people who live in this subculture of poverty but also to "us." "We," the social elite, will pay a price in the future for this devastation. The devastation costs "us" money. The argument is not only moral but also utilitarian; that is, if we pay now, we will save later in terms of social costs. It is a combination of language that will call forth not only guilt—over historical abuse and responsibility—for the present devastation of our inner cities but also a means-end rationality, which by the calculus of a cost-benefit analysis says that it will benefit us in the long run if we pay now.

A part of Buchanan's challenge is a call to give from an abundance, a place of privilege, to those who have less and are suffering. It is an ideology of noblesse oblige. This is not a call to deconstruct social boundaries of status, nor is it a call for radical egalitarianism. It both legitimates this status group and calls forth the good intentions of those in privilege.

A sermon that was printed in the *Chicago Sun-Times* is emblematic of this perspective. In the sermon Buchanan described how Americans have become people with a sense of entitlement; people who think in the short term rather than the long term; people with "a feeling that government programs to assist the less fortunate are an unnecessary burden, while government subsidies of their own affluence are a right. . . . We have come to tolerate a new and frightening income gap between the rich and the poor" (Buchanan, 1993). Buchanan clearly drew his own symbolic boundaries: America must be a place where all are included socially and culturally. Individual rights are at the heart of American liberal democratic culture, but those who are privileged are responsible for all people, no matter their status.

Buchanan's social analysis is limited in two respects. First, challenging those with privilege to give to the poor misses the recent social perspective that calls the poor to responsibility and asserts that welfare reinforces dependency instead of creating opportunity.[37] Of course, since the poor are not members of the congregation, Buchanan has little opportunity to challenge those who are less fortunate. Second, there is an implicit zero-sum equation in Buchanan's interpretation of the devastation of African American families and the social decay of their environment. The history of the segregation of African Americans reveals that upper-middle-class Protestants were not alone in the creation of African American ghettos. Protestant elites actually did little directly to create the ghetto, though they did even less to stop it.

The trajectory of Buchanan's preaching is finely tuned to the thinking of lay liberalism. Social status is challenged, not to be overturned but to become aware of the common good and the wider responsibilities of citizenship. The church exists for the world, as Buchanan says repeatedly, and service to the world is its purpose.

Sociodicy of Good Fortune

There is an implicit theodicy or "sociodicy" of good fortune in Buchanan's preaching.[38] The groundwork for this sociodicy is laid in a November 6, 1988, sermon entitled "Christ and Wealth." Buchanan used the Mark 10:23b text to speak about the dilemma of wealth in the light of Christ's saying "How hard it will be for those who have riches to enter the kingdom of God!" Buchanan addressed the issue in four points: (1) do not feel guilty about being upper-middle-class Christians; (2) do not deny your wealth; (3) Jesus did not condemn wealth per se; and (4) the problem is personal.

For Buchanan wealth is not inherently evil; evil is "greed" or "over-possessiveness" of money. In this sociodicy of good fortune, goodness does not produce wealth, but one's wealth is deserved and thus legitimate. Wealth is personalized and a function of the individual's prerogative. This narrowing of symbolic boundaries to individual subjectivity limits the possibility of challenging the social inequalities that are inherent in the Gold Coast social setting. Boundaries of social dominance are naturalized, but this reification is not theologically rationalized. That is, Buchanan, unlike his predecessors, never assumes that wealth is a blessing from God or that wealth implies class superiority. Nonetheless, Buchanan does nurture the elite; he is aware that it is precisely these individuals who have the power, capital, and leadership capabilities to challenge the sources of inequality of race and class in Chicago. There is thus a compromise with the reality of an unequal socioeconomic system—a strategy that enables Buchanan to speak to those who have the power to move the system toward greater equality and justice.

Theological Boundary Work

Buchanan is a champion for liberal Protestantism; for him conservative Christianity is a source of self-righteousness, theological arrogance, and a theology that rationalizes the exclusion of the marginalized in modern society.

In November 1993 an ecumenical women's conference called "Re-Imagining" caused a storm of controversy in the Presbyterian Church (U.S.A.).[39] The Presbyterian General Assembly received fifty overtures, two commissioner reports, and more than three thousand letters about the conference. Most were negative. In June 1994 at the 206th General Assembly in Wichita, Kansas, the General Assembly Council heard fervent critiques and ardent testimonies concerning the conference. The General Council Review was chaired by Buchanan, who wrote much of the report in response to the hearings. The report was overwhelmingly approved by the more than five hundred delegates from across the church; there were only four dissenting votes.

The gist of the report was twofold. First, church funds and the activities of General Assembly staff members must be monitored and supervised more carefully. That the Presbyterian Church (U.S.A.) gave the Re-Imagining Conference $66,000 was judged as a lack of institutional accountability because the request for funds did not go through all the proper channels. Second, theology matters to the church. The report strongly upheld the traditional view of the Trinity, God's incarnation in Jesus Christ, Christ's resurrection for salvation, and the affirmation that the Scriptures are the authoritative witness to Jesus Christ. Conservatives charged that the conference had been rife with heresy, including the celebration of homosexuality, the rejection of Christ's atonement, and the worship of the goddess "Sophia," which the report said "implied the worship of a divine manifestation distinctly different from the one triune God" (Buchanan, 1994:3).

Buchanan's role in this conflict was to reconcile the two parties. His theological vision may be liberal, but he has always pushed for the reconciliation of the warring theological factions within the Presbyterian Church (U.S.A.). From the fall of 1994 to the spring of 1995 Buchanan spent a great deal of his time negotiating with conservatives, such as the Presbyterian Layman, a group that seeks to radically change the direction and tenor of the Presbyterian Church (U.S.A.). Buchanan sees his role as a mediator between divergent opinions of the left and right in the church. Buchanan, however, is clearly more sympathetic to the liberal wing (Buchanan, 1996; Davies and Buchanan, 1996).

For Buchanan the Reformed tradition is an essential backbone of Western liberties and freedoms. Liberal Protestant values of the Reformed tradition have been like "seasoning in this culture, . . . pluralism, diversity, inclusiveness, tolerance, equal justice, free inquiry, freedom of expression, freedom of choice, compassion," as he put it in his February 8, 1987, sermon, "To Become the Whole World's Seasoning." For Buchanan these values are "under assault." The vehicle of this attack is conservative Christianity. Conservative Christianity, with its absolutist claims and moral self-righteousness, is the most potent force against a liberal culture. For Buchanan the values of tolerance and diversity run deep in the Reformed tradition. "Even at our most belligerent," he exclaimed in his May 21, 1989, sermon entitled "A Reforming Faith for a Changing World," "we never claimed to be the only church, the only answer to the truth, or the only way to worship or express the faith."

Buchanan fully accepts the historical-critical method of biblical criticism, as evidenced by his perspective on Scripture. "Fortunately we Presbyterians believe that the Bible is a human document which God uses, so we are not stuck with the appalling notion that it's all inspired and that the Holy Spirit dictated instructions," he observed in his April 21, 1991, sermon, "In the Presence of My Enemies." He is not willing to forego the findings of modern science and modern literary interpretation for the sake of maintaining biblical inerrancy. This puts him at odds with the more conservative-minded in the Reformed tradition. But it places him comfortably in the rationalist tradition of critical modernism (Farley, 1990).

Buchanan firmly believes in the power of the liberal tradition, supported by liberal Protestantism, to promote a just, democratic society. It is out of this tradition of a liberal and tolerant society that Buchanan asserts that justice calls congregants to include those who are different. This ideology of liberal democracy was the object of his May 28, 1989, sermon entitled "On Speaking and Hearing," which interpreted the scriptural story of the tower of Babel. Buchanan asserted that the building of the tower of Babel was not a sign of Promethean hubris but a symbol of a desire to exclude others: "Instead the people are trying to secure their future, their safety and well-being by clinging together, remaining exclusive." That God would cause them to have different languages and be spread across the world is, for Buchanan, a sign that

"God is the scatterer. God's intent here is for people to move out, settle the whole earth, become different. God is a pluralist. God does not think much of racial and political and social homogeneity."

Buchanan consistently approaches God as one who creates diversity and mystery. "What the Christian Church needs," he declared in his January 15, 1995, sermon entitled "To See God," "is a little theological modesty, a little self-deprecating humor in the middle of our intense representations of the absolute truth of God." Buchanan speaks in the tradition of lay liberalism with the sense that truth may be one but there are multiple ways to approach it. This truth is not dogmatic; it is dynamic and thus cannot be put into precise doctrinal statements or in the traditional forms of Puritan moral rules and regulations. Moral sanctions depend on the situation, though they must always be guided by love and justice. Self-righteousness is the ultimate sin. Theology is a humble movement toward the radical inclusive vision of a God who loves the world, a God who demands that followers love the world as well. God is not far off but is close and involved in the world. Scripture is a human document that guides interpreters toward a vision of life as radically inclusive. Sin is the arrogance of thinking that one has the truth and the only truth. As Buchanan explained, "I was very taken by Hans Kung's argument that he has no problem affirming the fact the Christ is the way, the truth and the life, but that also he has no problem affirming this truth can come to another human being in other ways" (Buchanan Interview, December 15, 1993).[40]

Critics of liberal Protestantism would say that this theological pluralist perspective is an accommodated form of Christianity that mirrors the kind of pluralist ideology common to modernist academies. Buchanan would say that these pluralist perspectives counter our cultural propensity, symbolized by conservative Christianity, to absolutize a narrow point of view and exclude others. The genius of American culture is its heterogeneity and its willingness to open itself to dissent and difference.

An Ethic of Beneficence

To be sure, Buchanan's symbolic boundaries are not countercultural in terms of the lay liberal tradition. The question remains, however, whether Buchanan challenges the social inequality of his Gold Coast congregation. Buchanan answers the question this way: "The ultimate point of human life is love and service. We are called to live risky lives and not just lives of security, comfort and accumulation. These values are strongly countercultural. Particularly when you are in a setting that the economy is God" (Buchanan Interview, December 15, 1993).

Because Buchanan mirrors the lay liberal position, there is no singular aspect to his preaching that is fundamentally transgressive. His preaching is powerful because it captures so well and thoughtfully the lay liberal point of view. He keeps in tension individuals' desires to maintain privilege and to step beyond their comfort zones to give to others. His preaching supports an altruistic ethic of beneficence that he outlines as central to human life.[41] He counters the competitive ethic of a dominant capitalist social order with a call to reach out to those who are left behind. Social dominance is legitimated, and distance from the needy remains, but at the same time a distinctively different standard of humanity is endorsed.

For Buchanan, as he claimed in his September 29, 1991, sermon, "Peculiar Victory," the purpose of the church is to serve others: "But Jesus taught that when you serve others in his name, you are in the presence of God; that the religious life is not sequestered from the world, but busy in the world, with its sleeves rolled up, holding out its arms to those no one else pays any attention to." The church is on a thoroughly this-worldly venture; moreover, serving the needs of others in relative anonymity and with no thought to one's salvation is the key to living the Christian life. "Jesus wants his followers to discover and define themselves in terms of service to people in need. Jesus—and this is stunning—wants us to forget about even our own salvation so he can save our souls," Buchanan declared in the sermon. Again, this altruistic ethic of beneficence is not incompatible with lay liberals' desire to serve others. Lay liberals are stridently this-worldly, and most view the world to come as a possibility but not the reason for their good works (Wuthnow, 1991). Christian life is thus defined as service to others—not the sharing of beliefs about faith or identification with the needy. Distance and compartmentalization are central to the liberal Protestant ethos and at the core of its religious values.

This ethic of beneficence is further developed in Buchanan's sermon "The Heart of the Matter," which he preached on October 21, 1990. Citing the Matthean text "Love God with all your heart, soul and mind, and your neighbor as yourself" (Matthew 22:37, 39), Buchanan defined the neighbor as the one in need. This is best exemplified by a letter that Buchanan received related to the tutoring program. The letter, from a Chicago City College professor, referred to several African American students in the professor's classroom who spoke about their success in life as a result of the tutoring program at Fourth Presbyterian. The professor commented to Buchanan, "A young woman said she believed she would have become pregnant thereby thwarting completion of high school, and college would have been a fantasy. I am convinced that Chicago City Colleges have students that are taking courses and succeeding in life due to your persistent care and well-conceived and directed outreach programs" ("The Heart of the Matter," October 21, 1990).

This letter paints the picture of those outside the social boundaries of the dominant class who find a way into the mainstream. It confirms the ideal of the lay liberal Protestant: all should have the opportunity to partake of the good life, in their own place and time. The challenge of Buchanan and the Fourth Presbyterian leadership is to open the boundaries of privilege to an ever-widening circle.

CONCLUSION

Fourth Presbyterian continued to attract many to its sanctuary in the 1980s and 1990s because it understood the social and symbolic boundaries of its members. Fourth Presbyterian's symbolic boundaries proclaim a message of inclusion even as its social boundaries attract a specific class and fail to draw those who are not educated and socialized into specific elite demographic categories. The symbolic worldview legitimates social privilege and at the same time calls for service to those left out.

Buchanan embodies in his leadership and his preaching the ethos of the lay liberal. His sermons reflect the message that God is a mystery. The only sure knowledge is that God loves us and seeks justice in the world. The church is a worldly institution that celebrates faith without denying other truth claims, an institution that attempts to include all and accept all, an institution that serves those left out. Buchanan triggers tensions over issues of class and race by continuing to challenge the congregation to open its social boundaries, while at the same time confirming and honoring privileged individuals. It is a deft balance between the need to secure privilege and the call to care for the outsider.

In this contemporary period Fourth Presbyterian models Niebuhr's Christ transforming culture. This Christ, however, is not the Christ of Christian conservatives but the Christ of Protestant liberalism, confronting inequality, demanding inclusion of those with the least in society, and building bridges across race and class. Fourth Presbyterian is a type of liberal, cultural Protestant church. The most explicit tension that arises culturally is with more conservative Christian communities. Conservatives assert the uniqueness and exclusiveness of the Christian way; belief is more fundamental than behavior, and dogma trumps action. Fourth Presbyterian reverses these priorities. Its symbolic boundaries are closer to liberal culture than to Christian conservatives. At the same time, Fourth Presbyterian continues to call forth service from the dominant social class. This challenge to the barriers of class and race are the chief marks of Fourth Presbyterian's cultural resistance. In the end the church embodies in a remarkably pure form lay liberalism as a new and distinctive religious type in the contemporary American religious market.

NOTES

1. In 1986 the total number of pledging units was 1,147 (units are an individual or household). The average pledge was $653. Total member giving was $749,176. In 1992 the total units were up to 1,370. The average pledge was $910. Total giving was $1,247,701. In 1998 the total units stabilized at 1,348 but the average pledge rose to $1,451. Total member giving was $1,929,000.

2. In 1995 there were numerous reports of private clubs closing on the Near North Side. As one manager put it, "The three-martini lunch is long past." The Union League Club remained stable because of its aggressive marketing.

3. The church's response was to create numerous outreach programs, including the Cabrini-Green tutorial program discussed in chapter 4.

4. The dramatic power of sports in American life is evidenced by the investment companies make on its behalf: "Statistics collected at the end of 1992 by International Events Group, Inc., would show that $2.1 billion was spent by North American companies on sponsorship of specific sports events—the figure dwarfing the $254 million spent on 'causes' by corporations and the $233 million spent on the arts" (Katz, 1994:27).

5. These statistics were taken from deVise (1993), which analyzed the 1980 and 1990 census data.

6. The per capita income of the fifty wealthiest areas in Chicago was $48,000, 3.7 times Chicago's average of $12,900 in 1990. In 1990 only 13 percent of the U.S. population made more than $50,000 annually.

7. Nicholas Lemann noted in 1994 that "the best intended liberal programs of economic redevelopment have failed because they miss the deeper structural changes that destabilize African-American inner-city culture—that is, the dramatic loss of population. During the thirty year period of urban renewal programs that Lemann reviewed, in Chicago alone 100,000 African-Americans had left the city. This is no loss for those who leave. It is the middle-class who move to the suburbs; those left behind are in a position of extreme economic and social vulnerability. Thus, the attempts at the creation of urban 'enterprise zones' often fail because there is little social or economic infrastructure to support the efforts" (Lemann, 1994:30).

8. Richard Sennett and Jonathan Cobb's work on the "hidden injuries" of class, particularly as they affect the working class, was a subtle revelation of the power of class

and status to structure certain individuals so that they not only are economically disadvantaged but also feel responsible for their failures (Sennett and Cobb, 1972).

9. In May of 1995 a Bible study and worship service, led by a combination of Fourth Presbyterian clergy, lay leaders, and Cabrini-Green residents, was meeting once a week. Only females from the housing project attended. A gang leader was invited to come but said that he was too busy. He told the director that he would send two of his lieutenants to the prayer service. Two young men did begin attending.

10. The *Chicago Tribune* ran an article on why Chicagoans were leaving the city. The top reason of the 3,000 who responded, most of whom were white middle-class families, was "a safer place to live." The third most frequent reason, after "a cleaner community," was "better schools" (Reardon, 1993:18).

11. Matthew J. Price and Elfriede Wedam provided some idea of the extent of these agencies: "The most striking feature of outreach to Cabrini-Green is its sheer scale. Let us begin with tutoring. A year ago we estimated that there were about 1,000 tutors and mentors serving the 2,204 5- to 14-year-olds in Cabrini-Green. We now believe that this is an underestimate, not of the number of children, but of the number of tutors, which could be close to 1,500. The organizations that we know of that are running tutor or mentoring programs are, Fourth Presbyterian, LaSalle St. Church's C.Y.C.L.E. ministry, the Montgomery Ward Cabrini Connections program, St. Chrysostoms's Episcopal Church, St. Luke's Church of God in Christ, St. Joseph's Parochial School, Holy Family Lutheran Church, and the Lower North Center. As well as the tutoring programs we have counted at least 40 agencies and organizations that work in the Cabrini area" (Price and Wedam, 1995:15).

12. The Fourth Presbyterian mission statement, which is examined in detail in this chapter, was developed during 1992, in consultation with the clergy and the leaders of the church.

13. The African American associate pastor left the church in February 1998 and was called as pastor of a Presbyterian Church in Michigan.

14. Women have been ordained into the Presbyterian Church (U.S.A.) only since 1957. Even as women have entered the ministry in large numbers, few have been called to be senior pastors in large churches. In 1994 the first minority pastor in Fourth Presbyterian's history was called to the church. Buchanan received support for this decision. In 1994 Buchanan was a part of the search committee that nominated Cynthia Campbell to be the president of McCormick Theological Seminary. She is the first woman president of any Protestant seminary in the country. Buchanan has aggressively pressed for the inclusion of women and minorities in the leadership of Fourth Presbyterian and in the Presbyterian churches in general.

15. I conducted a church survey of Fourth Presbyterian in April 1994. The survey was an eight-page, self-administered questionnaire consisting of four sections: (1) church and religious life, (2) personal religious beliefs, (3) personal worldview, and (4) social and political life. A random sample was sent out to 684 congregants from age twenty on up. The sample return was 317, a return of 46 percent. Two-thirds of the return

sample was female and a third male, which parallels the membership of the church in 1994. The mean age of the sample was forty-six. This section's conclusions are based on results of the church survey. Appendix A presents a detailed summary of the survey results.

16. In the church survey approximately 80 percent of congregants came from mainline Protestant backgrounds, 7 percent from evangelical backgrounds, and another 5 percent from the Roman Catholic Church.

17. To become a member of Fourth Presbyterian is a perfunctory process. One attends a new-members meeting for three hours and comes to a session meeting an hour before the 11:00 A.M. worship service in which one is installed into church membership. This method is clearly less demanding than the membership requirements during Stone's and Anderson's tenures.

18. I tested the means of males and females using an independent t-test procedure. I determined significant difference between the sexes at a .05 level, using a one-tailed test, where justified by the hypotheses.

19. Males' and females' responses to questions B1, B2, B3, B4, B5, B7, and B11 (see Appendix A for specific questions) were statistically different at the .05 level of significance.

20. Using an independent t-test procedure, I also compared the means of lower- and higher-income groups. I determined significant difference between the sexes at a .05 level, using a one-tailed test, where justified by the hypotheses.

21. This difference between 1967 and 1994 reflects not only change at Fourth Presbyterian but also a shift in American economic realities in the last thirty years. In the 1990s there were simply higher demands on senior executives, less loyalty within corporations, and the need, because of advances in competition, technology, and communication, to make decisions faster, produce products more efficiently, and lower overhead. All of this meant less job security, greater independence of workers, and less need for middle managers (Bridges, 1994:17).

22. In 1992 the Fourth Presbyterian session approved a motion to oppose the proposed casino gambling and entertainment complex for Chicago. This resolution of opposition was forwarded to the mayor's office (Session Minutes, May 15, 1992).

23. Throughout Davies's twenty-four years of ministry a similar percentage of revenue to mission work was maintained. During Davies's tenure, however, the average total revenue was half a million dollars, whereas during Buchanan's ministry the church's budget increased by almost sixfold. Davies did expand the endowment funds of the church significantly during his time. In 1961 the church endowment was more than $2 million; in 1985 it had increased to more than $11 million.

24. A personal autonomy index was created to interpret the degree of privatization in the congregation. The autonomy/communitarian index was based on responses to five statements: (1) To be a good Christian it is necessary to attend church; (2) Individual persons should seek out religious truth independent of any church's doctrines; (3) When making value judgments, the final authority is a person's conscience; (4) My

faith is a private matter; and (5) It is important to me to be able to do what I want in my life. The index was based on a scale from one to five, one meaning strongly agree, five meaning strongly disagree. The overall sample on the personal index averaged two on the scale. Specifically, the majority of respondents did not think it necessary to attend church to be a good Christian. Sixty-seven percent thought one should seek truth independent of any church's doctrines. Two-thirds of the sample thought that faith is a private matter. Seventy-seven percent agreed that it is important to be able to do what they want in their life.

25. Statistically significant correlations were obtained between the autonomy scale and the following questions in the survey: B1, B2, B3, B4, B6, B8, B10, and B11 (see Appendix A for the specific questions). That is, as personal autonomy increased, greater tolerance for other religious traditions also increased.

26. I asked in the church survey, "How important is it for you to integrate your personal faith and professional life?" Forty-six percent of the sample said that this integration was either critically important or very important. The percentage went up to 78 percent when the category "somewhat important" was included.

27. In 1990, as a part of the twenty-fifth anniversary of the tutoring program, a survey was taken of tutors in the program. Ninety-five percent of the tutors were between the ages of twenty-three and forty. Seventy-two percent of the tutors were women. Two occupations were predominate among the tutors: 35 percent were in advertising, and 25 percent were in financial services. Perhaps the most surprising finding was that 80 percent of the tutors were not members of the church. My 1994 investigation of the tutoring program confirmed these statistics.

28. The *Chicago Sun-Times* published a series of articles called "The Great Divide: Racial Attitudes in Chicago" in January of 1993, which used an opinion poll conducted by Metro Chicago Information Center and the Public Opinion Laboratory of Northern Illinois University. The sample included 1,116 whites, 279 blacks, 99 Latinos, and 79 Asian/other. African Americans strongly believed that Chicago is racist, whereas whites were much less apt to make this judgment. In answer to the question, "Do you believe Chicago is one of America's most racist cities?" 72 percent of blacks agreed with the statement, while only 30 percent of the whites agreed (Hayner and Johnson, 1993:22–25).

29. Fourth Presbyterian has recognized the existence of racial boundaries and its obligation to break them down. In 1992 the Racism Task Force at Fourth Presbyterian reported, "From what we have learned in the year-long Task Force process, from our colleagues and from our own experiences, it is apparent that, for example, an African American person believes that he or she will inevitably confront barriers in life that prevent equal participation in access to society's facilities. The barrier may come early in life in school or at a community club. It may come later at the doors of a college fraternity or in front of a corporate personnel office. It may not come until the American Dream seems only a short grasp away, at a country club gate or an executive washroom. All of us must be educated to recognize the existence of these barriers (whether

to African Americans, Hispanics, Jews, Arab, Native Americans, Asians, whomever) so that they may be dismantled" (T. Miller and Watson, 1992).

30. In national surveys in 1988, done by the Gallup Organization for Independent Sector, Inc., 45 percent of all Americans were involved in some kind of voluntary service to others (Wuthnow, 1991:6).

31. This outreach does not come out of an ethos of self-sacrifice. Only 34 percent of the Fourth Presbyterian sample agreed or strongly agreed with the statement, "An essential part of my Christian faith is to sacrifice myself for the sake of others." Self-sacrifice is not the norm for middle- and upper-middle-class Americans (Wuthnow, 1991:219).

32. Each Christmas the tutoring program sells Christmas cards with original designs and sayings by Cabrini-Green children in the program. These cards have wide distribution throughout the Chicago metropolitan area. The 1994 fund-raiser raised $15,000 for the tutoring program's budget, and that figure rose to $35,000 in 1998.

33. The purpose of the tutoring focus groups was threefold: one, to learn more about the tutoring program; two, to analyze further the church's relations with the students from Cabrini-Green; and three, to understand the motivations and thinking of tutors involved in this program.

34. On October 25, 1992, following the shooting death of Dantrell Davis at Cabrini-Green, Bob Greene had written a column in the *Chicago Tribune* entitled "Here's Your Chance to Make a Difference." It described the needless death of Dantrell Davis and how through Fourth Presbyterian's tutoring program individuals could make a difference in the lives of others. The Fourth Presbyterian telephone number was printed in the column. Fourth Presbyterian received more than 1,600 calls to volunteer. Fourth Presbyterian put together a volunteer conference, and 600 individuals, mostly young adults, showed up to hear about and sign up for various volunteer opportunities across the city.

35. This sentence alludes to Alex Kotlowitz's *There Are No Children Here,* which tells the story of two young boys growing up in the Henry Horner Homes, a public housing project on the West Side of Chicago. A protected childhood in this social context is an oxymoron. Kotlowitz asks Lafeyette, one of the boys in the book, what he wants to be when he grows up. He says, "'If I grow up, I'd like to be a bus driver,' he told me. If, not when. At the age of ten, Lafeyette wasn't sure he'd make it to adulthood" (Kotlowitz, 1991:x).

36. Buchanan preaches approximately forty times each year. His sermons are typed and archived immediately after he preaches. I read and analyzed all of his sermons from 1985 to 1998.

37. As Alan Wolfe succinctly put it, "Liberals cannot expect government to be in the business of helping people without recognizing that the beneficiaries have an obligation to behave responsibly. Conservatives cannot go around telling people how to behave if they are unwilling to make the plight of the unfortunate their business" (Wolfe, 1993:64).

38. Pierre Bourdieu's work is the source for the use of the word *sociodicy,* defined as the attempt to understand the social sources of social privilege and poverty: "The question of the origin of evil . . . which, as Weber recalls, becomes a questioning of the meaning of human existence only in the privileged classes—always in search of a 'theodicy of their good fortune'—is fundamentally a social interrogation of the causes and reasons for social injustices and privileges: theodicies are always sociodicies" (Bourdieu, 1991:16).

39. The conference was originally planned in response to the 1988 World Council of Churches' "Ecumenical Decade: Churches in Solidarity with Women, 1988–1998." The Re-Imagining Conference was an interdenominational and international conference. Women theologians from ten denominations, twelve countries, and eight racial-ethnic backgrounds were invited to address aspects of the theme of "re-imagining."

40. Hans Kung preached at Fourth Presbyterian after the 1993 Parliament of the World's Religions, which produced a document called *The Declaration of a Global Ethic* that did not use the word *God* because it would offend certain religious traditions.

41. I define *beneficence* as the "obligation to do good and prevent harm." Altruism is related to beneficence in that it means that we sometimes want to do something for another regardless of the consequence to ourselves. Thus beneficence can involve self-sacrifice. Both ethical principles disregard the consequence of actions, whereas a utilitarian ethic seeks the "greatest possible balance of good over evil." The calculation of results is implicit in a utilitarian ethic (Frankena, 1973:45–46).

FINDING A NEW CENTER:
THE FUTURE OF THE LIBERAL
PROTESTANT MAINLINE

States of pluralistic ignorance and anxiety, rather than consensus and sureness, characterize liberal congregations precisely because liberalism tries to maintain congruence with the wider culture at the same time that it tries to be Christian.

—R. Stephen Warner, *New Wine in Old Wineskins: Evangelicals and Liberals in a Small-Town Church,* 1988

For though I am free with respect to all, I have made myself a slave to all, so that I might win more of them. To the Jews I became as a Jew, in order to win Jews. To those under the law I became as one under the law (though I myself am not under the law) so that I might win those under the law. To those outside the law I became as one outside the law (though I am not free from God's law but am under Christ's law) so that I might win those outside the law. To the weak I became weak, so that I might win the weak. I have become all things to all people, that I might by all means save some.

—1 Corinthians 9:19–22, *New Revised Standard Version*

R. Stephen Warner's notion of "pluralistic ignorance and anxiety, rather than consensus and sureness," is an acerbic summary of Fourth Presbyterian in its lay liberal incarnation.[1] Critics who examine the church from the perspective of its tension with culture find fault with Fourth Presbyterian and liberal Protestant churches in general because they have accommodated to the wider culture and insinuated the principles of elite intellectual thought in their symbolic worldviews. In other words, they say little more than what is heard on any university campus and from most academics. This rhetoric beats to the rhythm of inclusion and tolerance, the rights of individuals, and the goal of democracy. Pluralism is understood as a gift and certainty as the companion of those who fear diversity.

I have argued in this study that it is in the theological nature of the Protestant mainline to accommodate to its cultural setting in order to witness and transform its environment. This tendency has always paid a price for its good intentions; too often mainline churches have done nothing more than reflect their cultural space. We witnessed the hegemony of the Protestant establishment early in the century when the Protestant ruling class commanded a cultural authority that is unimaginable at the turn of the century. It also mirrored the class and race inequalities of its time. The present Protestant mainline in comparison with its former self is a muted image of liberal Protestant cultural religion. American culture has left it behind, and the Protestant mainline's task is to find its prophetic voice in the midst of a pluralistic culture and religious situation. Fourth Presbyterian struggles to meet the needs of its Gold Coast clientele and to challenge them to move beyond exclusive boundaries of class and race.

To be sure liberal and mainline Protestants are not the only churches that labor with the vicissitudes of accommodation to culture. Mark Shibley argues in *Resurgent Evangelicalism in the United States* that the new growing evangelical churches succeed partly because they mirror contemporary cultural patterns in their style of worship, use of language, and the therapeutic nature of their theological discourse (Shibley, 1996:136). Evangelicals argue that to make the gospel relevant and attractive to an unchurched generation, a church must use cultural forms to reach out to this new potential constituency.

The challenges facing mainline and evangelical churches are therefore not entirely distinct. As has been noted, Christian conservatives move to the right on social values, are laissez-faire on economic issues, and defend a nationalist agenda. Liberals tend to be progressive on social norms and in favor of governmental intervention for the poor and some regulation of corporations. Of course, there are degrees and variations all along this spectrum. Fourth Presbyterian is libertarian on personal morality but follows evangelicals in affirming the autonomy of the market, though it would reject the nationalistic fervor of some evangelicals. This simply underscores the point that accommodation is not the sole temptation of liberals but is a struggle for conservatives as well.

The mainline Protestant mission is to reflect the culture to, in the words of St. Paul, "save" it. This is no longer the rhetoric that Protestant mainline leaders use to explain their perspective on the world, but it does go to the heart of the issue. This is the conversation of Christ and culture, accommodation and resistance, comfort and challenge, priest and prophet, which has been the focus of this study. This tension and balance has changed over the twentieth century for the Protestant mainline and at Fourth Presbyterian, but it continues to be the mission of the church to engage and critically reflect on its place in the cultural terrain. As David Tracy summarized in *Pluralism and Ambiguity,* this critical inquiry is the call of authentic religion:

> For religions do claim, after all, that Ultimate Reality has revealed itself and that there is a way of liberation for any human being. But even this startling possibility can only be understood by us if we will risk interpreting it. It is possible that some interpreters may have encountered the power of Ultimate Reality. They may have experienced, therefore, religious enlightenment and emancipation. But these claims can be interpreted only by the same kinds of human being as before: finite and contingent members of particular societies and cultures. They demand our best efforts at rigorous, critical, and genuine conversation. They demand retrieval, critique, and suspicion. (Tracy, 1987:86)

The difficult challenge of the Protestant mainline is to approach culture without being seduced by it; to speak to power without being implicated in it; to reach out to the victims of social structures without patronizing them; and to communicate for the voiceless without disempowering them. It is no easy task. Moreover, in the face of massive social change, it is even more difficult for the church to negotiate the tension between Christ and culture. It calls for creativity from Protestant mainline leaders to discern the spirit of culture and to speak words of resistance. As we have seen in Fourth Presbyterian and Protestant mainline history, the discourse of resistance has taken multiple forms throughout the twentieth century. This is precisely the challenge of liberal Protestantism: to keep alive the structures and language of resistance, resistance that embodies a vigilant critique of inequality and injustice, whether it comes in the shape of race or class. The Protestant mainline church has often failed in this obligation. It has too often embodied the very social boundaries that it should confront, but this does not negate its responsibility to continue to engage the culture in dialogue.

CHURCH AND SOCIETY

Patterns in Christ and Culture

Fourth Presbyterian's ministers in the twentieth century took distinctly different theological and ideological perspectives. John Timothy Stone, a nineteenth-century American evangelical, believed that the role of the church was to bring individuals into a personal relationship with Jesus Christ. This meant for him that one was saved for eternal life. The promise and the threat of an afterlife gave leverage to evangelists seeking to save souls for eternity. Stone was a charismatic and forceful preacher. He believed in revival and called his congregants to lift the banner for Christ wherever and whenever it was possible. Stone was not a social prophet; he ignored racism in Chicago and avoided the controversial issues of labor and capital. He did, however, confront the wealthy in his congregation by calling them to invest their resources for the sake of Christ's mission in the world. He was not afraid to call his congregants to serve the church's evangelical cause. For Stone progress was the Christianization of the Near North Side and the world. It was the Christ of culture, baptizing the social and symbolic forms of the Protestant establishment in the name of Jesus Christ. It was a quintessential form of cultural Protestantism.

Stone's exclusivist proclamation asserted that all must come to know Christ if they were to find salvation. Stone's evangelical style was sophisticated, but he was not shy about pushing his evangelical agenda. Paul Knitter in *One Earth Many Religions* outlined various frameworks for interreligious dialogue. Stone embodies the exclusivist model:

> Here on Earth, within history as we know it, God wills that all Hindus, Buddhists, Muslims, primal religious believers, and yes, Jews, become Christians. There is to be one religion. . . . Asked about the salvation of the millions before and after Jesus who through no fault of their own have never heard of him, the exclusivists will not, generally, affirm their perdition—but neither will they affirm their salvation. That's God business, they will say, perhaps to be carried out in a transhistorical realm; in the meantime, here in earthly history, it is the business of Christians to roll up their sleeves and make other Christians. (Knitter, 1995:27)

Harrison Ray Anderson took over for Stone and was tireless in his efforts to carry on the mission that Stone had established. Anderson concentrated on nurturing his congregation. Evangelism continued to be a priority for Anderson but not at the same level that it had been for Stone. Anderson believed in salvation, but he interpreted the concept of eternal life as a this-worldly quality of existence. Anderson took up the cudgel of civic righteousness under the banner of the Protestant ethic and in the spirit of a Puritan prophet. Progress for Anderson was the eradication of taverns from Rush Street, the elimination of parades celebrating religious holidays, and the restraint of all impious behavior in public and private life. An anti-Catholic spirit pervaded the ministries of Stone and Anderson. For them the Roman Catholic Church admitted some of the worst aspects of popular culture, allowing religion to become a part of the more ribald aspects of cultural celebrations. Under Anderson it was the Christ of culture in tension. Since culture had become corrupt, it had to be confronted before it could be Christianized and converted to the gospel. Anderson would not acquiesce to popular trends. Christ transformed the world not for the sake of liberation but for the task of disciplined struggle and moral order in every aspect of life. The church should march to the will of God regardless of swings in social tastes. Nonetheless, in the spirit of traditional cultural Protestantism, Anderson argued that if people led moral lives and worked diligently in their vocations, God would bless their work. A profound link between moral righteousness and economic success thus suffused Anderson's public rhetoric and ministry. He did not resist the moral self-righteousness of his privileged class. In his ministry this unwavering belief in the Protestant ethic combined with a moral perspicacity that would allow no excess without judgment, no privilege without just warrant, no wrong without repentance, and no moral corruption without moral outrage. This attitude led the church to be a crusader against all forms of moral corruption, whether publicly or privately conceived. Anderson's program was ill-prepared, however, for the moral upheaval of the 1960s.

In Elam Davies Fourth Presbyterian appropriated a more complex vision of the relation between Christ and culture. He did not push his congregants to evangelize others, nor did he favor political or social activism in the form taken by either Anderson or Buchanan. Davies believed profoundly in a vision of God whose grace was powerful enough to love the world in its most perverted and corrupt forms. God could redeem the darkness of the city and find salvation even in its most immoral impieties. This did not mean that all would be well—human life was a struggle only redeemed by God's mysterious grace. Davies vision lacked the triumphalism of Stone and the absolute certainty of Anderson. His vision of human life had a tragic aspect that could be redeemed only by God's grace. Nonetheless, Davies loved the privilege of his Protestant elite church and at the same time saw his position as an opportunity to challenge social boundaries of class and race. Progress for him was to serve the poor by bringing them into the church; progress also meant a profound experience of grace and acceptance of one's humanity. In Davies's theological vision the crucified Christ, rather than the incarnate Christ, was always primary. Christ died for the sin of the world. The world was therefore a place of sin and suffering redeemed only by the cross of Christ. He was far from certain that human agency could make a difference in the world or that one could know one was following God's will. Society could be transformed only by the act of God's grace. Davies distrusted the self-righteousness of do-gooders, whether on the right or the left. Nonetheless, Davies did more to start social services to the poor than did Stone, Anderson, or Buchanan. At one angle his model was

Christ transforming the world, and yet it was more fundamentally Christ and culture in paradox. Davies was never quite sure which side God was on; theologically, God was on everyone's side. To say that the church embodied righteousness and that the world was profane therefore struck Davies as wrongheaded. The church could not and should not claim the mantle of God's righteousness. The belief that God would necessarily bless those who followed God's way was thus discarded. God's mercy was for all, no matter what their moral, financial, or social status.

Stone and Anderson were christologically exclusive. Davies was more tolerant and willing to listen. Knitter's model calls this the inclusivist form (Knitter, 1995). Davies once said that Christ is like a light that shines through a "diamond through which colors refract and interact; one sees differences but there is a single light as the source" (Davies Interview, January 18, 1994). All religions reflect a degree of the truth; the Christ of the gospels is at the heart of the universe, the touchstone for all truth. Knitter summarized the inclusivist position this way:

> The theological grounding for the inclusivist model is found in its christology— the way these Christian communities understand Jesus Christ. Some will hold that in view of the New Testament witness, Jesus is constitutive of salvation; that is, God's offer of truth and saving grace has been brought about, or made possible, by the historical life, death, and resurrection of Jesus. Therefore, whatever truth or presence of the Spirit is found in other faiths is in some way "anonymously"— Christian without a name—caused by and directed toward fulfillment in Jesus and his community. (Knitter, 1995:28)

Davies refused to push his faith on anyone. He rebelled against the imperious nature of the Welsh preaching of his childhood. These experiences implanted in him a deep suspicion of absolutist thinking of any kind. It gave him the ability to doubt the righteousness of any cause that claimed moral superiority. This did not, however, keep him from envisioning the gospel as a majestic source of grace that could redeem all who called upon Christ's name.

In John Buchanan the church tapped someone who believes in an activist model of the church—theologically, socially, and administratively. The church is to serve the city and its neighborhood. For Buchanan God created the world and loves the world in all its diversity. God is a pluralist, and God's followers should tolerate difference and love it. Under Buchanan's ministry Fourth Presbyterian created the "Light in the City" mission statement, and Buchanan led a $14 million capital campaign for the expansion of the church and its social outreach ministries. Under his leadership the church has increased its ministries to the poor of the city. In the 1990s the church created the Center for Whole Life that is located in the midst of Cabrini-Green; it also helped build new housing for the poor. Buchanan is a liberal Protestant who believes that God calls a congregation to work on behalf of those who are less fortunate. While Buchanan does not assume that the privilege of class is a sign of God's blessing, he fully believes in the power of human agency to make a difference in the lives of others. Progress for Buchanan is to conceive, create, and implement as many programs of service to others as is possible.

At the core of Fourth Presbyterian is the worship service. It is the pivot around which all the programs of the church gather. It is the sacred hour where the church stops to worship, to listen, to pray, and to be challenged to go out to serve others. The Sunday services embody a traditional, sober, and aesthetically serene style; there are no surprises. In every way it mirrors the forms of middle- and upper-middle-class aesthetic values and profoundly ratifies the class structures of the Gold Coast. The irony of this form of worship and the symbolic world that Buchanan creates is that it does exclude specific groups from the congregation. As was mentioned, the traditional aesthetic forms and the subdued emotional style of the worship are uninteresting to most African Americans. This sober and laconic style appeals to Anglo- and European-Americans and has little attraction for other racial-ethnic groups. Moreover, Fourth Presbyterian's symbolic boundaries that advocate a libertarian moral ethic are repellent to Christian conservatives. African Americans and Korean Americans in particular find this progressive moral perspective unacceptable. Fourth Presbyterian thus engages in exclusivist practices despite its emphasis on inclusion in its symbolic worldview. At the same time, these symbolic boundaries give the church its distinctive identity, theologically and ideologically, without which the church would lose its institutional vitality.

Buchanan is not apologetic about Fourth Presbyterian's style of worship or about his liberal Protestantism. He believes that Christ transforms the world through service to others in need. The church's task is therefore not to Christianize the world or to confront it in its corruption but to be an agent of care to those who are marginalized and left out of the circles of privilege. The church is not more righteous than the world, nor does the church have the absolute truth; the church reminds all of the need to show love on behalf of those who have been left behind. The gospel of Christ, then, is not superior to other religions; it is one religion among many. The Christian faith calls one to serve others and to lead people into a relationship with God. The church therefore maintains a pluralist vision that does not deny the importance and the uniqueness of the Christian tradition; indeed, it recognizes its truth without having to judge other faith traditions as inferior to it. The Confession of 1967, in the *Book of Confessions* for the Presbyterian Church (U.S.A.), approaches the pluralist theme this way:

> The Christian finds parallels between other religions and his own and must approach all religions with openness and respect. Repeatedly God has used the insight of non-Christians to challenge the church to renewal. But the reconciling word of the gospel is God's judgment upon all forms of religion, including the Christian. The gift of God in Christ is for all men. The church, therefore, is commissioned to carry the gospel to all men whatever their religion may be and even when they profess none. (Confession of 1967, 9.42)

The Confession of 1967 is a theocentric rather than christocentric portrayal of the Christian faith. The Christian faith itself, as embodied in the church, is thus under God's judgment. God is transcendent over humanity and all its creations. This allows for a pluralistic perspective on world religions, including Christianity, as approximations of God's work in the world.

Contesting Social and Symbolic Boundaries

The question of how Fourth Presbyterian has contested and resisted boundaries of race and class has been a consistent theme throughout this study. I have argued against any simple understanding of class and race in the light of the complexity of these issues. Social and symbolic boundaries have been employed to understand the power structures negotiated by the church in relation to the culture and social systems of Chicago. I have clarified in the main body of the study that the construction of public housing in Chicago was not a class-caused phenomenon alone. That is, this process of social stratification was not the end product of a zero-sum game in which the actions and beliefs of the Protestant establishment produced public housing. The Protestant elite was one among many agents in the eventual construction of the second ghetto. To be sure, Fourth Presbyterian, particularly in the first half of the twentieth century, symbolically expressed and sanctioned social hierarchy. That is, the pastors of Fourth Presbyterian interpreted the church's economic and social privilege as a God-given blessing, and the church was to be a steward of this wealth. This theological rationalization formalized a position of social dominance. Nonetheless, there were distinctive elements in the ministries of Stone and Anderson that went against class interests and challenged the status quo. Stone confronted his ruling-class Protestants at the heart of their economic security by questioning the reproduction of their wealth in passing on inheritance to their children. Anderson was less apt to challenge privilege, but he did excoriate his congregants for their lack of moral rectitude and for their habits of class complacency. Davies, the most contradictory figure of the four ministers, nurtured class privilege but also used his withering rhetoric of judgment against his Protestant elite congregation for accommodating to segregation and class inequality. Davies brought the poor close to this privileged status group, something no one else had done. None of these actions by the ministers improved their status positions. Indeed, they were at some risk in taking these stands.

A class analysis of Fourth Presbyterian does not capture the complexity of the church's adaptation and response to the changes in American culture or the growth of Chicago's second ghetto. The empirical study of Fourth Presbyterian shows a more nuanced and complex process in the way symbolic systems interact and affect the expression, maintenance, and transgression of social boundaries. That is, symbolic forms express but also transform social structures by competing with institutional logics in parallel social settings. For the Gold Coast, status and economic ambition are powerful logics that impinge on the lives of individuals in the Fourth Presbyterian congregation. They are potent to those who possess them outright but also to those who experience them vicariously through a close proximity to this status and wealth. From the pulpit these logics are recognized and debated in the symbolic messages of the ministers' public rhetoric. That is, an ethic of responsibility that considers the means and ends of action contests a logic of technical rationality by confronting the unintentional consequences of the sole pursuit of status or profit.[2]

Nonetheless, the classic argument between Marx and Weber over the priority of structure and culture, social and symbolic boundaries, is in the end unresolvable. Culture and social structures work in tandem to shape each other. A class analysis that prioritizes structure over culture is not an adequate model to explain symbolic patterns used by Fourth Presbyterian clergy and the church's lay leadership. It overlooks the complexity with which symbolic and social boundaries interact and are in tension with one another. Fourth Presbyterian as a religious institution invites dialogue and conflict between various institutional logics. Its symbolic world does not pursue or promise consensus and certainty, particularly in the ministries of Davies and Buchanan. The ambiguity and confusion of social reality are a part of the rhetorical mix. These multiple logics speak to the disparate kinds of characters in the congregation, including status-minded young executives, activist-oriented lay liberals, pious business-people, upper-middle-class African Americans, profit-centered entrepreneurs, and working-class families. They are invited to clash in the symbolic world created by Buchanan. What brings stability to this blending of pluralistic logics is that the dialogue happens in an orderly matrix of formality that gives the institution its formal coherence. This commingling of traditional ritual life with a progressive public discourse creates a space for negotiating modern life and the norms and narratives of the Christian tradition.

This rhetorical and symbolic mixing of institutional logics has led to less doctrinal strictness, yet the requirements of time, service, and financial resources remain considerable. Furthermore, the cognitive challenges of the church's rhetorical messages may be too challenging for those who seek a plain message of good news. Fourth Presbyterian offers no uncomplicated therapeutic antidote for building self-esteem and ratifying one's internal sense of equilibrium. Instead, Fourth Presbyterian presses listeners to attend to the complexity of the social and political life of the world and to question and think about the relationship between faith and society. This message is followed by many opportunities to serve those less privileged. One must deal with ambiguity and face the problems of racism and inequality, issues that impinge on members of Fourth Presbyterian as they negotiate life in a complex and diverse urban setting.

As a religious institution, Fourth Presbyterian is a conflict-free, nondogmatic, formalistic church that throughout the twentieth century nurtured a tension between accommodation to upper-middle-class social and economic boundaries and a symbolic system that contests status and class. This negotiation has changed over the tenures of the four pastors, and the church has been able to adapt its approach depending on its cultural milieu. These adaptations illustrate the ways that the Protestant mainline has also had to fashion itself in the face of enormous cultural and social challenges. Fourth Presbyterian is an illuminating example precisely because it faced many of the fundamental dilemmas of the century, including dramatic social and cultural change; economic expansion and depression; urban flight and urban renewal; the construction of the new underclass; race riots and the deterioration of specific racial-ethnic groups; the theological controversies in the Protestant mainline churches; and the decline in status and numbers of these same religious institutions.

With the new millennium the Protestant mainline and particularly liberal Protestantism face enormous challenges in creating new religious forms. Fourth Presbyterian presents a dramatic counterexample of Protestant mainline decline. It substantiates the arguments that liberal Protestantism is no equation for failure, that dogmatic strictness is no key to a successful congregation, and that institutional identity creates religious vitality.

THE SHIFTING CENTER OF THE
PROTESTANT MAINLINE

Elements in Fourth Presbyterian's Adaptation

Fourth Presbyterian's ability to adapt to changes in its cultural and social setting has depended on three factors. First, Fourth Presbyterian is located at the
center of a thriving upper-middle-class neighborhood; it has consistently had
a strong pastor and lay leaders who have constructed social and symbolic
boundaries that accommodate and challenge this status group; and it is in close
proximity to a poorer neighborhood, which facilitates social outreach. Second,
the church has a strong institutional identity that nurtures core values and
qualities that are admired and reproduced. Third, the senior ministers have
been forceful as well as expert in negotiating and avoiding conflict.

Fourth Presbyterian from the beginning has been fortunate in its demographic context. The Near North Side expanded economically throughout the
twentieth century. The Gold Coast was the wealthiest area in metropolitan
Chicago in the 1990s. Not only is the area affluent, but it has consistently attracted young professionals and thus has maintained its dynamism in its economic, social, and cultural base. Demographically, Fourth Presbyterian has an
ideal religious market to draw on for its congregation. Moreover, the leaders
have been effective and sophisticated about marketing the church in its cultural milieu. Beginning with Stone, the sanctuary and club rooms were built
to appeal to a specific class and social ethos. People who were already a part
of the establishment and those who wanted to become so came to the church
and were socialized into a sophisticated but comfortable atmosphere. Anderson continued this appeal to the ruling class and created more church buildings to attract and serve the needs of young people. Davies, through his charismatic preaching, captivated his congregation by sermons that were pastoral,
challenging, and entertaining. Davies was a man of cultural sophistication who
drew men and women of social and economic distinction close to him. Davies
made it clear that he admired a Protestant ruling class that was successful,
urbane, modest, and willing to give to the church. Buchanan has continued
this tradition of appealing to high-status individuals. The recent capital campaign that renovated the sanctuary and church buildings had a middle and upper middle class in mind. These church leaders were aware that the aesthetics
and style of the church would continue to appeal to a sophisticated and professional clientele.

The environmental ecology of Fourth Presbyterian is unique not only because of the prosperity of its particular neighborhood but also because of its

close proximity to poorer areas in the city. The opportunity to serve others and to reach across social boundaries is not just an ideal but is close at hand, literally one mile west of the church. This has been an advantage to Fourth Presbyterian, particularly in the last half of the twentieth century when its social service programs to disadvantaged neighborhoods expanded dramatically. Each of the four pastors preached on the importance of service to the poor, in the ideological framework of noblesse oblige. Stone challenged the upper class to fund foreign and home missions and to Christianize the rooming-house district of the Near North Side. Anderson urged the ruling class to set the moral climate and standard for American culture, including those in the working class who needed the direction of their cultural and moral *superiors.* Davies encouraged Protestant leaders to reach beyond social boundaries to serve African Americans and to give them opportunities to develop themselves. Buchanan conceives of social service in less paternalistic terms, although he continues the tradition of challenging the rich to serve those with less. Buchanan understands that lay liberals, who make up the majority of the congregation, need an outlet for their charitable impulses and desire to help others. Each pastor has developed specific strategies to nurture an elite climate and at the same time invite those who are secure to serve others.

The second major factor in Fourth Presbyterian's institutional adaptation has been its strong identity as a church. It has always supported a specific set of core institutional values that have changed little over the years. The first is decorum. The church values sobriety and order in worship. This means a sense of formality, predictability, and rationality in its worship service. Excellence is expected from the professional staff; the church prides itself on the quality of the performance in worship and the efficiency of its programs in education and in service. Under all four ministers the administrative arm of the church has been unwavering in producing excellence. Fourth Presbyterian, while traditional in format, has always emphasized the importance of civic responsibility. For Stone and Anderson it was fighting alcohol, organized crime, and moral corruption. For Davies Fourth Presbyterian became a setting for serving the needy of the Near North Side, whether the emotionally distraught, the morally corrupt, the underprivileged poor, or the marginalized minorities. Buchanan has continued decorum and excellence in worship and social activism among the poor.

Other values prized throughout the twentieth century were tolerance and inclusiveness. Stone was open to revivalism and conservative Christian theological beliefs, but he was able to support people on both sides of the modernist-fundamentalist controversy. Stone was passionate about helping new immigrants establish churches in Chicago. Anderson reached out to Japanese Americans despite pressure against doing so, and he supported progressive and liberal theological leadership even as he saw himself as an evangelical. Davies went against popular opinion in the pews to serve African Americans; he viewed himself as an evangelical with liberal leanings on issues of service to others. Buchanan is the most symbolically challenging in his messages of inclusion and tolerance, even as he preaches against conservative Christianity and its traditional stringent moral message.

The third factor that has facilitated Fourth Presbyterian's stability is the style of leadership of its senior ministers. Stone, Anderson, and Davies were all autocratic leaders who made decisions and then rallied their leadership behind their vision. Several elders during Anderson's and Davies's leadership considered the session meetings times to rubber-stamp the decisions of the pastor. There were few signs of conflict in any of the public records that I came across during the tenures of Stone, Anderson, and Davies. Stone, like Davies, was a charismatic figure. Many spoke of these men as exceptional talents and as dynamic and unique leaders. Stone dominated his environment; no one in his leadership balked at his directives. At the same time, Stone did not invite controversy. In theological and political debates he took a mediating role, supporting people on both sides of the ideological spectrum. He disarmed conflict by befriending the adversaries and making a relationship with Christ the only absolute standard. His personal piety was simple and evangelical, and he refused to be drawn into fights over theological doctrines.

Anderson was a bureaucrat, and he was strong and forceful in the pulpit. He, like Stone, wanted to reconcile differences, and throughout his tenure at Fourth Presbyterian he worked tirelessly for reunion between the northern and southern Presbyterian churches. The only recorded conflicts were ones that Anderson spoke of late in his tenure. He described an upper-class clique that wanted to take over early in his ministry; later on there were conflicts with groups that represented more conservative and more liberal theological perspectives. Anderson found his strength in his elders, who, he said, stood by him like a "wall of fire" during the conflict in which a conservative elder went after Anderson but found himself alone against the rest of the session.

The only report of conflict during Davies's era came in the interviews I had with him and with one of his closest associates on the staff. Davies told me, "I packed my bag after being here for two years, and I always kept my bags packed" (Davies Interview, January 18, 1994). He felt that he was always on the edge of losing his position because of his controversial social programs and sermons. The session minutes from 1963 through 1966, however, recorded that

Davies received standing ovations after each year's annual meeting. Davies liked the role of an outsider, although he was clearly close to several of the most powerful men in his congregation. Davies did not lack political skills and connections. He could be harsh with people who did not believe in the direction of his ministry. He removed several men from the ruling boards, and they never served again. In the early 1970s he suspended a fellowship group that he thought was destructive to the congregation. Davies undermined all adversaries by muzzling them.

Stone, Anderson, and Davies handled conflict with great discretion; conflicts did not become public. This style of leadership foreclosed explicit strife and kept schisms from occurring. Moreover, none of the twentieth-century pastors was a controversialist; each was a mediator to a degree and nondogmatic in his religious beliefs. Buchanan, the most theologically liberal of the four, dealt with dissent in somewhat more democratic ways. Buchanan, through the force of his personality and the use of committees, pushed forward several major changes with little or no public conflict. In both the modification of the worship service and the $14 million capital campaign Buchanan processed every decision through a committee, to gather as much input as possible, and then only with restraint made a decision. Buchanan is a productive leader but has the wisdom of a bureaucrat who brings others along in the process. He does not move faster than his congregation. According to interviews with congregational leaders Buchanan's more democratic style of leadership is highly regarded. Nonetheless, behind the scenes and out of the public eye Buchanan has distanced his critics and moved them out of positions of leadership. Along with Stone, Anderson, and Davies, Buchanan has guarded the public peace of Fourth Presbyterian with vigilance and care.

Resolving conflict before it becomes public is a critical element in Fourth Presbyterian's adaptation to external changes in American culture and in the social setting of the Gold Coast. Because of this lack of discord and the positive and productive programs of worship and outreach, few criticize the church's staff. Less than a handful of congregants in my interviews had any negative comments about the church; most were extremely positive. When I asked congregants about what made them remain at Fourth Presbyterian, they would often say they were "proud of all the things the church was doing for others." That so many feel good about the church's identity enables the church to preserve institutional energy for its social outreach and the effective functioning of the overall church program.

Thus the key elements that have enabled Fourth Presbyterian's adaptation are the leadership's accommodation and outreach in its social setting, a strong institutional identity, and leaders' ability to keep conflict out of the public eye. Moreover, the church has creatively adjusted to two larger changes in American culture. First, the Protestant Puritan moral ethos that was powerful through the early 1960s has dramatically declined in its ability to persuade and affect private and public belief and behavior. Anderson's puritanical and patriarchal perspectives had little or no place in the symbolic world of the 1990s, at least in upper-middle-class American culture. Anderson's ascetic Protestantism was fundamentally displaced by a thoroughly this-worldly religion and popular culture centered on consumption. Second, and this is related to the first, the Protestant establishment that was so powerful in Chicago at the beginning of the century lost much of its cultural and social hegemony. Even as it remains powerful in the realms of finance, the Protestant mainline elite no longer sets the cultural or social agenda.

Some see these changes as signs of secularization. This is true only in the sense that the vocabulary and moral norms of the Protestant mainline are no longer taken for granted in American culture. The cultural space to make decisions about moral norms and religious ideals is more open. This does not mean, however, that the American people are less religious; it only means that they have more options and exercise these options under less constraint from public institutions. The religious market is wide open; there are no longer any natural monopolies. To thrive or even survive, religious institutions must market themselves to the consumer, because Americans have little or no denominational loyalty.

Fourth Presbyterian knows that it is in a competitive market and that it needs to continue to make itself attractive. As we have seen, Stone, Anderson, Davies, and Buchanan created the religious goods that appealed to large numbers of individuals and, at the same time, galvanized them to serve others and to expand their exclusive social boundaries. Fourth Presbyterian has expressed and shaped its social setting through its ability to accommodate and resist the symbolic and social boundaries of its setting. It has contested the status quo by being a pocket of qualified resistance to the Gold Coast's unremitting focus on maximizing profit. Indeed, it is precisely the church's accommodation that has enabled it to keep a voice of opposition alive in the midst of a profit-centered culture and economy.

The New Reality of Protestant Denominations

The kinds of churches that are growing in the United States point to little consensus concerning the American religious market. It has been suggested that few churches in the Protestant mainline understand this and that many are floundering in this competitive environment (Hadaway and Roozen, 1995). The Protestant mainline church is no longer taken for granted in the American cultural mix. Protestant mainline denominations no longer define the kind and quality of religion that is practiced in Protestant churches in the United States. Churches outside the mainline denominations now grab the attention and imagination of the media and the public. Willow Creek Church in South Barrington, Illinois, is just one example of how the new independent mega-churches have garnered the loyalty of many followers who seek something new and appealing in a church (Pritchard, 1995; Hunter, 1996).

The American denominational structures have changed dramatically over the last thirty years. The Protestant mainline is only one thread in a larger American tapestry of denominations. Denominational movement churches of the Pentecostal/Holiness tradition, such as the Assemblies of God and the Church of God, have grown more rapidly in recent decades than their main-line counterparts. Churches in the Pentecostal tradition seek to convert, tend to be otherworldly, and are movementlike in their group orientation. The ten-sion between Christ and culture is highest in these religious groups; Niebuhr's model of Christ against culture describes this type of religion. Conservative churches, including the Southern Baptist Convention, the Lutheran Church, Missouri Synod, and the Christian Reformed Church, have grown as well (Hadaway, 1995:25). They are more institutional and goal-oriented and lack the sectlike traits of the denominational movement churches. There is less tension with culture in these conservative groups, but clearly they are attempting to create independent cultural enclaves where moral plausibility structures form the values and behaviors of the group. Independent churches, such as Willow Creek, are also experiencing tremendous growth. The best estimates indicate they have more than three million members (Hadaway and Roozen, 1995:33).

Donald Miller's book, *Reinventing American Protestantism,* is an in-depth study of these independent churches, or what he calls "new paradigm" or "postdenominational" churches. Miller focuses on three movement churches, Calvary Chapel, Vineyard Christian Fellowship, and Hope Chapel. All origi-nated in California but have rapidly spread across the country and the world. These new paradigm churches have not put forth a strong political agenda. On the basis of his surveys, Miller describes them as conservative politically and morally but quite liberal on civil rights and service to the poor (D. E. Miller, 1997:108). These new paradigm churches fail to fit the typical culture war theory because they are more complex in understanding of culture, morals, and poli-tics. In a sense they are reminiscent of Anderson's ministry at Fourth Presbyterian—that is, Christ and culture in tension—a thoroughgoing conservatism that confronts moral corruption in society but reaches out to those who are left out. Of course, they would have deep differences with Anderson's theology. New paradigm churches are millenarian in their belief in the imminent end of the world and the return of Christ. Again, this does not keep them from active social outreach to the less fortunate (D. E. Miller, 1997:108). The localism of these independent churches is well adapted to an American culture that is mobile and lacks loyalty to traditional denominational ties. In a sense these churches are perfectly pitched to the realities of late twentieth-century American culture. They use the informality and populism of contemporary popular culture to reach out to the baby boomer generation. They are intensely aware of the need for programs for children and youth, and they are adept at using the media and popular music to appeal to a younger generation. Like the liberal churches, new conservative movement churches struggle with the problem of accommodation to culture and the degree of tension with culture that is acceptable to their new constituents.

The decline of Protestant mainline denominations parallels an increase in localism among all American Protestant denominations. Because of this growing localism, the strength of Protestant mainline national governing bodies has diminished. Time will tell, however, how much power local congregations will have in negotiating decisions made at the national level. With the passage of the "fidelity and chastity" amendment in the Presbyterian Church (U.S.A.) in 1997, the standards for ordination in the church have become stricter. Sexual relations outside of heterosexual marriages are stringently forbidden in an explicit way. This new legalism of the Presbyterian Church may move it further in the direction of conservative Protestant denominations.

There is no evidence from experts on church growth or church historians that standards of strictness will lead to church growth; indeed, the opposite is the case (Longfield, 1991; Luidens, 1990). To be sure, strict doctrine and dogmatic principles are not what the baby boomer generation is calling for in the church. Baby boomers are looking for inspiration in worship, a friendly congregational environment, and a church that can help them raise their children. I have used the term *lay liberal* to describe these kinds of individuals, and I have argued that they are a majority of the American population. Wade Clark Roof's *Generation of Seekers* distributes the baby boomer generation along these theological boundaries: "13% fundamentalist-leaning, 21% evangelical moderates, and other 66%. This breakdown is not all that different than for the population in the country as a whole today" (Roof, 1993:99). The question for the Protestant mainline is, what is the appropriate response to this lay liberal generation and to the many unchurched who no longer know any religious tradition whatsoever? How the church adapts to this new cultural terrain is one of the challenges for the new century.

We thus return to the tension between accommodation and resistance to the consumerist and therapeutic trends of the contemporary culture as the central challenge of Protestant mainline churches, a task made more difficult because of the decentered nature of the Protestant mainline and the pace of change in American life. At the same time, it can be argued that because of the embattled condition of the Protestant mainline, it is an opportune moment for it to speak with an authentic voice to the new centers of power in American culture. That is, since the church lacks any real political and cultural force, it can address more fearlessly the drift toward racial and class inequality in society. The question of how to galvanize lay liberals and to be prophetic in the culture is the continuing challenge for American Protestant churches.

The Contemporary Market of the Protestant Mainline: Lay Liberals

Fourth Presbyterian is a church for lay liberals, who find within it the freedom to question, to search, and to come to their own conclusions about the Christian faith. As my study has shown, few are dogmatic about Christian doctrine, and even fewer believe that one has to attend church to be a good Christian. Not many fit in a conservative Protestant frame. They seek a church that is sophisticated and speaks to the ambiguity and diversity of the culture in which they live. They do not want foreclosure on debate over controversial issues, they do not seek clear guidelines on personal morality, and they do not want to be told what to think about religious, political, or cultural issues. They want to be inspired by worship and guided in their thinking on difficult topics relating to Scripture and Christian tradition. Moreover, they want a vehicle for giving and volunteering.

In Roof's study of the baby boomer generation—76 million of them—he found a generation that is suspicious of institutions and committed to the development of their own spirituality: "For many, maybe even the majority of boomers today, personal faith and spirituality seem somehow disconnected from many of the older institutional religious forms" (Roof, 1993:30). More than half chose to be alone when asked whether they preferred to worship with others or meditate alone; less than a third said that they would like to be with others when they worship (Roof, 1993:70). This generation as a whole, even those who are on the conservative side of religious faith, tends toward a more individualistic form of religion: "Nine out of ten say one can be a good Christian without attending church; well over two-thirds say an individual should arrive at his or her own religious beliefs independently of any church or synagogue" (Roof, 1993:159).

This same determination to remain true to one's self spills over into the area of moral choices. It is a generation committed to coming to decisions based on one's own conscience, not on an external authority: "The overwhelming majority of religious boomers—whether theological liberals or theological conservatives—prefer a church that is tolerant and leaning in the open direction rather than overly strict in its attitudes toward people's lifestyles. . . . the fact that almost half of conservative Protestant boomers oppose absolute morality in favor of a more individualistic, conscience-first approach at morality is itself a telling observation" (Roof, 193:185–86).

It is a generation that takes pluralism for granted and is steeped in the values of tolerance. The liberal logic of inclusion constrains judgment and the exclusion of others based on external standards, whether religious or cultural. Roof's book is a meditation on the beliefs and assumptions of lay liberalism and a window into the lives of most who attend the Fourth Presbyterian Church. The challenge of liberal and moderate churches is how to maintain a sense of conviction about belief, when half of all baby boomers believe that all religions are equally true and good (Roof, 1993:72).

According to the analysis of Robert Bellah and his colleagues in *Habits of the Heart* lay liberals are expressive individualists who have brought about a decline of civility and a profound misunderstanding of the common good in American culture (Bellah et al., 1985). From the perspective of C. Kirk Hadaway and David A. Roozen typical baby boomers are sophisticated consumers whose personal needs and desires are subtle and refined. To attract and keep them, the church must come up with programs, buildings, sermons, and music that will draw their attention, sustain their interest, and engage their loyalty. As Hadaway and Roozen comment, this is not an easy task. Typical lay liberals are the most difficult to attract and are the least likely of all types to commit to a congregation. They are suspicious of institutions and most interested in their own spiritual life (Hadaway and Roozen, 1995).

It is in vogue to be suspicious of lay liberals and to blame them for their lack of support of institutions and their apparent betrayal of the common good. But there are other voices that blame the mainline churches or at least hold them partly responsible. Jeffrey H. Boyd in *Reclaiming the Soul* (1996) argues that mainline churches have lost a generation largely because they have not spoken to the spiritual needs of this group. To be sure, researchers on church growth assert that it is not the liberal politics of the church bureaucrats or clergy that have turned many away from churches, as many have suspected. Boyd's point is that Protestant leaders have simply stopped speaking to the complex spiritual needs of laypeople in their congregations. Moreover, Protestant academic theologians tend to analyze power structures and the symbol systems that oppress or segregate various populations. Most Americans are not interested in this analysis. Americans are interested in seeking meaning and value in their lives. What has taken the place of churches and clergy in this discussion is the therapeutic community. Clergy often imitate the language of this group. The success of this strategy is mediocre at best. To be sure, it is an accommodation to the contemporary language and ethos of the culture, and various secularized forms of psychological religion have achieved enormous popularity in American culture. Thomas Moore is the most notable purveyor of this psychological religion. His *Care of the Soul* (1992) and *The Enchantment of Everyday Life* (1996) were national bestsellers. *The Soul's Code* (1996) by James Hillman, Moore's intellectual mentor, was also on the bestseller list. Again, it is a psychological analysis of individuals that uses mythological language to revivify archetypal themes in the lives of individuals. Hillman provides a religious psychology without any reference to a transcendent metaphysic. It is apparent that many Americans are seeking spiritual engagement that is relevant to their lives. They find that the church fails to meet their needs for spiritual content that engages them on a deeper level.

Fourth Presbyterian, as we have seen in this study, attempts to meet the needs of lay liberals while avoiding the literalism of conservatism or the political correctness of liberalism. It delivers messages that deal with the complexity of American society without simplification. Through a myriad of groups it tries to help individuals struggle in their personal lives with questions of faith and how it relates to daily life. It constructs ministries to help the marginalized in society and to empower them to rise above their desperate situations. It does accommodate to the contemporary cultural terrain, yet it remains cognizant of the need to challenge the consumerist trends that are so much a part of contemporary American culture.

Hadaway and Roozen's book *Rerouting the Protestant Mainstream* is an empirically based and insightful book on revitalizing the mainline. Their answer to the plight of liberal churches describes the ministry of Fourth Presbyterian:

> The final group of growing mainstream churches provides greater source of hope for denominations struggling with a loss of identity and decline in members. These are the spiritually oriented mainstream churches. Such churches are

unapologetically liberal and heavily involved in community ministry, with a clear focus on social justice. Yet the social and moral agenda of these churches is anchored in a deep, meaningful worship experience. We believe that churches like this type provide one "answer" to mainstream decline. (Hadaway and Roozen, 1995:81)

Hadaway and Roozen emphasize, as Roof also pointed out, that liberal churches must give people the sense that worship is about experiencing God's presence. Baby boomers are attentive to subjective experiences and are much less invested in organizations or bureaucracies, whose purpose is to maintain the functions of the organization. The authors assert that the loss of the denominational superstructure may provide an opportunity for mainline denominations to grow. For this growth to occur, however, they must become more like religious movements than denominations. Denominations tend to be judged by how they perform for the consumer. Religious movements create their own momentum and thus a sense of urgency and loyalty in followers. This transition from a denomination to a movement cracks the core of any entrenched bureaucracy and opens organizations to a more entrepreneurial spirit. This is not an easy task. Denominations tend to nurture their bureaucracy and alienate those willing to risk new ventures. The challenge of the mainline is to nurture within its structures individuals alive in the faith, passionate about ministries of justice and inclusion. To do so, it must have leaders who have the wisdom to recognize the need to accommodate and the courage to resist when the social boundaries of the culture drift toward inequality and injustice.

At the end of Don Miller's book on new paradigm churches he reflects on what mainline churches can learn from this powerful new phenomenon in American religious culture. He paints a picture of his own liberal Protestant Episcopal Church in California, All Saints, as a growing mainline church. In certain ways it is similar to Fourth Presbyterian. All Saints has developed a powerful yet traditional worship service and a prophetic ministry of social justice and activism in its social setting. The congregants tend to be well educated and upper middle class, not very different from those at Fourth Presbyterian. Miller sees hope for the mainline in these kinds of churches, yet he also strikes a cautionary note. These liberal Protestant churches are not very effective at bringing young people up in the church. There is a noticeable absence of high-school-age young people at All Saints and Fourth Presbyterian, although in 1997 Fourth Presbyterian did call an associate pastor for youth and young adults.

Miller stresses two major areas that the Protestant mainline needs to address. First, as has been alluded to earlier, they must give more leadership to the laity and support leadership as it rises within the church. The bureaucratic steps for clergy preparation in the Protestant mainline do not nurture the most creative leadership for the church. The process has failed to produce innovative leaders in the church (D. E. Miller, 1997:188).

Second, the liberal Protestant mainline must move in a new direction in making room for experiencing the sacred. It is clear in research cited above that spiritual experience is critical in the lives of baby boomers and the following generation. There is a deep distrust of bureaucratic systems and authority figures. Nonetheless, there is a longing for what Miller refers to as the "primal" experience of the sacred in everyday life. That the church should nurture the experience of the sacred is stunningly obvious to outsiders but often simply forgotten by those in the ecclesiastical systems. Congregants come to encounter the sacred, not simply to go through the motions. Signs of change through creative liturgical worship and practice are beginning to bubble up in the return to contemplative spiritual practices (Miller 1997:189; Bass, 1997). There is a movement within the liberal Protestant mainline to rediscover the dynamics of sacred experience and religious practice.

Miller suggests that Protestant seminaries need to become decentralized and attached to churches, where theological education is grounded in the life and experience of laypeople. This turn toward church-affiliated seminary education is mirrored in John Buchanan's interest in hiring a theologian-in-residence at Fourth Presbyterian. Buchanan has spoken of creating theological classes and seminary student residences on Fourth Presbyterian's campus. The Academy for Faith and Life at Fourth Presbyterian, opened in 1998, is the first step in these new initiatives in theological education. All of this is in its initial stages but reflects important new enterprises in the adaptation of the Protestant mainline to American religious life.

The liberal Protestant mainline has been jolted into these new initiatives by the dramatic changes in its own status in the American religious market. It has had no choice but to adapt to the new reality of its cultural terrain. As has been noted, many bemoan the Protestant mainline church's decline, but the establishment has been dislodged and decentered throughout the history of American religious life. Fourth Presbyterian has been a model of adaptation through which we have witnessed the manifold possibilities for creative adjustment to the future. The continuing tension of accommodation to contemporary life and resistance to inequality is the story and task of the Protestant mainline at the turn of the century.

CONCLUSION: THE FUTURE CHALLENGE OF THE
PROTESTANT MAINLINE

The challenge of the Protestant mainline in the twenty-first century is to proclaim a gospel that is full of conviction but radically open and inclusive. American culture is too complex and dangerous to deny difference and foreclose debate and dialogue. Other religions and faiths exist and are as numerous as ethnic groups and peoples. The call of the liberal Protestant mainline is to recognize that it is possible to believe in the truth of one's Christian faith without denying the authenticity of another's perspective and belief system. The vision of the church should be not to make all people the same but to believe in a gospel that is good news, liberating one to love and accept others but also calling individuals to lives of justice and reconciliation. Hadaway and Roozen call churches to a vision that is "spiritually alive, radically inclusive and justice-oriented" (Hadaway and Roozen, 1995:89). This is the challenge of the church in the twenty-first century: to understand the depth of people's needs, the desire for spiritual experience, the complexity of our cultural and religious diversity, and the ambiguity of the global ethical situation and, in the midst of this, to speak words that accommodate and resist our cultural setting. This is the tension between Christ and culture that has been examined in this study. There is no equation whereby the tension can be fixed. It is a moving target that must be continually negotiated in the ever-changing place of the church in society.

Fourth Presbyterian is a Protestant mainline church that has served as a lens through which we have witnessed the adaptation of the Protestant mainline to the multiple changes in American culture and religion. It is illuminating in that it responded to many of the most demanding problems in the twentieth century. It negotiated the tension between Christ and culture, seeking to be faithful along this axis. At times, as has been shown, it failed to address and resist the powers of inequality and racial segregation. At other times, it stood against injustice and worked for reconciliation along lines of class and race. In its contemporary incarnation it models a form of lay liberalism that speaks to a new generation and keeps alive the prophetic voice of the Christian tradition. I have argued that Fourth Presbyterian has been faithful to its calling to proclaim the gospel and serve the poor. It has done this by pursuing a course that both confirms and contests the status quo. As St. Paul said, "I have become all things to all people, that I might by all means save some." The peril and possibility of accommodation and resistance is the precipice that the Protestant mainline must continue to negotiate. It is the space where the church continues to mediate the gospel to the culture in conversation and critique.

NOTES

1. Warner's later comments on American religion were less critical of liberal Protestantism. He asserted that any religious organization, no matter what its ideological spectrum, that is able to achieve some congruence between what is said in the pulpit and what is heard in the pews has the potential for organizational vitality (Warner, 1993:1063–64).

2. Rational choice theory, which shares certain assumptions about human behavior with Marxist and structuralist thinking, asserts that all human behavior is motivated by economic maximization and that even ethical decisions are basically ways of building capital and staking out status positions. Amartya K. Sen's "Rational Fools: A Critique of the Behavioral Foundations of Economic Theory" (1990) is a widely cited critique of this theoretical perspective.

APPENDIX A:
SURVEY RESULTS

There are 317 cases for all frequency counts, unless otherwise indicated. The number of cases used to compute any mean or standard deviations is located next to the standard deviation ("Std Dev") calculation in the *N* column.

A. CHURCH AND RELIGIOUS LIFE

A1. About how often do you attend worship at Fourth Church?

	Frequency	Percent
Not at all	25	7.9
About once or twice a year	42	13.2
About once or twice every three months	51	16.1
About once a month	49	15.5
About two or three times a month	95	30.0
Four times a month or more	52	16.4
No response	3	0.9

A2. How long have you been a member at Fourth Church?

	Frequency	Percent
Less than a year	30	9.5
One to five years	101	31.9
Six to ten years	84	26.5
Eleven to fifteen years	32	10.1

A2. continued

Sixteen to twenty years	21	6.6
More than twenty years	48	15.1
No response	1	0.9

A3. In how many Fourth Church organizations, committees, and groups do you hold membership, besides congregational membership?

	Frequency	Percent
None	199	62.8
One	50	15.8
Two	38	12.0
Three	20	6.3
Four or more	9	2.8
No response	1	0.3

A4. Has your involvement in Fourth Church increased, remained the same, or decreased in the last three years?

	Frequency	Percent
Increased	75	23.7
Remained the same	143	45.1
Decreased	89	28.1
No response	10	3.2

A5. If your participation has increased, which one of the following is the most important reason for your greater involvement?

	Frequency	Percent
More time available	14	18.7
Due to children	5	6.7
Accepted office/responsibility in the church	26	34.7
More positive attitude toward the church	8	10.7
Moved closer to church	6	8.0
Stronger faith	15	20.0
No response	1	1.2
	75	100.0

A6. If your participation has decreased, which one of the following is the most important reason for this decrease in involvement?

	Frequency	Percent
Less time available	35	39.3
Children are less involved	1	1.1
Given up office/responsibility in the church	7	7.9
More negative attitude toward the church	10	11.2
Moved away from church	31	34.8
Decreased faith	1	1.2
No response	4	4.5
	89	100.0

A7. How would you describe Fourth Church theologically? (Scale: 1 = "Very" to 4 = "Not Very")

	Mean	Standard Deviation	Number
Liberal	2.15	.72	288
Conservative	2.83	.83	256
Evangelical	2.92	.95	251
Fundamentalist	3.57	.74	238

A8. If Fourth Church did not exist, what kind of church would you attend instead?

	Frequency	Percent
More liberal	97	30.6
More conservative	92	29.0
No response	128	40.4
More evangelical	72	22.7
Less evangelical	97	30.6
No response	148	46.7
Similar	277	87.4
Dissimilar	12	3.8
No response	28	8.8
Less demanding	79	24.9
More demanding	71	22.4
No response	167	52.7
Larger	27	8.5
Smaller	177	55.8
No response	113	35.6
More formal	60	18.9
Less formal	123	38.8
No response	134	42.3

A9. Have you made a financial pledge to Fourth Church within the last year?

	Frequency	Percent
Yes	230	72.6
No	81	25.6
No response	6	1.9

A10. Approximately how much does your family household contribute to Fourth Church per year? (If single or widowed, you as an individual)

	Frequency	Percent
Under $99	41	12.9
$100 to $249	54	17.0
$250 to $499	56	17.7
$500 to $749	33	10.4
$750 to $999	19	6.0
$1,000 to $1,499	44	13.9
$1,500 to $2,499	23	7.3
$2,500 to $4,999	24	7.6
$5,000 and up	10	3.2
No response	13	4.1

A11. Where do you rate Fourth Church as a priority compared with other charitable and social institutional involvements in your life? (Scale: 1 = "Highest" to 4 = "Lowest")

	Mean	Standard Deviation	Number
Time	1.88	.96	300
Money	2.31	1.05	297

A12. What was there about Fourth Church that led to your initial and further involvement? (Scale: 1 = "Most Important," 2 = "Second Most Important," 3 = "Third Most Important")

	First Choice	Second Choice	Third Choice
Initial Involvement			
Location	74	76	55
Style of worship	53	78	50
Business opportunities	0	1	4
Architecture	3	11	13
Friendship	4	18	25
Mission/outreach programs	9	17	26

A12. continued

Bible study	0	2	5
Fellowship group	12	12	10
Preaching	101	54	33
Music	4	31	33
Meeting a partner or spouse	8	8	10
No response	49	9	53
Further Involvement			
Location	33	35	36
Style of worship	18	37	22
Business opportunities	2	2	5
Architecture	0	3	7
Friendship	17	46	33
Mission/outreach programs	27	41	33
Bible study	5	7	6
Fellowship group	15	17	12
Preaching	94	44	25
Music	12	23	29
Meeting a partner or spouse	4	5	12
No response	90	57	98

A13. How would you rate Fourth Church on these categories? (Scale: 1 = "Very" to 4 = "Not Very")

	Mean	Standard Deviation	Number
Inviting	1.74	.79	304
Formal	1.84	.68	304
Status conscious	2.40	.88	296
Impersonal	2.94	.91	293
Outreach oriented	1.50	.75	301
Ritualistic	2.44	.80	291
Place to meet friends	2.35	.92	296
Demanding of resources	2.87	.81	286
Demanding of time	2.94	.85	284

A14. Do you feel you "belong" at Fourth Church? (Scale: 1 = "Strongly" to 4 = "Not at All")

	Mean	Standard Deviation	Number
Response	1.94	.82	311

A15. Have you found a job as a result of being involved in Fourth Church?

	Frequency	Percent
Yes	9	2.8
No	303	95.6
No response	5	1.6

A16. Have you found a partner as a result of being involved in Fourth Church?

	Frequency	Percent
Yes	22	6.9
No	289	91.2
No response	6	1.9

A17. Has Fourth Church changed the way you thought about these areas of your life? (Scale: 1 = "Profoundly," 2 = "Some," 3 = "Little," 4 = "Not at All")

	Mean	Standard Deviation	Number
Self	2.10	.74	302
Work	2.71	.91	300
Relationships	2.31	.84	300
Spiritual life	1.97	.84	310
Family life	2.57	.86	297
Social/political life	2.44	.80	291

A18. Are you currently involved in any charity or social activities, such as helping the poor, the sick, or the elderly?

	Frequency	Percent
Yes	165	52.1
No	144	45.4
No response	8	2.5

A19. If yes, do you participate in these charitable and social activities through the programs of Fourth Church?

	Frequency	Percent
Yes	67	21.1
No	133	42.0
No response	117	36.9

A20. How important is it for you to integrate your personal faith and professional life? (Scale: 1 = "Critically Important," 2 = "Very Important," 3 = "Somewhat Important," 4 = "Not Very Important")

	Mean	Standard Deviation	Number
Response	2.57	1.00	301

A21. What has been the history of your involvement in general?

	Frequency	Percent
From childhood I have consistently been involved in the church	175	55.2
As a young adult I left the church and I only returned as an adult	108	34.1
I was not involved in the church as a child; I only became involved as an adult	24	7.6
No response	10	3.2

A22. At what age did these events (if they occurred at all) happen to you?

	Mean	Standard Deviation	Number
Lost faith in God	18.7	8.15	31
Left the church	19.2	5.83	108
Had first religious experience	11.8	8.46	123
Became active in church again	30.2	8.25	144
Changed denominations	30.5	11.31	149

A23. During your high school or college years were you ever active in Youth for Christ, Campus Crusade for Christ, Inter-Varsity Christian Fellowship, or a similar Christian student group?

	Frequency	Percent
Yes	95	30.0
No	208	65.6
No response	14	4.4

A24. When you were in high school how did you identify yourself?

	Frequency	Percent
Presbyterian or other mainline Protestant denomination	248	78.2
Roman Catholic	17	5.4
Evangelical	23	7.3
Fundamentalist	4	1.3
Nonreligious	12	3.8
Don't know	5	1.6
No response	8	2.5

A25. How often do you pray?

	Frequency	Percent
Daily	154	48.6
Two or three times a week	61	19.2
Once a week	37	11.7
Infrequently	53	16.7
Never	4	1.3
No response	8	2.5

B. PERSONAL RELIGIOUS BELIEFS

The possible responses to these statements are: 1 = "Strongly Agree," 2 = "Agree," 3 = "Undecided," 4 = "Disagree," and 5 = "Strongly Disagree."

	Mean	Standard Deviation	Number
B1. The only true faith is in Jesus Christ	2.78	1.40	303
B2. Jesus Christ is Savior of the world	2.04	1.09	300
B3. Only followers of Jesus Christ and members of his church can be saved	3.79	1.24	303
B4. Jesus Christ was a religious leader and teacher like Mohammed or Buddha	2.78	1.38	300
B5. The primary purpose of the human being in this life is preparation for the next life	3.44	1.18	300
B6. Humans should live with the assumption that there is no life after death	4.17	1.05	298

	Mean	Std. Dev.	Number
B7. I believe in divine judgment after death where some shall be rewarded and others punished	2.97	1.25	301
B8. The Bible is the inspired word of God	1.84	0.90	301
B9. The Bible is the actual word of God and to be taken literally	3.95	1.15	303
B10. All great religions of the world are equally true and good	3.05	1.20	302
B11. All people are born into original sin	3.12	1.32	303

C. Personal Worldview

The possible responses to these statements are: 1 = "Strongly Agree," 2 = "Agree," 3 = "Undecided," 4 = "Disagree," and 5 = "Strongly Disagree."

	Mean	Standard Deviation	Number
C1. People generally bring suffering upon themselves	3.30	1.11	303
C2. To be a good Christian it is necessary to attend church	3.50	1.17	307
C3. To be a good Christian it is necessary to care for the poor	2.60	1.14	308
C4. Independent persons should seek out religious truth independent of any church's doctrines	2.33	1.01	305
C5. When making value judgments, the final authority is a person's conscience	2.59	1.26	304
C6. A person needs to take care of oneself before they can help others	2.43	1.11	305
C7. To succeed at my profession is one of my most important values	2.55	1.08	300
C8. My faith is a private matter	2.49	1.16	303
C9. It is important to me to be able to do what I want in my life	2.23	0.96	305
C10. To help a person in need is one of my most important values	1.97	0.75	306
C11. When you help someone in need, you get as much from it as they do	1.76	0.82	308
C12. An essential part of my Christian faith is to sacrifice myself for the sake of others	3.05	1.02	294

D. Social and Political Life

The possible responses to these statements are: 1 = "Strongly Agree," 2 = "Agree," 3 = "Undecided," 4 = "Disagree," and 5 = "Strongly Disagree."

	Mean	Standard Deviation	Number
D1. The use of marijuana should be made legal	3.54	1.19	307
D2. Abortion should be legal for any woman who wants one	2.01	1.21	309
D3. In general, premarital sexual relations between persons committed to each other are morally appropriate	2.51	1.16	307
D4. We are spending too little money on welfare programs in this country	3.67	1.10	305
D5. Men and women are equal; there should be no role differentiation related to gender	2.09	1.18	304
D6. Although African-Americans may have achieved legal equality, I believe affirmative action should be used to help them achieve actual equality	2.91	1.22	305
D7. Gays and lesbians should be integrated into all areas of the military, with no reference to their sexual preference	2.69	1.38	304
D8. A man or woman who admits that he or she is a homosexual should be allowed to be ordained as a Presbyterian minister	2.56	1.36	301
D9. Because of the violence in America, Christians should support greater gun control	1.99	1.27	304
D10. Congress should pass an amendment to the U.S. Constitution that would allow prayer in the public schools	2.93	1.31	303
D11. In a country based on religious freedom such as ours, it is inappropriate for Christians to try to impose their beliefs and values on others	2.56	2.13	302

D12. Land-based casino gambling in Chicago would be an effective economic strategy for the city	3.72	1.19	305
D13. The death penalty is an appropriate punishment for a murderer	2.43	1.21	304

E. PERSONAL AND CULTURAL BACKGROUND

E1. Gender

	Frequency	Percent
Male	114	36.0
Female	196	61.8
No response	7	2.2

E2. Race

	Frequency	Percent
White	302	95.3
Other	7	2.2
No response	8	2.5

E3. Age

	Frequency	Percent
Twenty to twenty-nine	44	13.9
Thirty to thirty-nine	80	25.2
Forty to forty-nine	65	20.5
Fifty to fifty-nine	46	14.5
Sixty to sixty-nine	39	12.2
Seventy to seventy-nine	18	5.7
Eighty and over	17	5.4
No response	8	2.5

E4. Marital status

	Frequency	Percent
Single	119	37.5
Separated or divorced	26	8.2
Widowed	22	6.9
Married	144	45.4
No response	6	1.9

E5. If married, is your spouse a member of Fourth Church?

	Frequency	Percent
Yes	77	24.3
No	79	24.6
No response	161	50.8

E6. If no, is your spouse a member of another church?

	Frequency	Percent
Yes	28	8.8
No	57	18.0
No response	232	73.2

E7. If married, is your spouse employed?

	Frequency	Percent
Retired	14	4.4
Full-time homemaker	18	5.7
Employed part-time	21	6.6
Employed full-time	100	31.5
No response	164	51.7

E8. Do you have children?

	Frequency	Percent
Yes	128	40.4
No	171	53.9
No response	18	5.7

E9. What is your highest level of formal education?

	Frequency	Percent
Less than high school	0	0.0
Some high school	0	0.0
High school graduate	3	0.9
Trade or vocational school	0	0.0
Some college	31	9.8
College degree	85	26.8
Postgraduate work	46	14.5
Graduate or professional degree	147	46.4
No response	5	1.6

E10. Are you

	Frequency	Percent
Retired	49	15.5
Full-time homemaker	20	6.3
Employed part-time	33	10.4
Employed full-time	202	63.7
No response	13	4.1

E11. If employed, what is the nature of your work?

	Frequency	Percent
Secretarial	13	4.1
Administrator	15	4.7
Transportation	1	0.3
Education	15	4.7
Health care	29	9.1
Publishing	4	1.3
Advertising/marketing	26	8.2
Banking/finance	25	7.9
Social work	1	0.3
Accounting	4	1.3
Government	4	1.3
Retail	3	0.9
Sales	17	5.4
Law	23	7.3
Laborer	1	0.3
Automotive	1	1.3
Manufacturing	4	1.3
Medicine	9	2.8
Other	50	15.8
No response	72	22.7

E12. What is your family income range?

	Frequency	Percent
Under $14,999	17	5.4
$15,000 to $24,999	22	6.9
$25,000 to $49,999	71	22.4
$50,000 to $74,999	45	14.2
$75,000 to $99,999	36	11.4
$100,000 to $149,999	46	14.5
$150,000 to $199,999	7	6.9

E12. continued

$200,000 to $299,999	12	3.8
$300,000 to $499,999	9	2.8
$500,000 and up	8	2.5
No response	44	9.1

E13. How long does it take for you to get to Fourth Church from your residence?

	Frequency	Percent
Less than five minutes	30	9.5
Six to ten minutes	56	17.7
Eleven to fifteen minutes	62	19.6
Sixteen to twenty minutes	43	13.6
Twenty-one to thirty minutes	45	14.2
Thirty-one to sixty minutes	47	14.8
More than sixty minutes	26	8.2
No response	8	2.5

E14. By what method do you usually come to Fourth Church on Sunday?

	Frequency	Percent
Taxi	19	6.0
Car	35	11.0
Bus	16	5.0
Walk	140	44.2
Train	90	28.4
No response	17	5.4

E15. How many times have you changed residences in the last five years?

	Frequency	Percent
None	115	36.3
Once	94	29.7
Twice	54	17.0
Three or more	49	15.5
No response	5	1.6

E16. How many job changes have you had since college?

	Frequency	Percent
None	34	10.7
Once	36	11.4
Twice	50	15.8
Three or more	186	58.7
No response	11	3.5

E17. How far do you live from your high school home?

	Frequency	Percent
Under twenty miles	43	13.6
Twenty to one hundred miles	63	19.9
Over one hundred miles	204	64.4
No response	7	2.2

APPENDIX B:
A SHORT HISTORY OF AMERICAN
PRESBYTERIANISM

American Presbyterians have their roots in the Reformed Protestant tradition of six-teenth-century Europe.[1] For Presbyterians the key figure is John Calvin. His *Institutes of the Christian Religion* (1559) is a cornerstone of Reformed faith and life. John Knox, the Scottish divine of the sixteenth century, contributed to Presbyterianism by estab-lishing a Presbyterian polity distinct from the English episcopacy. Another building block of the tradition is English Presbyterianism. The British Parliament called the Westminster Assembly of Divines together in 1643. The Westminster Confession of Faith, Shorter and Larger Catechism emerged from this assembly (Balmer and Fitzmier, 1993; Leith, 1977). From this rich theological background unique tenants of Reformed belief and doctrine have guided Presbyterianism throughout the centuries.

The first and most important is the sovereignty of God. God is independent, omni-scient, omnipotent, and sovereign over all things. Implied in the focus on the doctrine of God is a reflexive understanding of the self in relation to the Creator. That is, knowl-edge of God implies a growing knowledge of one's limitations and need for salvation through the work of Jesus Christ on the cross. In the generations following Calvin Reformed theologians interpreted the doctrine of God's sovereignty along two distinct lines. One held that God foreordained salvation, which led to the belief in a predesti-nation of some to hell and others to heaven. The second, a subgroup within Reformed thought known as Covenant theology, accepted God's judgment of humanity but also emphasized God's initiative in salvation, which allowed God's sovereignty to work subjectively in the lives of individuals, leading them to redemption in Jesus Christ. This covenant theme took on greater social and political meaning in the early American Puritan "Bible Commonwealths," which were organized around the covenant principle and a reciprocal and accountable relationship in human communities (Balmer and Fitzmier, 1993:13–14). This tension between the independence and sovereignty of God and the agency of humanity would be negotiated throughout the history of American Presbyterianism. For some the cooperation of humanity became critical in the work of salvation, whereas for more traditional Calvinists the divine sovereignty would remain dominant in the fate of individual souls.

The Scottish, Scots-Irish, and English Presbyterians came to the New World and established the first Presbyterian stronghold in the middle colonies, focusing especially in Pennsylvania and New Jersey. Francis Makemie, the "father of American Presbyterianism," helped establish churches in Newark and Elizabeth, New Jersey, and in Philadelphia, Pennsylvania, in the second half of the seventeenth century. In 1706 Makemie created the first presbytery, called the General Presbytery. The Scots-Irish of the middle colonies and the Presbyterians from England and New England developed tensions early in the eighteenth century. The Scots-Irish remained loyal to a strict creedal understanding of the Westminster Confession, while the New England Presbyterians emphasized the importance of religious piety and the centrality of the Bible. The reliance on doctrinal precisionism would lead, or so the New Englanders thought, to a rationalistic faith rather than a warmhearted piety.

In the midst of the Great Awakening the two sides reached a compromise with the Adopting Act of 1729. The act distinguished between the essential and nonessential standards of the Westminster Confession. Candidates for ordination could present reservations about particular articles of the Westminster Confession to the presbytery, the governing body composed equally of clergy and elders. This body would then judge whether the question could be mitigated by the broader theological scope of the Reformed confessional tradition. This debate foreshadowed the pattern of conflict over Presbyterian doctrines in the eighteenth and nineteenth centuries.

A schism occurred between what were called the New Light and Old Light Presbyterians in the 1740s. The New Lights represented Presbyterians who supported the evangelical forms and style of revivalism sweeping the countryside. Led by Gilbert Tennent, New Light Presbyterians advocated for the importance of a experiential piety and a felt call to ministry. The New Light leadership was forced from the Presbyterian Church by the Synod of Philadelphia in June 1741. The New Light Presbyterians began to form their own training schools and send missionaries to the American frontier. The New Light/Old Light designation in the decades that followed came to be called the Old School and New School. The Old School Presbyterians represented traditional Presbyterians who sought full subscription to the standards of the Westminster Confession. The New School movement emphasized the experiential piety of the individual. The New School reached its peak with the election of Jonathan Edwards, a New School minister, to the presidency of the College of New Jersey in 1758. The school would later become Princeton University. Within just weeks of his arrival, Edwards fell ill and died. In subsequent months the New Side and Old Side Presbyterians reunited (Balmer and Fitzmier, 1993:25–34). John Witherspoon, a moderating force in the tension between the factions, became president of the College of New Jersey in 1766. Witherspoon brought a period of stability and peace to the Presbyterians, but he also actively advocated for American independence and eventually became the only clergyman to sign the Declaration of Independence.

In May 1789 the Presbyterian Church in the United States of America held its first General Assembly. It was composed of four synods (New York and New Jersey; Philadelphia; Virginia; and the Carolinas), made up of 16 presbyteries, 177 ministers, 111 probationers, and 419 congregations. The date was remarkable in part because during this same week the first Congress of the United States commenced its work in New York City. Some have suggested that the Presbyterian Church gave to the United States its early model of representative government. Critics of this thesis, however, have found little evidence for it and assert that Presbyterians and colonial political leaders were equally aware and influenced by Enlightenment political ideas in Revolutionary America (Balmer and Fitzmier, 1993:39).

Early in the nineteenth century fewer graduates of the College of New Jersey went on to the ministry. In response a new school for theological training was opened in 1811 called Princeton Theological Seminary. Under the powerful leadership of Archibald Alexander and Charles Hodge, Princeton shifted its loyalty from the New School and became the leader of orthodox Calvinism and Old School Presbyterianism (Balmer and Fitzmier, 1993:51–52). Hodge and his followers became a force in American Presbyterianism in the nineteenth century.

What in 1800 was a single Presbyterian Church had splintered into half a dozen different Presbyterian denominations by the end of the nineteenth century. The broad tensions between the New School and the Old School continued to plague the Presbyterian Church. Added to this tension were various ethnic and regional differences that included a growing division over slavery and the place of African Americans in American culture. As the Union fractured, so too did Presbyterians. There is, however, no easy distinction between the Old School and New School Presbyterians on the issue of slavery; the Old and New School had representatives in the North and the South. In point of fact, the Old School and the New School found their greatest strengths in the mid-Atlantic states. For the Old School it was New Jersey and eastern Pennsylvania; for the New School it was New York. In 1861 the Presbyterian Church in the United States of America (an Old School General Assembly) passed the Gardner Spring Resolution affirming the support of the Union. This passed over the protest of Charles Hodge, who deemed it an unfortunate entry of the church into matters of state. In response the Presbyterian Church in the Confederate States of America was formed by Southern Old School Presbyterians. New School Southern Presbyterians formed the United Synod of the South. Both Southern Presbyterian churches supported the Southern cause. In 1864, as the Civil War drew to a close, the Presbyterian Church in the Confederate States of America merged with the United Synod of the South to form the Presbyterian Church in the United States. This Southern Presbyterian body remained intact for more than a century (Balmer and Fitzmier, 1993:61–82).

Northern Presbyterians were active in developing strategies to include northern blacks as a part of the denomination, particularly during the antebellum period. However, following emancipation, these efforts ceased to a large extent. Black congregations in general sought independence for themselves, in preference to a Presbyterian denomination that was largely white and segregationist. Southern Presbyterians, like Methodists and Baptists in the South, developed ecclesiastical segregation. Blacks congregations and their ministers were not given equal status and thus soon joined northern blacks in seeking independent churches and denominations (Balmer and Fitzmier, 1993:74).

The battle over modernism was exacerbated by the publication of Charles Darwin's *Origin of Species* in 1859 and the growing use of the historical/critical methodology in interpreting the Scripture. Charles Hodge argued against Darwinism in his *What is Darwinism* (1874). Not all Presbyterians agreed with Hodge. Charles Briggs of Union Theological Seminary in New York rejected the idea that the Holy Spirit inspired every of word of Scripture and asserted that the Bible contained error that could not be readily explained (Balmer and Fitzmier, 1993:57). He was brought to ecclesiastical trial and found guilty, which led to the suspension of his ordination in 1893. In response to these proceedings in 1892 the General Assembly of the Presbyterian Church U.S.A. declared that the original manuscripts of the Bible were "without error." The reaction to modernism continued in 1910 with the adoption of the "five points" of fundamentalism. These doctrines included the inerrancy of the Bible; the virgin birth of Christ; substitutional atonement; Christ's bodily resurrection; and the authenticity of miracles. On May 21, 1922, Harry Emerson Fosdick preached a sermon entitled "Shall the Fundamentalists Win?" at the First Presbyterian Church of New York City. This sermon argued that liberalism was a legitimate form of Christianity and that fundamentalists "are giving us one of the worst exhibitions of bitter intolerance that the churches of this country have ever seen" (quoted in Balmer and Fitzmier, 1993:87).

J. Gresham Machen of Princeton Theological Seminary led the conservatives' counterattack, claiming that liberal Christianity was not a form of the authentic faith but a new religion. Moderates in the denomination gathered and signed the Auburn Affirmation in 1924, which affirmed the "five points" but allowed for alternative formulas for explaining these doctrines and called for toleration in the denomination. Machen's contentions were repudiated during the next several general assemblies. Southern Presbyterians were less affected by the controversy since liberal opinions on Scripture and doctrines were rare in their ranks (Balmer and Fitzmier, 1993; Loetscher, 1954; Longfield, 1991).

The official debate between modernists and fundamentalists was temporarily put aside in the northern Presbyterian Church in the late 1920s. The ramifications of the conflict, however, would continue to have enormous effects on the northern and southern Presbyterian churches throughout the century. In 1930 a commission to study mission in the Protestant church, led by William Ernest Hocking, a professor at Harvard University, issued a one-volume summary of its work called *Re-Thinking Missions*

(1932). The project was funded by John D. Rockefeller Jr., the benefactor behind Fosdick's Riverside Church in New York City. The report, which criticized missionaries for their "rigidity," urged greater sensitivity to the integrity of other religions and called for a more stringent standard in selecting missionary candidates. The report's effect was mixed: it solidified the conservative rejection of modernism but, over the next half century, became the basis for much of the contemporary mission work in the Presbyterian churches in the North and South (Balmer and Fitzmier, 1993:94).

At midcentury the Presbyterian churches were the fourth largest Protestant family in the nation. In 1958, the Presbyterian Church U.S.A. merged with the United Presbyterian Church of North America (the denomination formed from two Scottish-American bodies, the Associate Reformed Church and the Associate Presbyterian Church) to form the United Presbyterian Church in the United States of America. At its height in 1965 the church's membership reached more than 4.0 million. Only ten years later the denomination had lost a million members, nearly a quarter of its membership, and by the mid-1990s, the percentage hovered around a 30 percent membership loss, with a total membership of 2.7 million. The war in Vietnam and the battle for civil rights deeply divided the Presbyterian Church. Many in the leadership, particularly in the 1960s, were deeply involved in the antiwar protest and even more so in the civil rights movement. This reached a peak in 1971, as the Council on Church and Race of the United Presbyterian Church U.S.A. gave $10,000 to the defense fund of Angela Davis. Davis, a philosophy professor at the University of California, Los Angeles, was a member of the Black Panthers and a self-avowed Communist. Individuals and churches throughout the denomination raised enormous objections to this move, underlining the distance between the liberal leadership of the church's governmental bodies and the conservative lay people in the pews. In response a group of twenty African American Presbyterians sent a matching gift to the United Presbyterian Church U.S.A. as a show of support for Davis (Balmer and Fitzmier, 1993:107–8).

Parallel with this movement toward social activism was an ecumenical emphasis, led by Eugene Carson Blake, stated clerk of the United Presbyterian Church U.S.A. In 1961 Presbyterians along with other mainline denominations—the Episcopal Church, the Methodist Church, and the United Church of Christ—joined in the formation of the Consultation on Church Union. Blake asserted the need to form a union of churches that was both "truly Catholic" and "truly reformed" (quoted in Balmer and Fitzmier, 1993:103). This ecumenical spirit of inclusion was concurrent with the acceptance of women as leaders in Presbyterian churches. In the northern Presbyterian Church, women were able to be ordained as elders on the session of local churches in 1921. The ordination of women to the office of minister of word and sacrament, however, came only in 1957 in the North and in 1964 in the southern Presbyterian Church.

Not only did the Presbyterian Church change on social issues, but it redefined its theological identity. The Confession of 1967 focused on the witness of the gospel on important social issues of the day, including racism, poverty, and the dangers of nationalism. Moreover, the confession was still responding to the fundamentalist-modernist conflicts of the early century. It subordinated the Bible to Christ as the ultimate authority for the life and faith of the church. Two years later, the United Presbyterian Church U.S.A. further solidified its confessional stance by compiling a book of confessions that included the Confession of 1967, along with eight other historic confessions: the Apostles' Creed; the Nicene Creed; the Scots Confession; the Heidelberg Catechism; the Second Helvetic Confession; the Westminster Confession of Faith; the Shorter Catechism; and the 1934 Theological Declaration of Barmen. Reunion talks between the northern and southern Presbyterian Church began in 1969. It took until 1983 for the two bodies to negotiate their differences; the final compromise incorporated the Larger Catechism into the *Book of Confessions.* The new church was called the Presbyterian Church (U.S.A.). A committee was formed to write a brief statement of Reformed faith. A Brief Statement of Faith was adopted in 1991 that enunciated the essentials of the theological tradition in a statement that used contemporary language to describe the traditional beliefs of the Reformed faith.

Presbyterians have remained committed to a belief in a sovereign God that is transcendent over creation yet intimately and personally involved in the redemption of the world. Presbyterians have consistently supported a representative ecclesiastical government and have continued their struggle to remain united in their witness to the Scripture and to its creeds in the midst of a diverse culture and a history of internecine church conflict.

NOTES

1. This is a much expanded version of my article "Presbyterianism," in *Encyclopedia of Religion and Society,* edited by William H. Swatos Jr. (Walnut Creek, Calif.: AltaMira Press), 376–78.

WORKS CITED

All references to the Fourth Presbyterian Church newsletters, session minutes, bulletins, correspondence, and the ministers' personal papers and sermons can be found in the archives of the Fourth Presbyterian Church.

Ammerman, Nancy T. 1997a. "Golden Rule Christianity: Lived Religion in the American Mainstream." In *Lived Religion in America: Toward a History of Practice*, edited by David D. Hall, 196–216. Princeton, N.J.: Princeton University Press.

———. 1997b. *Congregation and Community.* New Brunswick, N.J.: Rutgers University Press.

Anderson, Harrison Ray. 1955. *God's Way: Messages for Our Time.* Westwood, N.J.: Fleming H. Revell.

Avella, Steven. 1992. *This Confident Church: Catholic Leadership and Life in Chicago, 1940–1965.* Notre Dame, Ind.: University of Notre Dame Press.

Balmer, Randall, and John R. Fitzmier. 1993. *The Presbyterians.* Westport, Conn.: Greenwood.

Baltzell, E. Digby. 1964. *The Protestant Establishment: Aristocracy and Caste in America.* New Haven, Conn.: Yale University Press.

Bass, Dorothy C., ed. 1997. *Practicing Our Faith: A Way of Life for a Searching People.* San Francisco: Jossey-Bass.

Becker, Penny Edgell, and Nancy L. Eiesland. 1997. *Contemporary American Religion: An Ethnographic Reader.* Walnut Creek, Calif.: AltaMira.

Bellah, Robert N., Richard Madsen, William M. Sullivan, Ann Swidler, and Steven M. Tipton. 1985. *Habits of the Heart: Individualism and Commitment in American Life.* Berkeley: University of California Press.

Berger, Peter L. 1961. *The Noise of Solemn Assemblies: Christian Commitment and the Religious Establishment in America.* Garden City, N.Y.: Doubleday.

Bergreen, Laurence. 1994. *Capone: The Man and the Era.* New York: Simon and Schuster.

Blau, Judith R., Kenneth C. Land, and Kent Redding. 1992. "The Expansion of Religious Affiliation: An Explanation of the Growth of Church Participation in the United States, 1850–1930." *Social Science Research* 21, no. 4:329–52.

Blau, Judith R., Kent Redding, and Kenneth C. Land. 1993. "Ethnocultural Cleavages and the Growth of Church Membership in the United States, 1860–1930." *Sociological Forum* 8, no. 4:609–37.

Bourdieu, Pierre. 1977. *Outline of a Theory of Practice.* Cambridge: Cambridge University Press.

———. 1991. "Genesis and Structure of the Religious Field." In *Comparative Social Research,* edited by Craig Calhoun, 1–44. Greenwich, Conn.: JAI.

Bourdieu, Pierre, and Löic J. D. Wacquant. 1992. *An Invitation to Reflexive Sociology.* Chicago: University of Chicago Press.

Boyd, Jeffrey H. 1996. *Reclaiming the Soul: The Search for Meaning in a Self-Centered Culture.* Cleveland, Ohio: Pilgrim.

Bridges, William. 1994. *JobShift: How to Prosper in a Workplace without Jobs.* New York: Addison-Wesley.

Bruce, Steve. 1990. *A House Divided: Protestantism, Schism, and Secularization.* London: Routledge.

———, ed. 1992. *Religion and Modernization: Sociologists and Historians Debate the Secularization Thesis.* Oxford: Clarendon.

Buchanan, John M. 1993. "We Must Look within Us for the Answers." *Chicago Sun-Times,* October 24.

———. 1994. *Resolution of the Assembly Commission on General Assembly Council Review in Regards to the Re-Imagining Conference, June 20, 1994.* Louisville, Ky.: General Assembly, Presbyterian Church (U.S.A).

———. 1996. *Being Church, Becoming Community.* Louisville, Ky.: Westminster John Knox.

Bullock, Robert H., Jr. 1991. "Twentieth-Century Presbyterian New Church Development: A Critical Period, 1940–1980." In *The Diversity of Discipleship: The Presbyterians and Twentieth-Century Christian Witness,* edited by Milton J. Coalter, John M. Mulder, and Louis B. Weeks, 55–82. Louisville, Ky.: Westminster/John Knox.

Carey, Joseph. 1984. "A Congregation to Be Watched." *U.S. News and World Report,* October 22.

Coalter, Milton J., John M. Mulder, and Louis B. Weeks. 1992. *The Re-Forming Tradition: Presbyterians and Mainstream Protestantism.* Louisville, Ky.: Westminster/John Knox.

———, eds. 1990. *The Mainstream Protestant "Decline": The Presbyterian Pattern.* Louisville, Ky.: Westminster/John Knox.

Comstock, Gary David. 1996. *Unrepentant, Self-Affirming, Practicing: Lesbian/Bisexual/Gay People within Organized Religion.* New York: Continuum.

Conn, Bruce C. 1975. *The Horror of Cabrini-Green.* Los Angeles: Holloway House.

Davies, Elam. 1964. *This Side of Eden.* Westwood, N.J.: Fleming H. Revell.

Davies, Elam, and John M. Buchanan. 1996. *Sermons for the City.* Foreword by Jack L. Stotts. Franklin, Tenn.: Providence House.

Day, Richard Ellsworth. 1946. *Breakfast Table Autocrat: The Life Story of Henry Parsons Crowell.* Chicago: Moody Bible Institute.

The Declaration of a Global Ethic. 1993. Chicago: Council for a Parliament of the World's Religions, September 4.

deVise, Pierre. 1993. "Chicago's Spreading Gold Coast and Shrinking Ghetto: Shifts in the Chicago Area's Geography of Wealth and Poverty 1980 to 1990." Chicago Regional Inventory Working Paper ii.103. Chicago: Committee on Population and Demographics, City Club of Chicago.

Dorsey, Gary. 1995. *Congregation: The Journey Back to Church.* New York: Viking.

Douglas, Ann. 1977. *The Feminization of American Culture.* New York: Anchor.

Douglas, Mary. 1966. *Purity and Danger: An Analysis of the Concepts of Pollution and Taboo.* London: Routledge.

Durkheim, Emile. 1957. *Professional Ethics and Civic Morals.* London: Routledge.

Erdman, Charles R. 1913. *William Whiting Borden: A Sketch of His Life and an Estimate of His Character and Service.* Reprint, New York: New York Committee of the Nile Mission Press from *Missionary Review of the World* (New York: Funk and Wagnells).

Ernst, Eldon G. 1987. *Without Help or Hindrance.* 2d ed. Lanham, Md.: University Press of America.

Farley, Ed. 1990. "The Modernist Element in Protestantism." *Theology Today* 47, no. 2:131–48.

Finke, Roger. 1990. "Religious Deregulation: Origins and Consequences." *Journal of Church and State* 32, no. 3:609–26.

———. 1992. "An Unsecular America." In *Religion and Modernization: Sociologists and Historians Debate the Secularization Thesis,* edited by Steve Bruce, 145–69. Oxford: Clarendon.

———. 1997. "The Consequences of Religious Competition: Supply-side Explanations for Religious Change." In *Rational Choice Theory and Religion: Summary and Assessment,* edited by Lawrence A. Young, 45–65. New York: Routledge.

Finke, Roger, Avery Guest, and Rodney Stark. 1996. "Mobilizing Local Religious Markets: Religious Pluralism in the Empire State, 1855 to 1865." *American Sociological Review* 61, no. 2:203–18.

Finke, Roger, and Rodney Stark. 1988. "Religious Economies and Sacred Canopies: Religious Mobilization in American Cites, 1906." *American Sociological Review* 53, no. 1:41–49.

————. 1989. "Evaluating the Evidence: Religious Economies and Sacred Canopies." *American Sociological Review* 54, no. 6:1054–56.

————. 1992. *The Churching of America, 1776–1990: Winners and Losers in Our Religious Economy.* New Brunswick, N.J.: Rutgers University Press.

Fitzmier, John R., and Randall Balmer. 1991. "A Poultice for the Bite of the Cobra: The Hocking Report and Presbyterian Missions in the Middle Decades of the Twentieth Century." In *The Diversity of Discipleship: The Presbyterians and Twentieth-Century Christian Witness,* edited by Milton J. Coalter, John M. Mulder, and Louis B. Weeks, 105–25. Louisville, Ky.: Westminster/John Knox.

Frankena, William K. 1973. *Ethics.* 2d ed. Englewood Cliffs, N.J.: Prentice-Hall.

Fry, John R. 1973. *Locked-Out Americans: A Memoir.* New York: Harper and Row.

Grant, Bruce. 1955. *Fight for a City: The Story of the Union League Club of Chicago and Its Times, 1880–1955.* Chicago: Rand McNally.

Greeley, Andrew. 1967. *The Catholic Experience: An Interpretation of the History of American Catholicism.* New York: Doubleday.

Green, Paul M., and Melvin G. Holli, eds. 1995. *The Mayors: The Chicago Political Tradition.* Rev. ed. Carbondale: Southern Illinois University Press.

Grimshaw, William J. 1992. *Bitter Fruit: Black Politics and the Chicago Machine, 1931–1991.* Chicago: University of Chicago Press.

Hadaway, C. Kirk. 1993. "Church Growth in North America: Religious Marketplace." In *Church and Denominational Growth,* edited by David A. Roozen and C. Kirk Hadaway, 346–57. Nashville, Tenn.: Abingdon.

Hadaway, C. Kirk, and David A. Roozen. 1995. *Rerouting the Protestant Mainstream.* Nashville, Tenn.: Abingdon.

————, eds. 1993. *Church and Denominational Growth.* Nashville, Tenn.: Abingdon.

Hadden, Jeffrey K. 1969. *The Gathering Storm in the Churches.* Garden City, N.Y.: Doubleday.

Hammond, Phillip E. 1992. *Religion and Personal Autonomy: The Third Disestablishment in America.* Columbia: University of South Carolina Press.

Handy, Robert T. 1984. *A Christian America: Protestant Hopes and Historical Realities.* New York: Oxford University Press.

Hatch, Nathan O. 1989. *The Democratization of American Christianity.* New Haven, Conn.: Yale University Press.

Hayner, Don, and Mary A. Johnson. 1993. "The Great Divide: Racial Attitudes in Chicago/Special Reprint." Series of articles originally published in January 1993. *Chicago Sun-Times,* February.

Heidebrecht, Paul H. 1989. *Faith and Economic Practice: Protestant Businessmen in Chicago, 1900–1920.* New York: Garland.

Hirsch, Arnold R. 1983. *Making the Second Ghetto: Race and Housing in Chicago, 1940–1960.* Cambridge: Cambridge University Press.

Hoge, Dean R., Benton Johnson, and Donald A. Luidens. 1993. "Determinants of

Church Involvement of Young Adults Who Grew Up in Presbyterian Churches." *Journal for the Scientific Study of Religion* 32, no. 3:242–55.

———. 1994. *Vanishing Boundaries: The Religion of Mainline Protestant Baby Boomers.* Louisville, Ky.: Westminster/John Knox.

Hoge, Dean R., and David A. Roozen, eds. 1979. *Understanding Church Growth and Decline: 1950–1978.* New York: Pilgrim.

Holifield, E. Brooks. 1994. "Toward a History of American Congregations." In *American Congregations: New Perspectives in the Study of Congregations,* edited by James P. Wind and James W. Lewis, 23–53. Chicago: University of Chicago Press.

Hunter, George E., III. 1996. *Church for the Unchurched.* Nashville, Tenn.: Abingdon.

Hutchison, William R. 1989. *Between the Times: The Travail of the Protestant Establishment in America, 1900–1960.* Cambridge: Cambridge University Press.

Iannaccone, Laurence R. 1994. "Why Strict Churches Are Strong." *American Journal of Sociology* 99, no. 5:1180–1211.

Ingersoll, Bruce. 1971. "Ousted Indians Find Temporary Shelter in Church." *Chicago Sun-Times,* July 2.

Johnson, Benton. 1982. "End of Another Era." *Journal for the Scientific Study of Religion* 21, no. 3:189–200.

———. 1990a. "From Old to New Agendas: Presbyterians and Social Issues in the Twentieth Century." In *The Confessional Mosaic: Presbyterians and Twentieth-Century Theology,* edited by Milton J. Coalter, John M. Mulder, and Louis B. Weeks, 208–35. Louisville, Ky.: Westminster/John Knox.

———. 1990b. "On Dropping the Subject: Presbyterians and Sabbath Observance in the Twentieth Century." In *The Presbyterian Predicament: Six Perspectives,* edited by Milton J. Coalter, John M. Mulder, and Louis B. Weeks, 90–108. Louisville, Ky.: Westminster/John Knox.

Katz, Donald. 1994. *Just Do It: The Nike Spirit in the Corporate World.* Holbrook, Mass.: Adams Media.

Kelley, Dean. 1972. *Why Conservative Churches Are Growing.* New York: Harper and Row.

Klass, Alan C. 1996. *In Search of the Unchurched.* Bethesda, Md.: Alban Institute.

Knitter, Paul F. 1995. *One Earth Many Religions: Multifaith Dialogue and Global Responsibility.* New York: Orbis Books.

Kohn, Aaran, 1953. *The Kohn Report: Crime and Politics in Chicago, a Preliminary Report of an Interrupted Investigation.* Popular edition of the famous Vol. 6. Chicago: Independent Voters of Illinois.

Kotlowitz, Alex. 1991. *There Are No Children Here: The Story of Two Boys Growing Up in the Other America.* New York: Doubleday.

Lamont, Michèle. 1992. *Money, Morals, and Manners: The Culture of the French and the American Upper-Middle Class.* Chicago: University of Chicago Press.

Leith, John H. 1977. *Introduction to the Reformed Tradition.* Atlanta: John Knox.

Lemann, Nicholas. 1994. "Rebuilding the Ghetto Doesn't Work." *New York Times Magazine,* January 9.

Leuchtenburg, William E. 1958. *The Perils of Prosperity, 1914–32.* Chicago: University of Chicago Press.

———. 1963. *Franklin D. Roosevelt, 1932–1940.* New York: Harper Torchbooks.

Lewis, James W. 1992. *The Protestant Experience in Gary, Indiana, 1906–1975: At Home in the City.* Knoxville: University of Tennessee Press.

Lippmann, Walter. 1969. *A Preface to Politics.* Ann Arbor: University of Michigan Press.

Loetscher, Lefferts A. 1954. *The Broadening Church: A Study of Theological Issues in the Presbyterian Church since 1869.* Philadelphia: University of Pennsylvania Press.

Longfield, Bradley J. 1991. *The Presbyterian Controversy: Fundamentalists, Modernists, and Moderates.* New York: Oxford University Press.

Luckmann, Thomas. 1967. *The Invisible Religion: The Problem of Religion in Modern Society.* New York: Macmillan.

Luidens, Donald A. 1990. "Numbering the Presbyterian Branches: Membership Trends since the Colonial Times." In *The Mainstream Protestant "Decline": The Presbyterian Pattern,* edited by Milton J. Coalter, John M. Mulder, and Louis B. Weeks, 29–65. Louisville, Ky.: Westminster/John Knox.

Lundén, Rolf. 1988. *Business and Religion in the American 1920s.* New York: Greenwood.

Machen, J. Gresham. 1923. *Christianity and Liberalism.* Grand Rapids, Mich.: William B. Eerdmans.

Marquette, Arthur F. 1967. *Brands, Trademarks, and Good Will: The Story of the Quaker Oats Company.* New York: McGraw-Hill.

Marty, Martin E. 1986. *Modern American Religion.* Vol. 1, *The Irony of It All, 1893–1919.* Chicago: University of Chicago Press.

———. 1991. *Modern American Religion.* Vol. 2, *The Noise of Conflict, 1919–1941.* Chicago: University of Chicago Press.

———. 1996. *Modern American Religion.* Vol. 3, *Under God, Indivisible, 1941–1960.* Chicago: University of Chicago Press.

Mayer, Harold M., and Richard C. Wade. 1969. *Chicago: Growth of a Metropolis.* Chicago: University of Chicago Press.

McLoughlin, William G., Jr. 1955. *Billy Sunday Was His Real Name.* Chicago: University of Chicago Press.

Miller, Donald E. 1997. *Reinventing American Protestantism: Christianity in the New Millennium.* Berkeley: University of California Press.

Miller, Robert Moats. 1958. *American Protestantism and Social Issues, 1919–1939.* Chapel Hill: University of North Carolina Press.

———. 1985. *Harry Emerson Fosdick.* New York: Oxford University Press.

Miller, Ted, and Robert Watson, 1992. *Report of the Committee on Racism.* Chicago: Fourth Presbyterian Church.

Moore, R. Lawrence. 1989. "Secularization: Religion and the Social Sciences." In *Be-*

tween the Times: The Travail of the Protestant Establishment in America, 1900–1960, edited by William R. Hutchison, 233–52. Cambridge: Cambridge University Press.

Morgan, Edward P. 1991. *The 60s Experience: Hard Lessons about Modern America.* Philadelphia: Temple University Press.

Morgan, Gloria Hayes. 1993. "Another Time: A Resident of One of Chicago's First Housing Projects Remembers the Good Years." *Chicago Tribune Magazine,* December 13.

Niebuhr, H. Richard. [1929] 1975. *The Social Sources of Denominationalism.* Reprint, New York: Peter Smith.

———. 1941. *The Meaning of Revelation.* New York: Macmillan.

———. 1951. *Christ and Culture.* New York: Harper and Row.

North, Frank Mason. 1905. "Where Cross the Crowded Ways of Life." In *Presbyterian Hymnal,* Hymn #408. Louisville, Ky.: Westminster/John Knox.

Olson, Daniel V. A. [1999]. "Religious Pluralism and U.S. Church Membership: A Reassessment." *Sociology of Religion* (forthcoming).

Olson, Daviel V. A., Roger Finke, and Rodney Stark. 1998. "Exchange on Religious Pluralism in the United States." *American Sociological Review* 63, no. 5:759–66.

Orsi, Robert Anthony. 1985. *The Madonna of 115th Street: Faith and Community in Italian Harlem, 1880–1950.* New Haven, Conn.: Yale University Press.

Pew Research Center for the People and the Press. 1996. "The Diminishing Divide . . . American Churches, American Politics." Washington, D.C.: Pew Charitable Trusts, June 25. http://www.people-press.org.

Powell, Walter, and Paul DiMaggio. 1991. Introduction to *The New Institutionalism in Organizational Analysis,* edited by Walter Powell and Paul DiMaggio. Chicago: University of Chicago Press.

Price, Matthew J., and Elfriede Wedam. 1995. "Class and Social Christianity: Community, Faith and Philanthropy in Restructuring Chicago." Paper presented at the Chicago Area Group for the Study of Religious Communities, University of Illinois at Chicago, Fall.

Pritchard, Gregory A. 1995. *Willow Creek Seeker Services: Evaluating a New Way of Doing Church.* Grand Rapids, Mich.: Baker.

Pyle, Ralph E. 1996. *Persistence and Change in the Protestant Establishment.* Westport, Conn.: Praeger.

Reardon, Patrick T. 1993. "More Chicagoans Find It Isn't Their Kind of Town." *Chicago Tribune,* November 28.

Reeves, Thomas C. 1996. *The Empty Church: The Suicide of Liberal Christianity.* New York: Free Press.

Reifsnyder, Richard W. 1992. "Transformations in Administrative Leadership in the United Presbyterian Church in the U.S.A., 1920–1983." In *The Pluralistic Vision: Presbyterians and Mainstream Protestant Education and Leadership,* edited by Milton J. Coalter, John M. Mulder, and Louis B. Weeks, 252–75. Louisville, Ky.: Westminster/John Knox.

Re-Thinking Missions: A Laymen's Inquiry after One Hundred Years. 1932. The Laymen's Foreign Missions Inquiry, the Commission of Appraisal, William Ernest Hocking, Chairman. New York: Harper and Brothers.

Roof, Wade Clark. 1993. *A Generation of Seekers: The Spiritual Journeys of the Baby Boom Generation.* New York: HarperCollins.

Roof, Wade Clark, and William McKinney. 1987. *American Mainline Religion: Its Changing Shape and Future.* New Brunswick, N.J.: Rutgers University Press.

Roozen, David A. 1993. "Denominations Grow as Individuals Join Congregations." In *Church and Denominational Growth,* edited by David A. Roozen and C. Kirk Hadaway, 15–35. Nashville, Tenn.: Abingdon.

Rose, Susan D. 1988. *Keeping Them Out of the Hands of Satan.* New York: Routledge.

Royko, Mike. 1971. *Boss: Richard J. Daley of Chicago.* New York: Plume.

Sandburg, Carl. 1994. *Chicago Poems.* New York: Dover.

Scroggs, Marilee Munger. 1990. *A Light in the City: The Fourth Presbyterian Church of Chicago.* Chicago: Fourth Presbyterian Church.

Sen, Amartya K. 1990. "Rational Fools: A Critique of the Behavioral Foundations of Economic Theory." In *Beyond Self-Interest,* edited by Jane Mansbridge, 25–43. Chicago: University of Chicago Press.

Sennett, Richard, and Jonathan Cobb. 1972. *The Hidden Injuries of Class.* New York: W. W. Norton.

Shepherd, William G. 1923. "John Timothy Stone: A Business Man in Religion." *Christian Herald: An Illustrated News Weekly for the Home* (New York), January 27.

Shibley, Mark A. 1996. *Resurgent Evangelicalism in the United States: Mapping Cultural Change since 1970.* Columbia: University of South Carolina Press.

Spielman, Fran. 1993. "Cabrini." *Chicago Sun-Times,* February 5.

Stamper, John W. 1991. *Chicago's North Michigan Avenue: Planning and Development, 1900–1930.* Chicago: University of Chicago Press.

Stark, Rodney. 1997. "Bringing Theory Back In." In *Rational Choice Theory and Religion: Summary and Assessment,* edited by Lawrence A. Young, 3–23. New York: Routledge.

———. 1998. "Catholic Contexts: Competition, Commitment and Innovation." *Review of Religious Research* 39, no. 3:197–208.

Stark, Rodney, Roger Finke, and Laurence R. Iannaccone. 1995. "Pluralism and Piety: England and Wales, 1851." *Journal for the Scientific Study of Religion* 34, no. 4:431–44.

Stark, Rodney, and Laurence Iannaccone. 1996. "Recent Religious Declines in Quebec, Poland, and the Netherlands: A Theory Vindicated." *Journal for the Scientific Study of Religion* 35, no. 3:265–71.

Stassen, Glen H., D. M. Yeager, John Howard Yoder. 1996. *Authentic Transformation: A New Vision of Christ and Culture.* Nashville, Tenn.: Abingdon.

Stevenson, Andrew. 1907. *Chicago: Pre-eminently a Presbyterian City.* Chicago: Winona.

Stone, John Timothy. 1936. *Winning Men: Studies in Soul-Winning.* New York: Fleming H. Revell.

Taylor, Mae Ross. 1947. "Why I Do Not Wish to Be Ordained." *Presbyterian* 117, nos. 27–28 (July 5–12): 7.

Terkel, Studs. 1993. *Division Street: America.* New York: New Press.

Thompson, Wayne L., Jackson W. Carroll, and Dean R. Hoge. 1993. "Growth or Decline in Presbyterian Congregations." In *Church and Denominational Growth,* edited by David A. Roozen and C. Kirk Hadaway, 188–207. Nashville, Tenn.: Abingdon.

Tracy, David. 1987. *Plurality and Ambiguity: Hermeneutics, Religion, Hope.* Chicago: University of Chicago Press.

Troeltsch, Ernst. 1931. *The Social Teaching of the Christian Churches.* 2 vols. Translated by Olive Wyan. New York: Macmillan.

Warner, R. Stephen. 1988. *New Wine in Old Wineskins: Evangelicals and Liberals in a Small-Town Church.* Berkeley: University of California Press.

———. 1993. "Work in Progress toward a New Paradigm for the Sociological Study of Religion in the United States." *American Journal of Sociology* 98, no. 5:1044–93.

Weber, Max. 1946. "The Protestant Sects and the Spirit of Capitalism." In *From Max Weber: Essays in Sociology,* edited by H. H. Gerth and C. Wright Mills, 302–22. New York: Oxford University Press.

———. 1958. *The Protestant Ethic and the Spirit of Capitalism.* Translated by Talcott Parsons. New York: Charles Scribner's Sons.

———. 1978. *Economy and Society.* Berkeley: University of California Press.

Williams, Rhys H. 1996. "Religion as Political Resource: Culture and Ideology." *Journal of the Scientific of Religion* 35, no. 4:368–78.

———. 1997. "Is America in a Culture War? Yes—No—Sort Of." *Christian Century* 114, no. 32 (November 12): 1038–39.

Williams, Rhys H., and N. J. Demerath III. 1991. "Religion and Political Process in an American City." *American Sociological Review* 56, no. 4:417–31.

Wilmore, Gayraud S. 1990. "Identity and Integration: Black Presbyterians and Their Allies in the Twentieth Century." In *The Presbyterian Predicament: Six Perspectives,* edited by Milton J. Coalter, John M. Mulder, and Louis B. Weeks, 109–33. Louisville, Ky.: Westminster/John Knox.

Wilson, William Julius. 1987. *The Truly Disadvantaged: The Inner City, the Underclass, and Public Policy.* Chicago: University of Chicago Press.

Winter, Gibson. 1961. *The Suburban Captivity of the Churches: An Analysis of Protestant Responsibility.* Garden City, N.Y.: Doubleday.

Wolfe, Alan. 1993. "The New Politics of Class in America: Middle-Class Moralities." *Wilson Quarterly* 17, no. 3:49–64.

———. 1998. *One Nation, After All: What Middle-Class Americans Really Think About.* New York: Viking.

Wuthnow, Robert. 1987. *Meaning and Moral Order: Explorations in Cultural Analysis.* Berkeley: University of California Press.

———. 1988. *The Restructuring of American Religion: Society and Faith since World War II.* Princeton, N.J.: Princeton University Press.

————. 1989. *The Struggle for America's Soul: Evangelical, Liberal, and Secularism.* Grand Rapids, Mich.: William B. Eerdmans.

————. 1991. *Acts of Compassion: Caring for Others and Helping Ourselves.* Princeton, N.J.: Princeton University Press.

————. 1997. "The Cultural Turn: Stories, Logic, and the Quest for Identity in American Religion." In *Contemporary American Religion: An Ethnographic Reader,* edited by Penny Edgell Becker and Nancy L. Eiesland, 245–65. Walnut Creek, Calif.: AltaMira.

Zorbaugh, Harvey Warren. [1929] 1983. *The Gold Coast and the Slum: A Sociological Study of Chicago's Near North Side.* Reprint, Chicago: University of Chicago Press.

INDEX

African Americans: Chicago history of, 65–66; Chicago riots and, 65; Dawson and, 86, 104; poverty and, 84, 87, 116n.10. *See also* Fourth Presbyterian Church, and African Americans

America First Committee, 116n.8

American religion: ethnography and, 19; Graham and, 117n.13; League of Nations and, 117n.14

Ammerman, Nancy T., 16, 19–20, 179

Anbari, Leslie, 131

Anderson, Harrison Ray: and African Americans, 81, 108; alcohol industry and, 103; background of, 89; Blake and, 108; Carnegie and, 92; Chicago's ghettos and, 84; Christ and culture and, 16; christology and, 200; Crowell and, 109–10; and the depression, 90–91; eternal life and, 81; evangelism and, 110–11, 118n.25; Hoover and, 83; Japanese Americans and, 100–101; leadership style of, 108–9; old-fashioned Christianity and, 93; parish plan of, 96; paternalism and, 92, 98, 101–3; Roman Catholics and, 93; social inequality and, 89, 91; social outreach of, 98; social reform and, 99; theology and, 111–13; and working people, 90

Baby boomers, 213

Baltzell, E. Digby, 26

Bellah, Robert, 215

Beneficence: definition of, 96n.41

Blair, William McCormick, 125, 126, 129

Blake, Eugene Carson, 30, 108

Borden, William Whiting, 2–3

Borden Library, 63, 77n.27

Bourdieu, Pierre, 153n.13, 196n.38

Buchanan, John: and African Americans, 183–84, 185; background on, 179–80; Christ and culture and, 16, 155; christology and, 202–4; on homosexuality, 4–5, 181–82; inclusive theology of, 182–83; lay leader rotation and, 169; preaching and, 180–81; Re-Imagining Conference and, 186–87; scriptural authority and, 187–88; social boundaries and, 184–85; sociodicy and, 185–86; on theological modesty, 188; women in ministry and, 192n.14

Cabrini-Green: and Fourth Presbyterian, 16, 18, 130, 134, 137, 139, 143, 152n.6, 158–60, 172–75, 176–78, 191n.3, 192n.9, 195nn. 32, 33, 203; *The Horror of Cabrini-Green,* 159; mission and, 177; 1990s demographics of,

157–58; public housing and, 122–24; social service agencies and, 192n.11. *See also* Public housing

Calvin, John, 236

Calvinism, 236–37, 238

Capone, Al, 82–83, 94–95, 116nn.4, 5

Chicago: government and public housing in, 123; 1950 demographics of, 106; population of, 88. *See also* Near North Side; Democratic machine

Christian Century, 25, 43

Christianity: definition of, 10. *See also* Evangelicalism

Christianization: dilemmas of, 62; social and subjective boundaries, 61; Stone and, 53

Church survey: outline of, 192n.15; personal autonomy index and, 193–94n.24; results of, 163–65, 169–71, 221–35

Coffin, Henry Sloane, 29, 52, 109

Compartmentalization, 170

Conservative Christianity. *See* Evangelicalism

Crowell, Henry Parsons: Anderson and, 109–110; background on, 51–52, 75nn.7, 11, 12, 13, 76n.21; Loesch and, 58, 77n.23; Stone and, 52–53, 57, 75n.10

Culture: definition of, 10

Culture wars, 164–65

Daley, Richard J.: ghetto and, 124; law and order of, 135; "shoot to kill" order, 147

Davies, Elam: and African Americans, 15–16, 18, 130–31, 137, 209; background of, 127; charisma of, 142–43; Christ and culture and, 16, 121, 149; christology and, 201–2; civil rights and, 18; church officers and, 124–5; class reconciliation and, 145–46; counseling and, 140; as evangelical liberal, 143–44; Fry and, 130; idolatry and, 150–51; King and, 147–48; on law and order, 146–47; leadership style of, 129–30, 138–39; oratorical style of, 141–42; pew rental crisis and, 128–29; political access of, 139; service agencies initiated by, 130; social activists and, 133–34

Davis, Angela, 30, 240

Davis, Dantrell, 159, 195n.34

Deaconess, 102, 131, 133

Democratic machine, 106–7

Douglas, Mary: *Purity and Danger,* 117n.16

Durkheim, Emile, 68–69

Eisenhower, Dwight, 18

Evangelicalism: Christ and culture in, 198; definition of, 22n.4; Fourth Presbyterian and, 164; political activism and, 31. *See also* National Association of Evangelicals

Farley, Ed, 38n.8

Fosdick, Harry Emerson, 28–29, 48, 73, 78n.29, 239, 240

Fourth Presbyterian Church: adaptation of, 207–11; advertising and, 62, 81, 97; and African Americans, 15, 16, 18–19, 63, 64, 66, 81, 87, 108, 115n.2, 124, 130–31, 135–37, 158–60, 165, 171–78, 183–85, 189–90, 194–95n.29, 203, 205, 208, 209, 240; Americanization and, 67; architecture of, 55, 160–61; Atrium Village and, 137; benevolence budget of, 118n.19, 21; bridging class and race, 137; budget of, 169, 191n.1; Center for Whole Life at, 158–59; civil rights movement and, 134–35; conflict and, 15, 209–10; endowment fund of, 118n.23, 152n.7, 193 n.23; evangelicalism and, 12, 203; free-riders and, 165; gender ideology and, 166; growth of, 53, 71, 206; law and order and, 135; lay exemplars at, 96; lower middle class and, 167; membership process of, 57, 193n.17; men's and women's clubs at, 58–60; missionary work of, 76n.16, 77n.26; Native Americans and, 139–40; 1990s congregational demographics and beliefs of, 163–67; 1990s elders at, 167–68; noblesse oblige and, 183–84; order of worship at, 162; patriarchal leadership of, 132; police corruption and, 104–7; racial groups and, 130; Racism Task Force and, 194–95n.29; single-room occupancy and, 174; social distance and, 172; volunteer activities in, 173. *See also* Church survey

Fundamentalist-modernist debate. *See* Modernist-fundamentalist debate

Gold Coast. *See* Near North Side
Golden rule Christianity. *See* Lay liberalism
Graham, Billy, 18, 29, 117n.13
Greene, Bob: Dantrell Davis and, 195n.34; tu-
    toring program and, 175

Hadden, Jeffrey, 31
Hammond, Phillip: on personal autonomy,
    27; personal autonomy and Fourth Pres-
    byterian, 169–70
Higginbottom, Sam, 61–62, 97
Hirsch, Ed. 85, 86, 122–23. *See also* Second
    ghetto
Hocking Commission, 62
Homogenization: isomorphism and, 78n.32
Homosexuality: American opinion of, 6; and
    ordination, 4–5, 181–82
Horror of Cabrini-Green, The (Conn), 159
Hutchison, William, 26

Ideology, 13–14
Interreligious dialogue, 200–204
Invitation committee: Stone and, 57–58;
    women's invitation committee, 60
Isomorphism. *See* Homogenization

Johnson, Elmer, 168–69

Kennedy, Robert F., 149
King, Martin Luther, Jr.: assassination of, 136,
    147; Chicago and, 135–36, 159; Davies and,
    147–48
Knitter, Paul, 200
Kohn Report, 105
Kotlowitz, Alex, 195n.35

Lamont, Michèle, 22nn.3, 5
Lay liberalism: characteristics of, 214–18;
    definition of, 16–17, 155
Leuchtenburg, William, 83
Liberal Protestantism: American religious
    culture and, 37; critique of, 178–79;
    definition of, 22n.4; Hadaway and Roozen
    on, 216–17; Johnson on, 33
Lippmann, Walter, 49
Loesch, Frank J.: and Capone, 82, 94–95,

116n.5; Chicago Crime Commission and,
    82, 117n.15; and Crowell, 77n.23; and
    Fourth Presbyterian, 58, 82, 83, 103; racism
    of, 94

Mainline Protestantism, 25–37; baby
    boomers and, 30; capitalism and, 62;
    growth and decline of, 31–32, 34–35, 72;
    missionary decline and, 68, 117n.17; 1920
    members and clergy in, 61; secularization
    and, 211; Supreme Court and, 32. *See also*
    Protestant establishment
Mathews, Shailer, 50–51
McCormick, Cyrus H., Jr., 54
McCormick, Nettie Fowler, 54, 78n.30
Men and Religion Forward Movement, 55
Menninger, Karl, 140–41
Miller, D. E.: church growth and, 218; on new
    paradigm churches, 212–13
Modernist-fundamentalist debate, 28–29,
    236–40
Money: Anderson and, 113; as incarnated
    spirit, 72
Moody Bible Institute, 51–52, 57, 77n.23, 109,
    112
Moore, Thomas, 216

National Association of Evangelicals, 29
Near North Side: class and, 157; description
    of, 22; 1910 demographics of, 54; 1920 de-
    mographics of, 41–43; 1990s demographics
    of, 157–58; 1920s North Michigan Avenue,
    80; 1990s North Michigan Avenue, 156–57.
    See also Zorbaugh, Harvey Warren
Niebuhr, H. Richard: Christ and culture and,
    9–12; critique of, 22; racial segregation
    and, 13
Niebuhr, Reinhold, 30; class conflict and, 91

Personal autonomy: and church, 27; and
    Fourth Presbyterian, 169–70; index of,
    193–94n.24; tolerance and, 194n.25
Petersen, Ann, 168
Pew rental system: description of, 12, 128;
    elimination of, 72, 128–29, 152nn.4, 5
Presbyterian Church: "fidelity and chastity"

amendment of, 213; history of, 236–41. *See also* Fourth Presbyterian Church

Presbyterian Layman, 187

Privatization, 169–71

Protestant denominations: new reality of, 211–12

Protestant establishment: Chicago Sunday Evening Club and, 47–48; class contradictions and, 81; Committee of Fifteen and, 48; decentering of, 73; description of, 26, 126–27; disestablishment and, 27; moral reform and, 48–49; ruling class and, 26. *See also* Mainline Protestantism

Psychological religion: Thomas Moore on, 216

Public housing: Chicago Housing Authority and, 85; Daley administration and, 87; multiple sources for, 123; urban renewal and, 85, 87. *See also* Cabrini-Green

Questionnaire, 21, 221–35

Racism Task Force, 194–95n.29

Rational choice theory: Finke and Stark on, 38n.4; Sen's critique of, 220n.2

Re-Imagining Conference, 186–87, 196n.39

Reston, James, 149

Roman Catholic Church: native-born Americans and, 82; postwar growth and decline of, 31; Protestant establishment and, 14; urban renewal and, 123

Roof, Wade Clark, 213

Roosevelt, Franklin D., 100; economic recovery and, 116n.7

Royko, Mike, 88; King and, 135

Sandburg, Carl, 21

Second ghetto, 15. *See also* Public housing

Secularization, 38n.8

Shibley, Mark, 198

Social boundaries: challenge to, 204–6; definition of, 12–13

Social inequality: Buchanan and, 188–90; Cabrini-Green and, 159; challenges to, 13; class boundaries and, 86; class interest and, 204

Speer, Robert E., 62; war and, 100

Stelzle, Charles, 53–54; background of, 76n.15

Stone, John Timothy: and African Americans, 64, 66; background of, 44–46; on business and religion, 50–51; Christ and culture and, 16, 41; christology and, 200; evangelizing men and, 55–56; family life and, 69; patriotism and, 66; and pew rental system, 72; preaching of, 46–47; prohibition and, 64; Protestant triumphalism and, 25; as Protestant virtuoso, 40, 43–46; Sabbath observance and, 70; social reform and, 64; Sunday's revivals and, 57

Strictness debate, 32–33; Finke and Stark on, 33; Hadaway and Roozen on, 33

Sunday, Billy, 57

Swenson, Norman, 136; Native Americans and, 140

Symbolic boundaries: challenges to, 204–6; definition of, 12–13

Symbolic labeling: race and ethnicity in, 95

Taylor, Mae Ross: as deaconess, 102; and women's ordination, 102–3

Terkel, Studs, 152n.8

Thompson, William ("Big Bill"), 50, 116nn.4, 6

Tracy, David, 199

Tutoring program: description of, 18, 160, 171–72; evangelism and, 174; focus groups and, 174–78; funding and, 195; 1990 tutor survey, 194n.27; social capital and, 176–77

Vanishing Boundaries (Hoge, Johnson, and Luidens), 33, 179

Warner, R. Stephen: liberal religion and, 172–73, 197, 220n.1; new paradigm research and, 19–20

Weber, Max: on charisma, 143, 153n.11; and Marx, 205; on Protestant ethic, 51, 79; on status group, 22n.6; on worldly asceticism, 114

Williams, Rhys: on cultural war analysis, 164–65; on culture and ideology, 13–14

Wilson, Orlando W., 107

Wolfe, Alan, 195n.37

Women: in Fourth Presbyterian's women's organizations, 132–33; ordination of, 131

Woods, Elizabeth: Chicago Housing Authority and, 116n.9

Wuthnow, Robert, 16

Zorbaugh, Harvey Warren: on Gold Coast, 40, 41–43, 121–22

JAMES K. WELLMAN JR. received his undergraduate degree from the University of Washington, his M.Div. from Princeton Theological Seminary, and his Ph.D. from the University of Chicago Divinity School. He is a Presbyterian minister and currently lectures in the Comparative Religion Program at the University of Washington. He is the coeditor of the *Power of Religious Publics: Staking Claims in American Society* (1999).

Typeset in 10.5/13 Minion
with Copperplate display
Designed by Dennis Roberts
Composed by Jim Proefrock
at the University of Illinois Press
Manufactured by Cushing-Malloy, Inc.